Aquariums

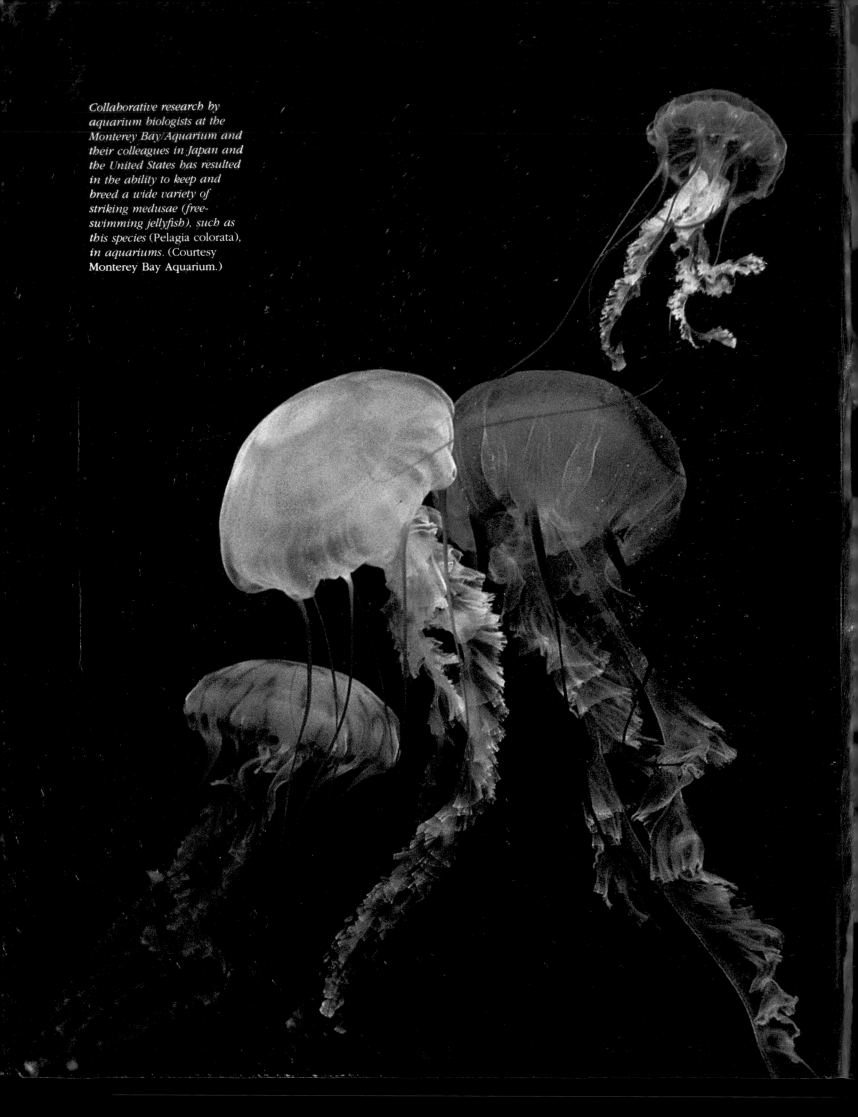

Collaborative research by aquarium biologists at the Monterey Bay Aquarium and their colleagues in Japan and the United States has resulted in the ability to keep and breed a wide variety of striking medusae (free-swimming jellyfish), such as this species (Pelagia colorata), *in aquariums. (Courtesy Monterey Bay Aquarium.)*

AQUARIUMS
Windows to Nature

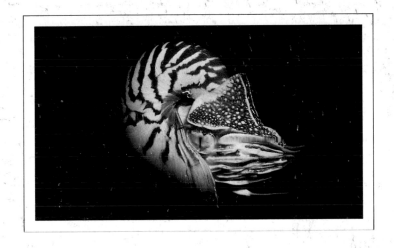

Leighton Taylor

Prentice Hall General Reference

New York   London   Toronto   Sydney   Tokyo   Singapore

Emperor penguin chick rests comfortably on its father's feet at Sea World's Penguin Encounter. (Courtesy Sea World of California.)

PRENTICE HALL GENERAL REFERENCE
15 Columbus Circle
New York, New York 10023

Library of Congress Cataloging-in-Publication Data

Taylor, L. R. (Leighton R.)
    Aquariums: windows to nature
    Leighton Taylor.
      p. cm.
    Includes bibliographical references (pp. 167-168) and index.
    ISBN 0-671-85019-9
    1. Aquariums, Public. 2. Aquariums, Public—Guidebooks.
  I. Title.
  QL78.T39   1993
  574.92′074—dc20   92-25083
                                                        CIP

Designed by Richard Oriolo

Manufactured in the United States of America

10 9 8 7 6 5 4 3 2 1

First Edition

Previous Page

Chambered nautiluses (Nautilus *spp.*) *provide a fine example of the advancement of aquarium biology. Twenty years ago these species were rarely displayed. Today they are on view in major aquariums throughout the world. Nautiluses raised from eggs produced in aquariums have been displayed side by side with their parents.* (Photo by Thomas Kelly.)

ACKNOWLEDGMENTS

After almost 25 years in the aquarium profession, I have had the support of more friends and colleagues than I can list. Some have helped me in the classroom, some at the sea surface, some five fathoms beneath it. Some have sent me photographs; others have sent me fish. Some have read my manuscripts and provided helpful rewrites. Some have shaped my career; others have held my hand. Some are human; many are not. All of them share a commitment to know nature and its ways, and to share our love for the sea with others. To all of my colleagues, wet and dry, my sincere thanks.

Special appreciation is extended to colleagues who reviewed the manuscript: Bruce Carlson, Waikiki Aquarium; Allen Eskew, Eskew Filson Architects; Chuck Farwell, Monterey Bay Aquarium; Lou Garibaldi, New York Aquarium; John McCosker, Steinhart Aquarium, California Academy of Sciences; Paul van den Sande, European Union of Aquarium Curators.

Thanks to Deirdre Mullane for supportive editing, Linda Taylor for manuscript production, Sylvia Earle for a wonderful preface and a wonderful role-model, and to the many colleagues who provided advice, support, comment, and help with illustrations, (including but certainly not limited to): Murray Newman, Gilbey Hewlett, Janet Atkinson-Grosjean, Vancouver Aquarium; Phyllis Bell, Laverne Weber, Oregon Coast Aquarium; Tom Otten, John Rupp, Point Defiance Zoo and Aquarium; Michael Demetrios, Dave DeNardo, Bill Meeker, Marine World Africa USA; John McCosker, Tom Tucker, Steinhart Aquarium, California Academy of Sciences; Kenneth Norris, University of California, Santa Cruz; Julie Packard, David Powell, Chuck Farwell, John Racanelli, Mike Pinto, Steve Webster, Tom Williams, Monterey Bay Aquarium; Jerry Goldsmith, Sea World of California; Don Wilkie, Matthew Kiwala, Cindy Clark, Scripps Institution of Oceanography; Steve Neudecker, Chula Vista Interpretive Center; John Hewitt, Aquarium of the Americas; Bill Flynn, Jackson Andrews, Tennessee Aquarium; Jim Stuart, Ed Bronikowski, Dena Leavengood, Florida Aquarium; Brad Andrews, Frank Murru, Sea World of Florida; Nick Brown, Bob Jenkins, National Aquarium in Baltimore; John Prescott, Paul Boyle, New England Aquarium; Lou Garibaldi, John Nightingale, Paul Sieswerda, New York Aquarium; Patricia Doyle, Cleveland Aquarium; Dan Moreno, Cleveland Metro Zoo; Bill Braker, David Lonsdale, Shedd Aquarium; Bruce Carlson, Daryl Imose, Carol Hopper, Tom Kelly, Susie Kelly, Marj Awai, Mary Morioka, Les Matsuura, Waikiki Aquarium; Steve Kaiser, Hawaii Sea Life Park; Liang-Shiu Lee, Lee-Sing Fang, National Aquarium of Taiwan; Yoshitaka Abe, Tokyo Sea Life Park; Senzo Uchida, Okinawa Expo Aquarium; Tsunesuke Nakayama, Ueno Zoological Gardens; Itaru Uchida, Nagoya Aquarium; U. Erich Friese, Sydney Aquarium; Stephane Henard, Nausicaa; Jim Peterson, Bios; John Swanson, Portico Group; Johnpaul Jones, Jones and Jones; John Schleuning, Rich Farrington, SRG Architects; Tony Gale, Fulton Gale Architects; Linda Rhodes, Vicki Dahl, John Christiansen, Rhodes/Dahl; Nestor Ramos, Pat Case, Enartec; Bob Stark Filters; Chuck Davis, Esherick, Homsey, Dodge, and Davis; Allen Eskew, Eskew Filson Architects; Peter Chermayeff, Cambridge Seven Associates; Frank Zaremba, Lyons/Zaremba; Richard Lyon, The Lyon Group; Hiroshi Nakamura, Mitsubishi Heavy Industries; Stan Bonillas, Exhibit Technology; Barry Taylor, Argo Plastics; Andy Anderson, Larson Company; Al Giddings, Kim Dodd, Rosa Chastney, Terry Thompson, Margaret Hall, International Images; Robert Kiwala, Slimeco Industries; Mark Shelley, Sea Studios; Dean Weldon Academy Studio; Ed Shallenberger; Bruce Beasley; Marty Wisner, and, for invaluable research support, Robert Eichstaedt, Eliza Manegold, Sayre Van Young, and Lex Salisbury, Lowry Park Zoo.

A major appeal of aquariums is the personal view they provide into the world of living creatures with which we share the earth and its waters. Here, beluga whales and the designer of their enclosure observe each other. (Courtesy The Portico Group.)

CONTENTS

The Lowry Park Zoo in Tampa, Florida, is home to the most advanced manatee rehabilitation center in the world. These docile aquatic mammals are protected but are subject to injury and death resulting from boating collisions. Biologists and veterinarians conduct research on manatee rescue and rehabilitation. (Courtesy Lowry Park Zoo.)

PREFACE

Dr. Sylvia Earle
Scientific Advisor to the
National Oceanographic and Atmospheric
Administration

For many, the first—and sometimes only—glimpse of what the world is like from the viewpoint of fish and other aquatic creatures comes from peering into the depths of an aquarium. My first eye to eye encounters with underwater creatures happened that way, through the glass of a beautiful, large freshwater tank that gave me a window on a world that I, as a terrestrial air-breathing mammal, might not otherwise have seen.

As a child, I witnessed tadpoles transforming into frogs, guppies bringing forth young, and brine shrimp emerging from long-dried eggs in assorted jars, bowls and tanks at home. Family visits to public aquariums further inspired my curiosity about life underwater, and in due course, led me to taking the plunge as a diving scientist in the "Big Aquarium"—the ocean.

Often, I have wished to be able to share with people everywhere some of the life-changing experiences I have had underwater, from swimming with whales and exploring kelp forests to encountering iridescent blizzards of small, diaphanous jelly creatures and getting to know the endearing, quirky ways of fishes.

For example, while piloting a small submarine alone, more than 500 meters underwater along the edge of a deep dropoff in the Bahamas, out of the darkness cruised a large, curious grouper. He was neither afraid nor aggressive; rather, he peered inside my "aquarium"—the submarine, and gently nudged the acrylic sphere. We visited for a while, two mutually curious creatures, he, the dweller of the deep sea where sunlight never shines, and I, the alien from above, bringing greetings from afar.

At present, few are able to visit the deep sea directly to meet giant grouper or see fish equipped with small, natural lights or get to know shrimp or clams or crabs. Most people enjoy such creatures only on a plate with lemon slices and butter. Even those who spend much of their life around, on, or even under the sea, are not likely to encounter giants such as the magnificent whale shark, largest fish in the ocean—or witness the behavior of beautiful small rainbow creatures that live in plankton, or have cutaway views of unexpectedly exciting action that takes place in sandy beaches, coral reefs and even marsh mud!

But thanks to growing number of aquaria, people of all ages and backgrounds have opportunities to do such things, to explore the waters of the world in a microcosm and to meet individual creatures that are, in a way, serving as ambassadors for their kind. Through these extraordinary places, people are now being inspired as never before to consider the nature of life underwater and the importance of water to all life, from the tiniest microbe to the largest squid or fish or whale, and certainly to all of humankind.

Creating such awareness is increasingly urgent. Astronauts who have viewed earth from above and aquanauts who have seen the planet from the inside out have

observed environmental changes caused by human activity that do not bode well for the future of fish or whales—or of mankind. Ecosystems millions of years in the making are being deliberately or sometimes unwittingly damaged or destroyed, squandered in a few decades by a single species—ourselves. Our dependence on natural ecosystems is clear; how to live harmoniously within them is not.

The many fine aquaria depicted here—and this book itself—are cause for hope that we are on the right track toward finding answers. The author of this volume, a highly respected marine scientist and a friend of many years (also a friend of many fish), brings together here for the first time a remarkable and timely portrait of special places that are making a difference concerning our understanding life on earth, and our place on this largely aquatic planet.

Their success can be measured in the expressions of children—and grandparents—enjoying the thrill of discovery, of fish watching people watch fish, of an awakening concern about the future health of the oceans as people begin to know more, and then care more, about life in the sea. Much that is good can come from this, including wiser policies and more protection for the natural world. Perhaps in so doing, we can win an enduring place on earth for starfish, small crabs, great turtles, whales, and deep sea grouper—and for ourselves.

Although today's advanced institutions emphasize the diversity of ecosystems and display a wide variety of organisms, including plants, invertebrates, mammals, and reptiles, fishes are still the keystone species of most exhibits. This school of blue lined snappers (Lutjanus kasmira) *was photographed just offshore of the Waikiki Aquarium in Honolulu. (Photo by John E. Randall.)*

Based on the success of institutions such as Sea World in breeding and rearing killer whales, some biologists have suggested that aquariums no longer need to collect orcas from the wild. Others believe that the genetic diversity of aquarium populations needs occasional additions to the breeding stock. (Courtesy of Sea World of California.)

Introduction

"We regard the institution of public aquaria as more or less
the result of the deeper interest now felt in the life-histories
of aquatic animals. . . . That they are a popular means
of education none will deny, and the success they
have everywhere met with leads us to hope they are
serving a good purpose."

—John Ellor Taylor,
The Aquarium (1876)

Widespread and abundant along the coastline of the northern Pacific Ocean, harbor seals (Phoca vitulina) *have long been a popular and adaptable marine mammal in zoos and aquariums. While sea lions have prominent ear flaps, true seals like these lack an exterior ear.* (Photo courtesy of Point Defiance Zoo and Aquarium.)

Aquariums, whether large or small, have been popular for centuries. Asian fish-fanciers kept colorful fish and green plants in ornate ceramic urns. Roman emperors maintained elaborate pools filled with live eels for the entertainment (both visual and epicurean) of their guests. Today, aquarium professionals maintain a wonderful variety of aquatic (a word that denotes any totally wet habitat, either freshwater or marine) plants and animals—from jellyfish to polar bears, from diatoms to giant kelp. The best aquarists do not limit their efforts to isolated species but rather attempt to establish healthy communities of organisms in order to simulate part of a natural ecosystem—a piece of the real world—within their aquariums.

When we hear the word *aquarium* used out of context and without qualifiers, we may be unsure what to visualize. The term equally describes a goldfish bowl and a major social institution complete with beluga, buildings, boats, and bay-front

restaurants. Unlike the mariner's aphorism that distinguishes the size of vessels—"A boat can be loaded on a ship but a ship cannot be loaded on a boat"—no such exactitude is provided by the statement "An aquarium can be put in an aquarium, but an aquarium cannot be put in an aquarium."

This book discusses both kinds, large and small. It focuses mainly on the educational and entertainment complexes that we still call "aquariums," but for which, perhaps, we need a new, as yet undetermined, label. Attempts to create new names have failed for the most part. There is also the question of the better plural: aquari*ums* or aquari*a*? Although some dictionaries approve the second, latinized version, most people who work in aquariums consider the word *aquaria* to be a needless affectation—and these are the same people who call a goldfish *Carassius auratus* without batting an eye.

The large and popular institutions that have been called *aquariums* since the word was first coined in 1854 can be found in almost every major city throughout the world in one form or another. These important social organizations rival the great museums of art and science in their popularity and influence. As civic institutions, they have their beginnings in England, continental Europe, and America in the last half of the nineteenth century.

Since then, and with accelerating change over the past three decades, aquariums have evolved to have very special characteristics. Traditionally, in Victorian England and expansionist America, a large public aquarium made an unmistakable architectural statement. The design and structure of the grand building were predominant; the exhibits were secondary. Society rejoiced in the belief that the rest of the world had been created for mankind's pleasure. Inside this great building, a creation of

Animals like this young raccoon (Procyon lotor) *at the Point Defiance Zoo and Aquarium are important members of aquatic ecosystems even though they spend much of their time away from the water.* (Photo by Leighton Taylor.)

When is a zoo an aquarium? We have come to expect brown-eyed, furry mammals in zoo enclosures, not aquariums. However, advancing aquarium technology has produced acrylic windows and improvements in water treatment systems, which allow us to observe these aquatic animals in surroundings that closely resemble their natural habitats. (Courtesy Jones & Jones.)

human labor and intellect, were contained selections of aquatic creatures displayed for popular instruction and amusement. All of the exhibits (save, perhaps, an outside reflecting pool near the entry, which might be filled with decorative carp, turtles, or, in rare cases, sea lions) were subordinated to the grand interior. The glass windows of aquariums lined the walls like so many paintings in a museum, or like windows in a train car touring an exotic region.

Today's aquariums are inherently very different, although some admittedly bear the tradition of architectural signature and civic monument. Such changes have come about in the last half of the twentieth century, when we have seen a vigorous blossoming of new institutions, especially in Japan and the United States.

In 1992 alone, four major aquariums opened in the United States (in Camden, New Jersey; Chattanooga, Tennessee; La Jolla, California; and Newport, Oregon), and one in Japan (Nagoya). The total annual attendance at American aquariums rivals that at sports events and certainly exceeds any single sport in ticket sales. Modern aquariums are at once entertainment attractions, education centers, economic successes, and agents of social change. Although some traditional features remain, today's best aquariums combine techniques from stagecraft, horticulture, marine biology, theoret-

River otters (Lutra canadensis) *are important animals in temperate riverine ecosystems. Traditionally, only the fishes from such areas have been exhibited. Increasingly, aquariums are focusing on complete presentations of habitats and are including such active mammals in their displays.* (Courtesy Jones & Jones.)

Fishes of coral reefs, like these raccoon butterflyfish (Chaetodon lunula), *are traditionally the most popular species in aquariums. However, fishes from many habitats—from polar to temperate regions—can be found in modern aquariums.* (Photo by John E. Randall.)

The imperial angelfish (Pomacanthus imperator), *like many reef fishes, has a different color pattern as an adult than as a juvenile.* (Photo by John E. Randall.)

ical and field ecology, materials engineering, educational theory, and many more disciplines and sources of knowledge about the world.

Old exhibits that once featured "the stingray" or "the rainbow trout" are now more likely to display the communities in which these species live. Stingrays are displayed and interpreted as members of the "sand flat community" along with burrowing clams, eelgrass, and many other organisms. Trout swim and feed in a simulated mountain stream complete with water ouzels (small birds that dive and walk along the stream bottom) and mayflies and a stream bank covered with ferns and rhododendrons. Surrounding the aquarium display are other exhibits that augment the information provided by live animals and plants. Such exhibits may be interactive

The popularity of aquariums is not new. Hundreds of thousands of visitors attended the aquarium displays at the Paris Exposition in 1900. (Collection of Leighton Taylor.)

Philadelphia commuters look to an informative landmark on the Delaware riverfront— the Thomas H. Kean New Jersey State Aquarium at Camden. The building's dome changes color to visibly forecast the weather. (Photo by Steve Walker.)

The Tennessee Aquarium adds a stunning riverside centerpiece to the cityscape of Chattanooga. It bears the distinctive architectural style of Peter Chermayeff, who has also designed the Osaka Ring of Fire Aquarium, the New England Aquarium, and the National Aquarium in Baltimore. (Photo by R. T. Bryant, Tennessee Aquarium.)

computer games, colorful panels combining text and illustrations, video projections of unusual aquatic behavior, and friendly guides answering questions and leading discussions, maybe even tying trout flies and demonstrating casting techniques

The modern aquarium is part zoo, part theater, part classroom, part nature center, part arboretum, part natural history museum—but uniquely an aquarium. Its success and popularity rely on a single element—the presence of living animals and plants—and the opportunity for people to make meaningful contact with another species.

Early aquariums attempted comprehensive surveys of the "Fishes of the World," something like stamp collections, featuring specimens from all continents and diverse habitats. The central theme, if there was one, was a celebration of the grandeur revealed by the great diversity of aquatic species—a great panoply of fish life, punctuated by the occasional invertebrate and hardy plant, and perhaps other aquatic vertebrates such as seals, snakes, and turtles.

While some contemporary aquariums, for example the Steinhart Aquarium in San Francisco and the Shedd Aquarium in Chicago, retain such a broad focus, traceable to their early origins, new aquariums (and older institutions seeking renewal) plan their exhibits around themes and regions. The Monterey Bay Aquarium focuses its permanent exhibits solely on the ecology of Monterey Bay. The Tennessee Aquarium has committed its program exclusively to the watershed of the Tennessee River. Other institutions have chosen broader themes. The Aquarium of the Americas in New Orleans features life of the Amazon and Mississippi rivers, the Gulf of Mexico, and the Caribbean Sea. In Osaka, the area of emphasis encompasses the entire Pacific Ocean contained within the geological boundary known as the Ring of Fire.

In Cleveland, Ohio, planning is underway for an aquarium devoted to "the Great Waters," which will include complex exhibits on Great Lakes (with Lake Erie as the centerpiece), Great Rivers (the Nile), and Great Oceans (the Great Barrier Reef). Cleveland will also add another dimension to its displays by including the human species as a member of the natural ecosystem. Natural exhibits usually exclude human beings or mention us only as intruders, bunglers, or fixers. Our species and our cultures have been deeply influenced by the waters on which we have lived, from Pacific islands to African lakeshores to the edges of melting glaciers. The aquariums of the next generation will be more comprehensive in their interpretation of living systems and their ecological dynamics.

The goal of designers and aquarists is to convey the feeling and look of another place, another kind of life, to lure and to startle the visitor into another view of the world. They are no longer satisfied to have the visitor stand detached and curious before a glass window. The moments of epiphany that have happened while staring through a clear window at a kelp forest or standing within a simulated rain forest or on a simulated coral-sand beach are made possible by immersing the visitor in the feeling of a place. This is a complicated and artistic task, as we'll see in chapter 2.

Most importantly, the raison d'être of today's best aquariums is arguably very different from the "good purpose" that John Ellor Taylor implied in his turn-of-the-century book, *The Aquarium*. Leading aquariums, following the model of well-managed enterprises, both commercial and nonprofit, declare themselves dedicated to well-defined and well-advertised mission statements. Consider, for example, the Waikiki Aquarium in Honolulu, Hawaii. Though it was founded in 1904 and is relatively modest in size, it is still a thoroughly modern institution in management and research, display and education. The declared mission (adopted in 1984) of the Waikiki Aquarium is "to help people of all ages to understand, to love, and to care for the life of the ocean."

A review of the mission statements of other aquariums, such as the Monterey Bay Aquarium, the New England Aquarium, and the Oregon Coast Aquarium, to name only a few, reveals a similar commitment to encouraging stewardship for nature. Managers of such institutions believe that they have a social obligation to educate and inspire their visitors about the natural world. Yet despite their good intentions and success with the public, aquariums, especially those that maintain cetaceans (porpoises and whales), find themselves the focus of increasingly vocal criticism. The complaint ostensibly finds cause in the ethics of removing animals from their natural environment and displaying them to the public. How do aquariums justify their actions?

In the best of all possible worlds we would not *need* aquariums. Species and habitats would not be endangered, and humans could easily observe any animal, plant, or ecosystem by visiting the place where it lived. But such a world does not exist. On the earth we share, nature is jeopardized. Only the most privileged can visit killer whales in Puget Sound, right whales in Patagonia, walruses in Lancaster Sound, or lionfish on a Balinese reef. And there is growing concern that such well-intentioned "ecotourists" are touring in such numbers that their very presence might further endanger once-pristine habitats and communities of plants and animals.

There is a dual justification for the maintenance and exhibition of elaborate ecosystems and unusual (and even familiar) species outside of their natural habitats. One of these may be ancient; the second is far younger. Jon Coe, the influential architect of such "habitat immersion" zoos as ZooAtlanta, has speculated that there is an ancient and perhaps inherent drive in human beings to relate closely to animals. He suggests, for example, that bear pits in Neolithic caves, and the symbiotic relationships between early human bands and some canid species, suggest strong inclinations in our species for intimate relationships with animals.

The popularity of modern zoos and aquariums, as well as the growing demand for travel experiences to areas rich in wildlife (which some have termed "ecotourism," or "environmental tourism"), provide further substantiation. If such a drive to be close to animals does indeed exist, it has sometimes been grossly distorted by human manipulation and exploitation of species. The menageries of ancient Rome and Victorian England seem to have been motivated by the human need to dominate the world rather than to understand it.

More recently, the professions of aquarist and zookeeper have been motivated by the need to save the natural world. Nowadays, the universal justification for placing animals in artificial environments, whether in zoos or aquariums, is that it helps people understand and appreciate the natural world so that their political and economic decisions will act to protect it. Aquarium proponents rely on their institutions to inspire stewardship for the natural world in their visitors.

Aquariums have two possible futures. One would continue the task of showing the wildness, diversity, and beauty of the world the way it is now and could continue if humans act responsibly. The other, far sadder, future is to display the world as it once was and can no longer be.

The noble justification of inspiring stewardship for nature in aquarium visitors is necessary but not sufficient. There is no substitute for conscientious and enlightened husbandry—the collection, maintenance, and display of living organisms in a state as close to their natural habitats as possible. This book explores some of those techniques and examines some case studies among a variety of species and habitats, from chambered nautiluses to penguins (see chapter 4).

Killer whales have had a long relationship with humans. Orca are sacred elements in cultures of the Pacific Northwest, yet they have been wantonly killed by angry and competitive salmon fishermen. Today they are esteemed as social, communicative, intelligent predators that thrill all who see them. (Photo by Flip Nicklin, Images Unlimited.)

The endangered Hawaiian monk seal (Monachus schauinslandi) *is limited to the northwest Hawaiian Islands, where its population numbers less than 2,000. These remote islands are closed to the public, so aquariums present the only opportunity to view live monk seals. The few animals on public display (at the Waikiki Aquarium and Sea Life Park in Hawaii) are important participants in research that supports the recovery of the wild population.* (Photo by George H. Balazs.)

The last four decades of the twentieth century have seen both a blossoming of great public aquariums and a widespread increase in interest and conservatorship for the life of the waters. The supporters of public aquariums claim a direct correlation between their institutions and a growing worldwide commitment to respect and protect the life of the seas, lakes and rivers. This book was motivated by these dual phenomena.

The mid-1990s seems an especially good time to look to both the past and the future of aquariums, and to survey the rich array of the aquariums of the world. Any such survey should admit at the outset that full comprehensiveness is impossible. In addition, the value judgments of one aquarium visitor, like a visitor to an art museum, are based on personal and subjective standards. It may be worthwhile, however, to list some of the criteria that most people agree provide the basic measurements for excellence in an aquarium; these will be found throughout the book. But one important point needs to be made at the outset.

A great aquarium does not have to be big to be good. Aquariums can be measured in many ways—annual attendance, volume of water contained, area of the building and grounds, numbers of species, sizes of animals, cost of construction and annual operation, number of staff. A great aquarium might have very high numbers in all these measurements, but a great aquarium can also be small. What counts is the institution's success at catalyzing within each visitor some personal, vivid, perhaps even life-changing vision of life.

Such experiences can be witnessed in good aquariums. Standing before the great window of the kelp forest in the Monterey Bay Aquarium, one senses the awe in each visitor's eyes as he or she looks up into the cathedral-like spaces—or shares the moment with a child, eye to eye with a spiny pufferfish at the Edge of the Reef exhibit at the Waikiki Aquarium.

A great aquarium touches the emotions and feelings of visitors while it engages their intellects. A great aquarium inspires love and concern for the natural world.

The building details of the architecturally distinguished Shedd Aquarium are exquisite. Cast-bronze doors feature a diversity of marine motifs. Mother-of-pearl lamps have been made in the shape of the chambered nautiluses with cast-bronze algae motifs in the lamp stand. When the Shedd Aquarium opened in 1930, nauilus seashells were familiar, but living specimens were unknown in American and European aquariums. It was not until the 1970s that aquariums like the Shedd began to display live nautiluses. (Photo by Leighton Taylor.)

1. The Nature of an Aquarium: History, Architecture, and Design

"This little volume is intended as a handbook to our public
aquaria, so as to render them still more effective as a means
of education. Their history, construction, and principles of management
[are] briefly described as also the natural history of the chief animals
which have been more or less successfully acclimatised."

—John Ellor Taylor,
The Aquarium (1876)

When the idea occurred to me to write a book reviewing modern public aquariums, I had not heard of John Ellor Taylor (who to my knowledge is no relation to my family, Taylor being a name almost as common as Jones). In the course of research on the history of aquariums, I encountered Taylor's book, *The Aquarium: Its Inhabitants, Structure, and Management,* first published in 1876. It was popular enough to warrant three subsequent editions through 1901. For anyone interested in the history of aquariums, large and small, it is indispensable. To my delight I found that Taylor had chosen a format similar to the one I had planned before picking up his small and excellent work. I found my own intents summarized in his preface. I can phrase them no better, so I will let his 117-year-old words above suffice for my own.

In addition to Taylor's book, there are a number of excellent reviews of contemporary aquariums from writers of the late nineteenth century. For the especially keen student of aquarium history, these are cited in the bibliography. To add a perspective from which to consider our "modern" aquariums, and to remind us that often what seems new is really venerable, comments from earlier writers appear throughout this chapter.

While modern aquariums such as the Texas State Aquarium and the National Aquarium in Baltimore may seem like inventions of the past decade, they have their origins in the England of Victoria and the United States of P. T. Barnum.

During the last half of the nineteenth century, the beaches and tide pools of coastal Britain, near seaside resorts such as Brighton, Scarborough, and Folkstone, were popular haunts of avid amateurs, men and women fascinated by natural history. Equipped with buckets and baskets, they assiduously collected live specimens (anemones, snails, and fish) for their parlor aquariums and plucked algae to press into display cards. For some, this interest may have been feigned and faddish, but for many it was a serious intellectual and recreational pursuit.

It is a far distance, not only geographically but also temporally and technologically, from the beaches and parlors of Victorian England to the carpeted galleries before the expansive windows behind which swim 20-foot-long sharks at the Ring of Fire Aquarium in Osaka, Japan. Contemplation of such a leap inspires a raft of questions about aquariums of the past and present.

The gentlefolk of Victorian England were rabid amateurs for "natural history." If they weren't collecting butterflies and ferns they were scouring tide pools for fish, snails, and anemones. In every pack was a copy of Philip Henry Gosse's book, The Aquarium, *a must for every collector and parlor aquarium keeper. (Collection of Leighton Taylor.)*

Who Invented Aquariums?

To look a swimming fish in the eye we need a window. Perhaps it is the tempered glass of a scuba diver's faceplate, the thin glass side of a fishbowl, a 1-inch-thick piece of polished plate glass in a 60-year-old aquarium, a 12-inch-thick piece of laminated acrylic in one of the newest aquariums, or a cast-acrylic porthole in a deep-sea submersible. These are all windows interposed between our human eye and water so that we can focus on creatures living within a medium far more viscous than air.

Even the interface of water and air at the surface of a tide pool or fish pond forms a window of sorts. But until the development of inexpensive glass or plastic, we really had no simple way to look into the natural world beneath the surface. The hand-blown glass of fishbowls provided the first such opportunity, but size was constrained by price and technique.

The grand aquariums of the late nineteenth century and the great aquariums of today owe their existence to the invention of the basic aquarium box with walls of relatively inexpensive glass. The lessons learned by amateurs and scholars working with these modest boxes formed the foundation for the principles used today in constructing even the largest aquarium tanks. Albert J. Klee, in a series of 22 articles published from December 1967 until September 1969 in *The Aquarium* magazine, provided the most comprehensive history of American aquariums both large and small and traced their English and European origins.

These small chambers began in the charming company of English butterflies and ferns. In her excellent book on the amateur pursuit of natural history in Victorian England, *The Heyday of Natural History 1820–1870*, Lynn Barber details the almost serendipitous invention of the glass tank in a chapter entitled "An Invention and Its Consequences." She awards the prize for the invention of glass boxes for the purpose of keeping live plants and animals to one Nathaniel Bagshaw Ward.

Like many surgeons of his day, Ward was an avid biologist and was careful to report his findings, although he did not always do so promptly. In 1829 he collected a chrysalis of a hawk moth and put it away in a bottle. When he came across the sealed jar again the following spring, he noticed green plants sprouting inside the chamber. He had unwittingly discovered the principle that green plants can sustain themselves within a sealed chamber containing only soil and moist air. The moisture respired by the plant into the contained air of the jar is reabsorbed as the liquid condenses at night and soaks back into the soil.

The sealed desk terrarium we may take for granted today has its discovery in Ward's early bottle. He reported his findings to colleagues and published a paper entitled "Improved method of transporting plants" in a botanical magazine in 1836. The article became the basis for his classic and influential book, *On the Growth of Plants in Closely Glazed Cases,* published in 1842.

Nurserymen were the first to recognize the value of this principle; they used glass boxes based on Ward's experiments to import exotic ferns, orchids, and the like from South America and Australia. As Barber points out, Ward's invention was quickly taken up by agronomists, who used these so-called Wardian cases to establish tea from China as a cash crop in India and rubber from South America in Malaya, thus adding two valuable commodities to the British Empire's resources. One could argue that a third commodity was also developed indirectly—the modern aquarium.

In the nineteenth century most glass was imported from France. When the Napoleonic Wars began a heavy tax was imposed, making glass a luxury item. After the wars ended in 1815, however, the tax was lifted, and Wardian cases could be made very economically. A nationwide fad for fern-keeping in the glass boxes (think of them as upside-down aquariums) spread rapidly throughout England. Although Ward had suggested that the cases could also be used to harbor animal life, it was the chemist Robert Warington who described the principle of using the glass cases for what we now would call an aquarium.

John Ellor Taylor's recounting of the evolution of aquarium from fern case reveals the scientific seriousness of his contemporaries:

> *Mr. Ward in 1842 published a little work . . . showing that animals and plants might be kept in airtight glass cases and that [the amount of each kind of organism] might be adjusted as to breathe in what the other breathed out.*
>
> *Ward [had] commenced his study in 1829 and the celebrated "Wardian Cases" for ferns, now to be seen in most drawing rooms, are the popular results. . . . In 1850, Mr. R. Warington, whose name is inseparably associated with the history of aquaria, reported on his own experience in keeping a fresh water aquarium . . . consisting merely of a glass globe of fresh water in which two goldfishes had been placed, together with some plants of Valisneria. . . .*
>
> *Two years afterward [Ward] and Mr. [Philip Henry] Gosse experimented after a similar fashion with sea water. This was the commencement of that rage for small marine aquaria which shortly afterwards set in. . . . Mr. Gosse first began with sea anemones, the easiest of all marine objects to obtain and keep afterwards in healthy order.*

A prominent natural historian, Gosse described his experiments in his very popular book, *A Naturalist's Rambles on the Devonshire Coast*, published in 1853.

Another Victorian author, William Simmons, writing in New York in 1874, made it clear that some avid naturalists did not wait for Warington's scientific paper to begin using glass cases for keeping aquatic animals:

> *The credit of the inventing of the aquarium proper has generally been given to Madame [Jeanette] Power . . . who, in the year 1832 and thereabouts, while studying marine animals on the coast of Sicily, brought into use the "water cage" to facilitate her investigations. . . . Since Madame Power began the study of marine animals by the aid of glass cases filled with water, in which she confined them, still almost our entire knowledge of aquatic zoology [has] been obtained through the [aquarium]. . . .*
>
> *But Mr. W. Alford Lloyd, the present Curator of the Crystal Palace Aquarium, London . . . says that the introduction into the "water-cage" of "plants for the avowed purpose of preserving the purity of the sea-water, and of sustaining the animals in health, is due to Mrs. Anna Thynne, who experimented in London in 1846 on living madrepores [corals]." It would seem that while to Madame Power belongs the credit of furnishing the clew to the scientific value of the aquarium, to Mrs. Thynne belongs that of inventing the aquarium itself.*

Mr. Lloyd's apparent quibble is based on the fact that when a Victorian aquarist used the term *aquarium* for a small system, he or she did not refer to the container but to the contained community—if only two fish and a plant. Victorians considered genuine aquariums to be "balanced aquariums," that is, almost self-sufficient tanks

FRESH WATER AQUARIUM.

This balanced freshwater aquarium, illustrated in Henry D. Butler's popular 1858 book, The Family Aquarium; or, Aqua vivarium, *is based on the original concepts of Nathaniel Bagshaw Ward.* (Collection of Leighton Taylor.)

containing both plants and animals, in which the carbon dioxide exhaled by the animals balanced the oxygen "exhaled" by the plants.

Taylor noted that work on aquariums was not limited to his own nation, observing, "One of the first notices we have of the establishment of aquaria on the modern basis of adjusting animal and vegetable life is that of Bordeaux commenced by M. de Moulins in 1830. This naturalist found that by keeping plants in the water where his fish and mollusca were, the latter were stronger and healthier for it." To confuse matters further, Philip Henry Gosse later attributed the invention of the aquarium to one Dr. George Johnston, who, in his 1842 work *History of British Sponges and Lithophytes,* mentioned the "formation of a little Marine Aquarium." "To Dr. Johnston therefore," wrote Gosse, "must be assigned the honour of the first accomplishment of this object."

Regardless of who deserves the honor of creating the first aquarium, the real popularity of the modern institution was triggered in 1854 by the publication of Gosse's widely read volume, *The Aquarium: An Unveiling of the Wonders of the Deep Sea.* The book, which was a Victorian best-seller, was instrumental in stimulating the founding of some early aquarium displays in public institutions as well as in private parlors.

Gosse himself had experimented with keeping an aquarium, bringing a small collection of marine invertebrates from Ilfracombe, in Devon, to London, where he kept them in "vases." Gosse approached the secretary of the London Zoological Society about his collection, and in 1851 the society transferred his "sea worms" to a new "fish house" in the zoological garden in Regent's Park. "This little collection," wrote Gosse, "thus became the nucleus and the commencement of the Marine Aquarium afterwards exhibited there." Soon after, another public aquarium was opened at the Surrey Zoological Gardens, while various public museums, notably one in Liverpool, exhibited small tanks or glass vessels containing animals and plants, fulfilling Gosse's hope that "my experiences may be useful to others in forming similar collections, either for public exhibition or for private study."

Touring the galleries of the Brighton Aquarium was a popular outing at Victorian England's popular seaside resort. (Mary Evans Picture Library.)

When droves of eager Londoners first thronged through the new, enlarged aquatic exhibits within the zoological gardens—the "London Zoo"—in 1853, Gosse's term *aquarium* was not yet in vogue, and the complex was christened the *aqua-vivarium*. Regardless of nomenclature, the attraction, described in the *Literary Gazette,* sounds as if it would have pleased today's aquarium visitors:

> *A living exhibition of the sea-bottom and its odd inhabitants is such an absolute novelty, that we must give our readers this week, at the risk of being charged with an undue partiality for natural history, some account of the elegant aquatic vivarium just opened to the public. On the borders of the flower-bed in the Zoological Gardens, Regent's Park, has been constructed, crystal-palace fashion, of glass and iron, a light airy building sixty by twenty feet in area, containing around its transparent walls fourteen six-feet tanks of plate glass. Eight tanks will, in the first instance, be devoted to living marine animals, and of these, six are ready for exhibition. They enclose masses of rock, sand, gravel, corallines, sea-weed, and sea-water; and are abundantly stocked with crustacea, starfish, sea-eggs, actiniae [sea anemones], ascidians [sea squirts], shelled and shell-less molluscs, and fish. . . . The whole are in a state of natural restlessness, now quiescent, now eating and being eaten.*

As popular as these early exhibits were, there was an impediment to establishing more of them: the problem of obtaining fresh seawater. To overcome this obstacle, Gosse developed a formula for manufacturing seawater simply by adding salts to pure fresh water. (Gosse's method is still usable today.) Soon, public aquariums opened in many cities in Europe, including Belfast, Galway, Edinburgh, Scarborough, Yarmouth, Vienna, Hamburg, Cologne, Le Havre, Brussels, Hanover, Boulogne, and Berlin. Of course, some of these were located near the seaside and were thus able to use natural seawater, but scientific breakthroughs like Gosse's formula encouraged the development of other, larger exhibitions and even freestanding "aquaria." The aquarium opened by the French Acclimatisation Society in the Bois de Boulogne in Paris, in 1861, was fitted with 14 tanks, each of which contained 200 gallons of water.

One of the greatest of Victorian England's popular aquariums was undoubtedly the Crystal Palace Aquarium, which opened in 1871. The Crystal Palace had originally been constructed for the "Great Exhibition of the Works of Industry of All Nations" held in Hyde Park in London from May 1 to October 15, 1851. The iron frame of the building, which covered almost 19 acres, was clad with more than 270,000 of the largest glass panels glaziers had yet produced, each measuring 4 feet long and an inch thick. After the exhibition closed, the huge glass-and-steel building was dismantled, moved, reerected outside London in Sydenham, and opened 20 years later as the Crystal Palace Aquarium. Sixty large exhibit tanks contained 200,000 gallons of seawater, while a storage reservoir held 100,000 gallons more. The largest of the tanks was 20 feet long and held 4,000 gallons of water.

This huge structure was soon outdone, however, by the ornately fitted Brighton Aquarium, which opened in 1872. The largest tank at Brighton measured 100 feet by 40 feet, and was "big enough," wrote Taylor, "for the evolutions of porpoises, full-grown sturgeons, sharks, sea-lions, turtles, and other marine animals." The tanks in the aquarium held more than 300,000 gallons of seawater, while storage reservoirs held more than another half million gallons pumped directly from the sea.

In 1896 an American ichthyologist, Bashford Dean, reviewed the public aquariums of the Continent, observing that "throughout Europe aquariums became fashion-

Public aquariums in Europe and the United States were formerly built with neoclassical façades. From the outside, these civic monuments were almost indistinguishable from libraries, art museums, and government buildings. (Collection of Leighton Taylor.)

able to a degree indeed which caused the great cities to vie with each other in their prompt efforts to build and equip them." Things, he clearly felt, had gotten out of hand. "These early aquariums were at first exceedingly popular," he wrote, "amply remunerating their stockholders when organized by private capital. Some of these, however, owing in nearly every instance to injudicious management, came later to deteriorate, and after becoming concert halls, or adding circus-like attractions, have ultimately failed." (Dean's sentiments may strike a chord in some modern aquarium professionals who are concerned about an apparent trend of commercialization.)

Across the Atlantic in New York City, P. T. Barnum added aquarium attractions to his American Museum as early as 1856. In 1861, Barnum purchased the pioneering "Aquarial and Zoological Gardens" in Boston (begun in 1859) and moved its collection of whale, shark, dolphin, and seal to New York. He constructed new tanks within the museum and provided seawater by directing harbor water that flowed in at high tide. Marine animals were a popular feature of the museum. Genuine, living, breathing (for a while at least), fresh-from-the-sea specimens of white (beluga) whales and rainbowed reef fish from the Florida keys shared the stage with the bogus contrivances for which Barnum is now more widely known. A famous hoax-specimen was the "Feejee Mermaid," a combination of a mummified spider monkey sewn into the mouth of a large sea bass. Spectacular and popular, it only remotely resembled the lovely, conch-breasted sirens that appeared in newspaper advertisements.

Barnum was so notorious for his outrageous promotions (and, it appears, even more popular as a result of them—people apparently liked to be fooled by a master) that some visitors believed the beluga whales to be fakes. In his autobiography, Barnum proudly reported that a satisfied woman customer complimented him on the cleverness with which the almost lifelike mechanical white whales had been crafted from rubber.

Part of Barnum's collection (it did include some genuine artifacts) helped establish the New York Aquarium, which opened in 1896 in Castle Clinton, part of the fort established before the War of 1812 to defend Manhattan. The New York Aquarium was an almost immediate popular success. In 1897 attendance was recorded at 1,635,252. Total visitor count for the first 14 years of operation exceeded 28 million people!

London's Crystal Palace housed one of the Victorian era's largest aquariums. The original structure stood in Hyde Park. The aquarium opened after the Palace was relocated and reconstructed in Sydenham. (Mary Evans Picture Library.)

P. T. Barnum, the American impresario famous for his promotion of such varied attractions as Jenny Lind (the "Swedish Nightingale"), Tom Thumb, and Jumbo the Elephant, was an early pioneer in public aquariums. In the 1860s he displayed tropical reef fishes and living beluga in his Manhattan museum. (Collection of Leighton Taylor.)

Like the New York Aquarium, the Berlin Aquarium (opened in 1869) is still with us, and both are excellent examples of aquariums that have persisted and improved over the years. Originally located on the Friedrichstrasse, the Berlin Aquarium was forced to move to the grounds of the Berlin Zoo in 1913. A contemporary observer wrote that the relocation was forced by "the increasing invasion of palatial hotels and office buildings." "The New Berlin Aquarium" was completely destroyed in World War II and was rebuilt on the original site according to the original specifications in 1950. Owing to the financial constraints of postwar Germany, cheap and inferior building materials were used. As a consequence, extensive reconstruction was begun in 1977, funded by money from the German lottery, and the aquarium reopened in 1983.

In 1941, the New York Aquarium was evicted from Castle Clinton by Park Commissioner Robert Moses, who planned a bridge to Brooklyn near the site. From 1941 to 1957 the Aquarium was housed in the old lion house at the Bronx Zoo. Finally in 1957, it moved to Coney Island, and by 1961, beluga whales were comfortably housed there. The Aquarium continues to make major exhibit improvements. In 1989 the 20,000-square-foot Discovery Cove exhibit and educational complex was opened, followed in 1993 by the Sea Cliffs complex, featuring seabirds, seals, sea lions, sea otters, and new homes for the aquarium's family of beluga. In the century and a third since Barnum "hosted" beluga whales in New York City, a sensitized public consciousness and advanced knowledge of biology and behavior have resulted in beluga that reproduce in aquariums and achieve levels of health and safety that exceed those of natural populations.

The success of the New York Aquarium inspired the establishment of public aquariums in other major cities, including Philadelphia, Chicago, and San Francisco. But the popularity of aquariums was not restricted to large metropolises. In 1904 the Honolulu Aquarium (operating today as the Waikiki Aquarium of the University of Hawaii) opened to great reviews, including that of visiting sailor Jack London, who (in 1908) expounded, "Never before have I seen such an orgy of color."

Fishes displayed at San Francisco's Woodward Gardens were collected in the rich coastal waters of northern California and displayed to more than a million people. According to an early guidebook, seawater was obtained offshore "to protect against impurities" (pollution was a problem even in the nineteenth century) and then "conveyed in large casks to the aquarium where it was dumped into underground reservoirs. . . . Artesian wells provided the water needed for freshwater fishes." (Courtesy San Francisco Public Library.)

Castle Clinton, the first home of the New York Aquarium in 1896, was built in 1807 as a fort to protect the New York harbor. After its military retirement it became a public center. In 1850 Jenny Lind presented concerts here. (Courtesy of New York Zoological Society.)

Although aquariums are great public attractions, many have found it necessary to promote themselves to ensure financial success. Compare this handbill for Woodward Gardens in 1875 to the advertisements for modern aquariums. (Courtesy San Francisco Public Library.)

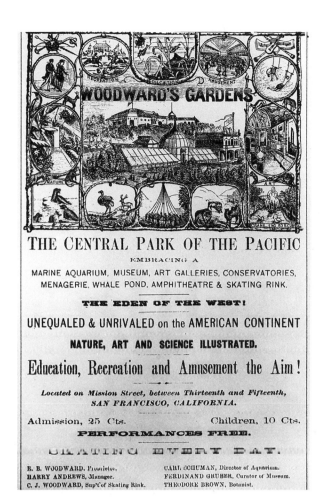

WOODWARD'S GARDENS

THE CENTRAL PARK OF THE PACIFIC

EMBRACING A

MARINE AQUARIUM, MUSEUM, ART GALLERIES, CONSERVATORIES, MENAGERIE, WHALE POND, AMPHITHEATRE & SKATING RINK.

THE EDEN OF THE WEST!

UNEQUALED & UNRIVALED on the AMERICAN CONTINENT

NATURE, ART AND SCIENCE ILLUSTRATED.

Education, Recreation and Amusement the Aim!

Located on Mission Street, between Thirteenth and Fifteenth,
SAN FRANCISCO, CALIFORNIA.

Admission, 25 Cts.   Children, 10 Cts.

PERFORMANCES FREE.

SKATING EVERY DAY.

R. B. WOODWARD, Proprietor.   CARL SCHUMAN, Director of Aquarium.
HARRY ANDREWS, Manager.   FERDINAND GRUBER, Curator of Museum.
C. J. WOODWARD, Sup't of Skating Rink.   THEODORE BROWN, Botanist.

The popularity of public aquariums was widespread at the turn of the century. This aquarium exhibition held in Philadelphia in 1900 featured many varieties of goldfish. (Collection of Leighton Taylor.)

By 1920 the success and popularity of public aquariums was securely established. In the United States, civic governments and wealthy philanthropists were ready to invest large sums in new institutions. The John G. Shedd Aquarium, which opened in parkland on Chicago's lakeshore in 1930, is a fine example of monumental civic architecture. Built in Beaux Arts style at a cost of $3 million (in 1930 dollars), the landmark building was underwritten by the philanthropic family of John Shedd, a vice-president of the Marshall Field department-store chain. Venerable though it may be, Shedd has continued to "stay modern" by improving its exhibits. In 1991 Chicago's lakeside aquarium opened a huge new marine mammal pavilion, built at a cost of $54 million (1991 dollars!).

Of course, governments and donors like to see impressive architectural monuments result from their investments. Major aquariums established in the early twentieth century are therefore dominant architectural statements. The live exhibits seem subordinated to the architecture, just as the paintings and sculptures within an art museum often appear secondary to the grandiose spaces in which they are displayed. Only recently have the design and construction of the building been subordinate to the exhibits and needs of the animals, and complementary to the vernacular architecture of the aquarium's surroundings. But, simultaneously, the tradition of creating monumental architecture to make a bold civic statement is still strong.

With the development of large outdoor oceanariums in Florida and California, huge outdoor tanks (viewed chiefly from the surface) became the major design elements. In these large outdoor parks, buildings provided support facilities but were no longer the chief features of the aquarium complex.

The John G. Shedd Aquarium, which opened in Chicago in 1930, is a beautiful example of Beaux Arts architecture. Filled with a panoply of exhibits of aquatic life from around the world, the building's exterior belied its contents. (Courtesy John G. Shedd Aquarium.)

In 1991 the Shedd Aquarium constructed a $54 million Oceanarium along the shore of Lake Michigan. This handsome addition connects the original Shedd Aquarium building both visually and philosophically to the world of water. (Architect: Lohan Associates. Photo by Hedrich Blessing.)

What Makes an Aquarium an Aquarium?

The nomenclature of the animals contained within an aquarium is precise and clear. Zoological names are based on a very specific set of rules (called the *International Code for Zoological Nomenclature*). Yet the taxonomy of the institutions that house aquatic life is loose and flexible. Today the word *aquarium* refers to something as small as a tabletop fishbowl and as large as a $150 million building. When Philip Henry Gosse first coined the word in his book *The Aquarium* in 1854, he argued that

> *a neat, easily pronounced and easily remembered, significant and expressive term is so advantageous, that it is worth taking some trouble to select the best. For the subject of this volume some have chosen the word Vivarium, and I have myself occasionally used it. The only objection to it is that it lacks distinctiveness of signification. It literally means any enclosure in which living animals are kept; and the ancients used it to signify a park, a rabbit-warren, and a fishpond; indeed, I am not sure whether our word "warren" is not "Vivarium" Saxonised. Thus it is quite as applicable to the whole Zoological Garden as to any particular house, yard, or tank in it.*
>
> *To avoid this indefiniteness, others have used the term Aqua-vivarium. The objection to this is its awkward length and uncouthness, which render it unsuitable for a popular exhibition or domestic amenity.*

Visitors to the Coral Reef exhibit at the Point Defiance Zoo and Aquarium, Tacoma, Washington, experience "diving" in a blue hole without getting wet. (Courtesy Michael Ian Shoppin for The Portico Group.)

   I have adopted the word aquarium, *as being free from the objections which lie against the other two, while it possesses the neatness of the former, and the definiteness of the latter. The term had already been in use among the botanists, to designate the tanks in which aquatic plants were reared; and the employment of the same term for our tanks is not forbidden by the character of the service to which they are put, since this is not an alteration, but only an extension. The growth of aquatic plants is still a most important and pleasing feature of our pursuit, and the addition of aquatic animals does not at all detract from the appropriateness of the appellation. Let the word* aquarium *then be the one selected to indicate these interesting collections of aquatic animals and plants. . . .*

At its coining, even though Gosse strove for "definiteness," the word was imprecise as to the size of the "interesting collections" to which it referred. The large buildings established for the display of aquatic animals in England and the Continent before 1900 were commonly designated by the name *aquarium,* which, as today, people pluralized as either *aquariums* or *aquaria.*

The name—as well as the concept—apparently caught on. In his review of European aquariums published in 1876, John Ellor Taylor referred to "the great public marine *aquaria* like those located at Hanover, Berlin, Belfast, Galway, Edinburgh, Scarborough, Yarmouth, Boston, Vienna, Hamburg, Cologne and Le Havre."

While it is now clear what the word *aquarium* indicates, there has always been a vague dissatisfaction with the indefiniteness of the term that persists to this day. Anyone who has visited a modern aquarium understands that the institution is not limited to just tanks of marine life. There is an increasing trend toward a mix of programs, including formal education and informal demonstrations. Exhibits mix techniques from natural history museums, science museums, arboretums, zoos, and even film, television, and theater. For example, the coral-reef exhibit complex at the Point Defiance Zoo and Aquarium near Tacoma, Washington, features a naturalist's cabin, a beach pathway and lagoon with a view to the far horizon, and a large collection of living coral-reef animals.

The modern institution we term an *aquarium* would thus seem to be much more than the name implies. No really satisfactory replacement has caught on, however, despite numerous tries. An examination of a list of North American "aquariums" reveals attempts to find a new name: Sea Life Park, Sea World, Underwater World, Gulfarium, Marineland, Ocean Park, Seaquarium, and the very complex Marine World Africa USA. Despite the inexactness, and the numerous attempts to replace Gosse's term, the public knows just what to expect when it hears "aquarium," so its formal use continues at such places like the Vancouver Aquarium, National Aquarium in Baltimore, and the Oregon Coast Aquarium.

Italy hosts both the oldest and youngest operating aquariums in Europe and has retained the name in both institutions (although rendered in Italian): the Naples Aquarium and the Genoa Aquarium. In France, a country with a language famous for its academic clarity, the two newest institutions devoted to marine science and exhibition have created original names, yet anyone would correctly call them "aquariums." Nausicaa is a marine center in Boulogne dedicated to the life of coastal France and to human interactions with the sea. Opened in 1990, the "aquarium" was named for the sea nymph who aided Odysseus in his struggles with the ocean. In Brest, Oceanopolis focuses on the life and geology of the continental shelf and the technology used to study and exploit it.

What about the term *oceanarium?* This word, coined in America in the 1930s, does not appear in the name of any institution. It has been used to describe more spacious, often outdoor, displays of marine life in parks of large acreage or in institutions that feature large-volume tanks for marine mammals. The first "oceanarium" was Marine Studios in Marineland, Florida. It was probably for this park, founded in 1936, that the name was originally coined. The studios were built as a facility in which to film underwater movies. (Sequences of *Creature from the Black Lagoon* were filmed there.) The park soon became a popular attraction for its bottlenose dolphins and large sharks as well, however, and the name was changed to Marineland of Florida. Under that name it still welcomes visitors. An entertaining history of Marineland's early days is found in Ralph Nading Hill's 1956 *Window in the Sea.* He refers to Marineland as the "towering oceanarium" of Florida.

Marineland of the Pacific at Palos Verdes, north of Los Angeles, was the first "oceanarium" on the Pacific Coast. Like the attraction that inspired it, Marineland of Florida, this park and subsequent "oceanariums" (such as Sea Life Park in Hawaii and the Sea Worlds of San Diego, Aurora, Orlando, and San Antonio) have large open tanks as the main architectural emphasis, with buildings subordinated to them. (Courtesy Donald Zumwalt.)

Craig Phillips, in his excellent review of the history of American aquariums (*The Captive Sea: Life Behind the Scenes of the Great Modern Oceanariums;* 1964), provided another definition: "In 1937, Marine Studios introduced the principle of the Oceanarium—the giant multilevel tank which displays various species of large and small fishes and other forms of marine life together, much as they are found in the open sea." By Phillips's definition, any modern public aquarium could also be called an oceanarium. Actually, the term *oceanarium* is losing any exactitude it may have had. Although the *American Heritage Dictionary* emphasizes its scale—"a large aquarium for the display of marine life"—it does not include the common connotation, added after Phillips's book, that an oceanarium includes marine mammals. The Vancouver Aquarium displays beluga and killer whales in large open-air exhibit areas designed to simulate the coastal Pacific Northwest. The Baltimore Aquarium displays marine mammals in indoor exhibits that exceed in size the original (outdoor) displays of Marineland of the Pacific, the second "oceanarium" to be developed in the United States. *Oceanarium* has also connoted operation by a profit-making enterprise (such as Marineland, Sea Life Park, or Sea World), in contrast to *public aquariums,* which are usually operated by noncommercial enterprises. However, the nonprofit Shedd Aquarium now advertises its beautiful new lakeside addition, opened in 1991, as "the world's largest indoor oceanarium."

How Big Is a Big Aquarium?

Aquariums of all sizes, from small (the 10-gallon tank in a dentist's waiting room) to large (50,000 gallons in the Tennessee Aquarium), can have a significant influence on how people feel about the natural world and can help them increase their knowl-

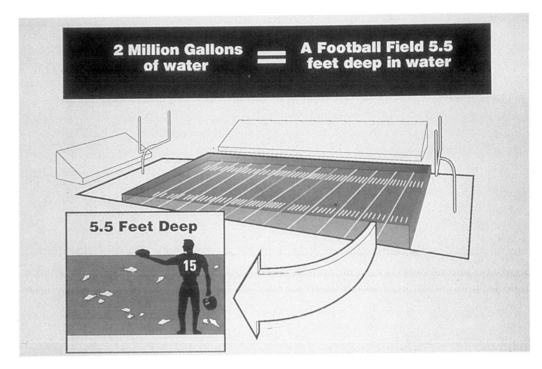

The volume of an aquarium is difficult for nonaquarists to visualize. A fish tank in the dentist's office usually holds 50 to 100 gallons. In contrast, the Living Seas exhibit at Walt Disney's Epcot Center in Orlando, Florida, holds 6 million gallons. Japanese aquariums measure the volumes of their large tanks in tons of water. This picture of an imaginary flooded football field shows the amount of space taken up by 2 million gallons of water. (Photo by Chris Krueger and Leighton Taylor.)

edge about it. Recent public aquarium projects have tended to be large, but even small ones, like the Waikiki Aquarium (Hawaii) and the Cabrillo Marine Museum (California), can be very influential.

The size of a public aquarium can be measured in a number of ways. It can be expressed as the total volume of water held in display and accessory tanks; the area of the building's "footprint," or the amount of ground and dock space covered by the building; the total area of a multifloor building; the annual attendance (expressed both in number of people and revenue derived from ticket sales); the capital costs of the building, support systems, and exhibits; or staff size.

In England and the United States, tank volumes are traditionally expressed in gallons, probably because early exhibits were relatively small. Early "large exhibit tanks" included Shedd's Coral Reef (100,000 gallons) and (in Hawaii) Sea Life Park's Coral Reef (300,000 gallons), but these are relatively small compared to today's huge exhibits, such as the 6 million gallons in Disney's Living World at Epcot Center in Florida, the 500,000-gallon Gulf of Mexico tank in New Orleans's Aquarium of the Americas, and others.

In Japan and Europe (perhaps more modest?) aquarists describe their tank volumes in metric tons. One metric ton of seawater (equal to about 1 cubic meter) comprises about 264 gallons. Thus, the large reef-exhibit tank at the Toba Aquarium (Japan), described as containing 820 metric tons, holds about 216,500 gallons.

To express the size of a really large aquarium like Osaka's Central Ocean Exhibit (1.5 million gallons), or Disney's Living World (6 million gallons), perhaps we need to invent a new dimension based on the large unit of measurement understood by most Americans—the football field. As the illustration above shows, 2 million gallons of water (7,575 metric tons) would cover a football field to a depth of 5½ feet, just reaching the chest pads of an NFL quarterback. We could name this measure a *candlestick*, after the San Francisco '49ers' home field, but in deference to size and the venerability of the New York Aquarium, perhaps we should call it a *giant*. Thus, the volume of the Osaka tank is 1.33 giants.

How Are Aquariums Created?

How is the idea of a public aquarium transformed into the complex, tangible institution that hosts hundreds of thousands to millions of visitors a year and accommodates hundreds of species of diverse aquatic creatures, ranging from microscopic to whale-size? Who creates aquariums? How are they conceived and built? Who accomplishes these myriad tasks? From where does the money come to support these complex buildings costing millions of dollars to construct and further millions to operate?

The establishment and operation of a public aquarium is a complex collaborative process, tantamount to the writing and production of a major motion picture or the establishment of a new corporation. In many cases it *is* the establishment of a new corporation, usually a nonprofit one. But even collaborative projects have their origin in a single mind, or at the most, in the minds of several kindred spirits. Every aquarium has its own unique history. All seem romantic in retrospect, yet they require years of planning, fund-raising, research, preparation, construction, and refinement. It is a long, hard way from the conception of an aquarium to throwing wide the doors on opening day.

Each project needs at least one champion, a "tender of the flame" who is devoted to the idea and mission of the institution. Such heroes have been diverse. The range includes politicians like Mayor Joseph P. Riley, Jr., of Charleston, South Carolina (the force behind the yet-to-be-built South Carolina Aquarium), and Mayor William Donald Schaefer of Baltimore, Maryland (the National Aquarium in Baltimore); researchers like Dr. William Ritter (who began programs in 1903 that resulted in what is now the Scripps Aquarium); the like-minded group of Stanford biologists who conceived the Monterey Bay Aquarium; and philanthropists who have both conceived and financed aquariums, such as Ignatz Steinhart, John G. Shedd, and David and Lucile Packard.

Such champions and the groups that form around them work hard to make a new institution a reality. And the work takes many forms, including raising public support and harnessing public opinion. As an example, consider the reasoned and emotional petition of William E. Simmons in 1874 for a public aquarium in New York. Twenty-two years before the New York Aquarium opened, Simmons appealed to the civic pride of New Yorkers in a lengthy article in *Popular Science Monthly* that began: "It is a subject for regret as well from a national as a scientific point of view that while London, Paris, Berlin, Hamburg, Naples, Brighton, in fact nearly every European city of note, has its aquarium, New York, the metropolis of the New World, is as yet without one."

Sometimes aquariums are championed by people and organizations with motives that are economic, like port commissioners and city councils. Others have their origin in aquarium societies and universities. Somewhere in their background successful institutions have the involvement of the minds and hearts of biologists who know well the diversity and fragility of the real world that will be displayed in the new institution.

The best aquariums are conceived and designed by a small team of creative yet practical people who guide the institution from conception (or shortly after) to opening day, and perhaps even during its continuous operation. Such a team includes architects, exhibit designers, biologists, curators, educators, and managers. Not every-

Careful planning and design support every successful exhibit. Talent and skills from many disciplines—art, biology, engineering, and construction all contribute to the finished habitat. From schematic drawing to scale model to the opening of the Arctic Canada exhibit at Vancouver's Public Aquarium, years of effort and complex programming were required. (Courtesy Vancouver Aquarium and Finn Larsen, Ursus.)

one subscribes to this collaborative team approach. Some strong-minded architects prefer to see themselves as the conductors of an orchestra of specialists and designers. Good aquariums have resulted from both methods. Increasingly, however, the team approach is becoming more common as its strengths are demonstrated in such excellent institutions as the Monterey Bay Aquarium.

The major proponent of the team approach is usually an architect by training, like Linda Rhodes of Rhodes/Dahl. Rhodes has acquired her expertise by managing the construction of the original Monterey Bay Aquarium, collaborating on the design and construction of the second phase of this aquarium, and facilitating and assisting the design process for numerous other projects, including the renewal of the Naples Aquarium, the Cleveland Aquarium, and the South Carolina Aquarium.

Outlining the team approach, Rhodes explained her ten-step process for the design and development of a new aquarium at a conference on aquarium design in 1992:

1. **Mission Statement.** The first step is for the champions and the supporters of the aquarium to honestly work out together what the purpose of the institution will be, to answer the question, "Why do this?"

2. **Market Research.** It is also essential to learn about the audience, what the size of the market is, where people will come from.

3. **Concept Plan.** The team then develops exhibit ideas, the architectural program (i.e., how big the building needs to be to include all the desired exhibits and visitor services), a study of the site, probable costs of building and operation, and the projection of management costs.

4. **Feasibility Study.** This crucial step tests the likelihood of the success of the institution. Representatives from market segments, and cooperating institutions such as universities, schools, and community groups, are interviewed. This estimate will dictate the building size required to afford a comfortable and safe visitor experience.

5. **Budget.** Estimates include preconstruction costs, fees, permits, site preparation, planning, construction costs and preopening expenses. This last category covers a variety of expenses such as animal collection and maintenance; advertising; salaries for employees hired before opening, such as aquarists; and, the most pleasant expense, the opening celebration.

6. **Fund-raising Feasibility Study and Fund-raising Program.** Attempts are now made to identify all, and the best, sources of funds, from bond sales to corporate gifts to individual philanthropy to construction loans.

7. **Design Process.** This lengthy and team-driven process includes actual architectural schematic design of the buildings, the exhibits, the support systems, the development of construction documents, the careful definition of costs, and the choosing of contractors.

8. **Construction.** This is the actual tangible creation of the buildings, the exhibits, and all of the support structures.

9. **Preopening Activities.** Expenses do not stop with construction. This vital series of activities includes the collection of animals; the development and introduction of educational programs, which begin even before the

building is opened; membership development; marketing and advertising; hiring and training of staff; development and recruitment for a volunteer program; and systems testing and evaluation.

10. **Opening.** An aquarium that has done its job well will open with a strong membership, will have created a pent-up demand in its market, and will already be well recognized as a community cultural resource. This last step is really not the end, but the beginning.

What follows these steps, however, may really be the most important. That is the continuing operation, constant renewal, and perpetual dedication to standards of excellence and visitor satisfaction. In fact, it is a well-recognized risk that institutions may fail to plan beyond opening day.

In addition, aquariums now in design, and those that have been opened in the past ten years, recognize that they can plan on a significant drop in admissions after the popularity of their first two or three years. To prevent such a drop and to encourage repeat attendance, most find it necessary to commit to a program of special exhibits that change periodically and stimulate return visits. In 1992, for example, the Monterey Bay Aquarium spent $500,000 to mount its heavily advertised and very successful exhibit featuring live jellyfish.

Fund-raising, feasibility studies, market research—these are all essential steps, but the really vital and creative process is design. Architects and teams who plan aquariums have four "clients" to please:

- The plants and animals that live within the displays

- The people who care for and educate the public about these living things

- The visitors who come to see them

- The owners (city governments, wealthy patrons, or nonprofit corporations) who pay for the buildings

Balancing the needs of each client group and ensuring that the resulting structures complement their surroundings present practical and creative challenges for design teams.

The design of an aquarium must be a collaborative process among the owners, exhibit designers, engineers, biologists, curators, landscape architects, educators, and architects, but it is the last group—architects   that traditionally holds the leadership role and receives the lion's share of the credit for the design.

The public aquarium is a unique project for an architect. An aquarium is not just a building with extra plumbing. It is, in a very real way, a living organism. Its design, construction, and continuing operation cannot be designed by formula or by reusing old blueprints. Despite their originality, enough aquariums have been built in the last twenty years to permit some definition and analysis of this "building type," as architects call specific kinds of structures (such as schools, hospitals, and libraries). Architect Allen Eskew, codesigner of the Aquarium of the Americas in New Orleans, was the first to conduct a systematic analysis of aquarium design.

Of the eleven aquariums built in the United States since 1969, the five largest have had the involvement of one of two architects. Chuck Davis of Esherick, Homsey, Dodge, and Davis in San Francisco designed the Monterey Bay Aquarium (1984) and is the codesigner with Gyo Obata of the Florida Aquarium, scheduled to open in Tampa in 1995, and the National Museum and Aquarium planned for Kenting, Taiwan.

He has acted as design consultant for the Aquarium of the Americas in New Orleans (1990) and has been selected as the principal architect for the Cleveland Aquarium (scheduled to open in 1998).

Peter Chermayeff of Cambridge Seven Associates in Massachusetts is credited with the planning and design of the pioneering New England Aquarium (1969), the National Aquarium in Baltimore (1981), and the Tennessee Aquarium (1992). His projects outside the United States include Osaka's great Ring of Fire Aquarium (1991), the Genoa, Italy, Aquarium (1992), and the yet-to-be-built Toronto Aquarium (Canada).

Both Davis and Chermayeff have spoken widely, often from the same platform, about the importance of collaboration in aquarium design.

Davis has described the architectural design of aquariums as:

. . . the most complicated, paradoxical projects we do. We must simulate what is real in a built environment. Much of the design process seems like

The Osaka Ring of Fire Aquarium provides visual excitement both inside and out. Its huge central tank hosts dozens of species, including whale sharks. At night the building's distinctive outline sparkles on Osaka's waterfront and attracts visitors to the adjacent shopping center. (Photo by Y. Matsumura; courtesy Cambridge Seven Associates.)

organizing chaos. There is so much input that it is hard to figure out what is needed and when to make a decision and go on.

The most important element is the quality of the design team and the ability of its members to listen to one another and to clients and advisors. The aquarium ideas really come from the biologists and the exhibit people. Our job as architects is to get the ideas down and wrap a building around it.

I design from the inside out and am convinced that the personality of the design team needs to be both argumentative and collaborative, working with the spirit and the passion for the project. There are no workbooks or handbooks for designing an aquarium. Review of the initial concepts by experts and specialists as well as experienced operators is extremely valuable and helpful in the design process. Every design schedule needs to provide time for such review, as well as time for the team to think and reflect on the ideas put forward by its own members. The best ideas come after the third or fourth cycle, and refinement makes the best product.

But really the best physical feature for an aquarium is a really good site. It is important to be on, next to, or closely associated with water. The visitors need to be able to walk outside and get those connections in their heads between the exhibit content and the real world.

Peter Chermayeff is particularly noted for his distinctive buildings, often crowned with the glass pyramids that some see as a Cambridge Seven signature or icon. While Chermayeff has said that "architecture can be a servant of exhibits," he also says that he works somewhat differently from Davis, who regards exhibit designers as almost equal members of his design team. Chermayeff describes his style: "I orchestrate the exhibit design. It's important to listen well and to seek a diversity of input from ecologists to fishermen."

Although some see his tour de force aquarium in Osaka as a very clear architectural icon, Chermayeff argues that it has been "designed from the inside out," that both interior and exterior sight lines "make the whole complex system legible. While some would say Osaka is an important architectural statement, I think the building's structure is secondary."

The biggest difference that industry observers have noted between Chermayeff's and Davis's designs is the pattern of traffic flow within the exhibit spaces. Chermayeff's design are often characterized as linear, and indeed, some begin with an escalator transporting visitors to the first exhibit experience. In contrast, Davis's designs are typically described as more random and free. Both styles have their partisans. Some argue that a linear style permits better crowd movement and control as well as a structured story line to the sequence of exhibits. Proponents of the more open flow believe that visitors have a more diverse experience. But while there are many ways of measuring visitors' satisfaction (few of which are used), there is no arguing that the premier measure of institutional success—high attendance—proves that both Davis's and Chermayeff's aquariums are very successful.

Although the architect receives most of the public recognition for designing an aquarium, a second, very important, contributor to the design team is the exhibit designer. Sometimes the architect tries to serve this role as well. Creative tension exists between the two roles: "The building exists to hold the exhibits," says the designer. The architect responds: "But the exhibits must fit within the building!" In the best cases, these two positions balance, and the building and the exhibits blend into a single significant experience for the visitor.

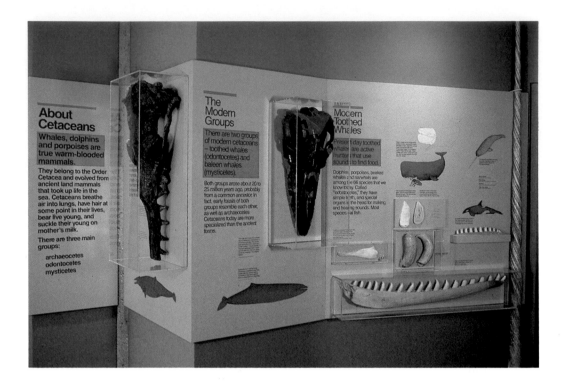

About
Cetaceans

Whales, dolphins
and porpoises are
true warm-blooded
mammals.

They belong to the Order
Cetacea and evolved from
ancient land mammals
that took up life in the
sea. Cetaceans breathe
air into lungs, have hair at
some point in their lives,
bear live young, and
suckle their young on
mother's milk.

There are three main
groups:

archaeocetes
odontocetes
mysticetes

The
Modern
Groups

There are two groups
of modern cetaceans
– toothed whales
(odontocetes) and
baleen whales
(mysticetes).

Both groups arose about 20 to
25 million years ago, probably
from a common ancestor. In
fact, early fossils of both
groups resemble each other,
as well as archaeocetes.
Cetaceans today are more
specialized than the ancient
forms.

Modern
Toothed
Whales

Present day toothed
whales are active
hunters that use
sound to find food.

Dolphins, porpoises, beaked
whales and narwhals are
among the 66 species that we
know today. Called
"odontocetes," they have
simple teeth, and special
organs in the head for making
and hearing sounds. Most
species eat fish.

Aquariums increasingly use the techniques of natural history museums to interpret their displays of living organisms. Writers and educators use the latest research findings to ensure that the information presented is accurate and engaging. These exhibits enhance the Arctic Canada gallery at the Vancouver Aquarium, adjacent to the spacious, naturalistic outdoor pool for beluga. (Courtesy Vancouver Aquarium.)

There are many excellent design firms in the United States, but only a handful have worked on more than one aquarium. These firms have been very influential in the development of newer aquariums. Every firm has its fans, just as architects have their partisans. But the real key to a successful project is the involvement of aquarium biologists and educators in the design process from its earliest conception. Serious errors can be made when a design firm, no matter how talented on their drawing boards, conceives of exhibits without a proper firsthand knowledge of the biology of the plants and animals they will be exhibiting.

In turn, good writers and educators—called *interpreters* in the aquarium field—are vital to assure that the information content about the plants and animals is entertaining, clear, true, and accessible. The profession of educational interpretation is a growing and important field. Allied to interpretation is the discipline of *evaluation,* the planning and testing to see whether exhibits work, whether visitors actually understand and value their exhibit experience.

Complementing exhibit design are landscaping, interior design and furnishing, the engineering of crowd control, and the provision of visitor services.

Well-designed projects are only as good as their tangible fulfillment—their construction. Building an aquarium involves a very complex set of tasks. Many aquariums are constructed near the water's edge, so site preparations like pilings, wharfs, and flood controls are usually needed. Aquariums depend on complicated life-support systems. Simply plumbing and wiring an aquarium are major projects. Construction time for large aquariums usually exceeds two years. Costs can reach $375 per square foot (in 1992 dollars) for the finished and furnished building and grounds.

There is a second vital element of aquarium construction: the building of the exhibits. This, too, is a complex task that involves everything from molding and fabricating artificial rocks (which look natural to visitors and feel natural to birds' feet and crabs' claws) to illustrating and silk-screening graphic panels that tell fascinating stories about crab-eating birds. There is a growing but still select field of exhibit fabricators. Some firms include the design process with the fabrication effort. They contend that given good design talents and the willingness to work with biologists, such doubly talented firms can produce excellent projects more efficiently because the designs are practical and can be made with less difficulty, given their experience in fabrication.

Where Do Aquariums Get the Money to Operate?

Although there are commercial facilities (such as Sea World, Marine World Africa USA, and Hawaii Sea Life Park), most modern aquariums are technically nonprofit and noncommercial institutions—either because they are tax exempt under federal law or, less frequently, are agencies of city governments. Some, a decreasing number, receive direct grants from municipal and state governments. Most of these institutions must earn revenues in excess of their operating expenses. Increasingly, new institutions may also be responsible for paying debt service on the bonds that capitalize them.

Technically, the excess revenue earned by a tax-exempt organization is not profit but is considered *retained earnings,* which can be used for a variety of purposes, all aimed at institutional improvement. Examples include new education programs, exhibit improvements, research, and even building expansion. Phase II of the Monterey Bay Aquarium, scheduled to open in 1995 and to include a 1-million-gallon open-ocean tank with schooling albacore tuna among other highlights, is financed by retained earnings accumulated since the aquarium opened in 1984. As in most aquariums, such revenues are earned in a variety of ways, principally through admission fees.

But money generated by retail sales is a vital part of any aquarium's income. The inclusion of a large, well-designed, and tastefully stocked gift- and bookstore is an essential element. Most successful aquariums view their shops as extensions of the visitor's exhibit experience. Shops are stocked and decorated in ways that stimulate browsing and create an amusing, interactive experience, regardless of whether one buys anything.

Most purchases extend the enjoyment and learning of the aquarium visit to the purchaser's experience after leaving the aquarium. The best aquariums ensure that even trivial items have educational value, either by their inherent content or by the informative tags attached to them. The best shops are managed by the institution itself, with considerable collaboration provided to shop management by educators, curators, and exhibit designers. Some aquarium professionals are concerned that new aquariums will relinquish their retail operations to unrelated commercial concessionaires. They believe this risks the loss of the educational and exhibit content of a shop and its inventory at the expense of added profits.

It is interesting to compare the inventory of a shop in a major American aquarium with its Japanese counterparts. Some, like Tokyo Sea Life Park, have very similar gift inventories. This institution has established a collegial arrangement with the Monterey Bay Aquarium for mutual assistance in research, collection, and staff training. So it is no accident that the Tokyo shop carries posters, T-shirts, and books featuring animals of Monterey Bay.

The Toba Aquarium has a large section of its retail space devoted to all manner of seafood items—dried squid, frozen crab, sliced tuna—most of which, in living form, are on view in exhibit tanks!

Philip Henry Gosse would probably be delighted with the shop at the Shima Aquarium. It features a section of home aquarium equipment—tanks, filters, lights, fish food—and books on aquarium keeping.

Architect's rendering of the interior mezzanine of the Tennessee Aquarium. (Courtesy Cambridge Seven Associates.)

2. From Fishbowl to Contained Ocean: The Technology and Design of Aquarium Systems and Exhibits

"The life of the sea has ever had a peculiar interest to people of every class and calling. The strange and bright-colored fishes, the sea stars and anemones, the rich forests of seaweeds, the ghostly and luminous jellyfishes, introduce to their observers a submerged world which bears with it every charm of the unreal and unknown."

—Bashford Dean, American scientist (1896)

To introduce observers to the submerged world within the constraints of a building (or even in an outside exhibit), and to do so in a convincing and natural manner, requires an impressive combination of art, science, technology, and craft. Of course, all visitors know intellectually that although the animals and plants are genuine and natural, they are looking at a contrived habitat—or do they? Surveys at the Monterey Bay Aquarium strongly suggest that many visitors are convinced that the windows of the large kelp-community exhibit provide a view into the bay that laps the building's pilings. Such a convincing success results not only from the quality

of the exhibitry but also from the fortunate location of the building. Other sites, in busy harbors, for example, require the willing suspension of the visitor's disbelief for an exhibit to be effective.

Such willingness depends heavily on design and technology. The carelessly or incompletely constructed exhibit risks looking fake and unnatural and creates discomfort and dissatisfaction in the viewer. Yet when skillfully realized, an aquarium exhibit can inspire, move, inform, and amuse.

In many ways, the windows to nature that invite an adventure in the "rich forests of seaweeds" are the essential secret to a modern aquarium's success. These magnificently expansive viewports through which millions of aquarium visitors view giant kelp, whale sharks, chambered nautiluses, and the grand diversity of ocean life, are now made of acrylic plastic—polymethyl methacrylate.

Designers have long struggled to demand the best results from their materials. Long before acrylic windows were developed, Bashford Dean reported on the aquariums of Europe in 1896. He admired the "cunning builders" of one aquarium who had taken pains to have the waterline higher than the windowlike opening of the tank, so that the water surface aided the effect. The eye of the visitor at a lower plane than the surface looked upward at the totally reflected images of the forms below. Dean also observed that the glass fronts of the aquariums were not "exceedingly large" in his turn-of-the-century judgment. He described their height as rarely more than 4 or 5 feet—a dimension dictated by the "danger of breakage through water pressure."

In contrast, Dean described the "great height" of the tanks at the Trocadero Aquarium in Paris, where, he said, "the water measures over 12 feet, giving a depth which results in enormous pressure upon the glass fronts of the aquaria. This dangerous strain, however, has been cleverly counterbalanced: instead of attempting to employ a [single] large plate of glass to resist the water pressure, the designers have prudently broken the front of the tank into a series of stouter panes, whose outlines are larger above, smaller below, framed massively by log-shaped beams of iron."

Although glass is still used in smaller windows, it is too heavy, color-flawed, and brittle to be used in the sizes and shapes that modern aquariums require. The commercial development of the clear plastic material that provides the wide and high view-windows through which to observe the sea began with more prosaic animals—dogs and cattle. The chemical and manufacturing techniques to produce these clear views into the ocean had their origin around 1900 in the collaboration of Otto Röhm, a chemist, and Otto Haas, a businessman. In 1901 Otto Röhm graduated from the University of Tübingen after completing his doctoral dissertation on acrylic acid and its derivatives. Before he had the opportunity to apply his doctoral work on acrylics, however, he became preoccupied with a more practical problem, an odor emanating from a tannery near the Stuttgart gasworks.

The tanning of animal hides is one of the oldest industries (perhaps even older than maintaining fish in ponds). But procedures used in 1904 were still those of ancient times. Röhm sought a reliable odorless synthetic substitute for the smelly fermented dog manure that was an essential ingredient in the traditional tanning process. The resulting successful new chemical products, and the organizational and marketing skills of Haas (working in both Germany and America), formed the basis of the Röhm and Haas companies.

By the 1920s the two colleagues had diversified their product lines and sought new markets. Röhm resumed his early work on acrylic-acid products. Early uses focused on the improvement of automobile glass through lamination, resulting in

The now-famous Giant Kelp exhibit, hallmark of the Monterey Bay Aquarium, was a marvelous innovation in 1985 when it began to grow to maturity. Although aquarists since the days of Gosse had maintained live algae in small aquariums, no one had ever re-created an entire California kelp-bed ecosystem with the hundreds of species that live within it. Many visitors liken the experience of standing before this marvelous display to standing in the apse of a cathedral and looking through the stained-glass windows. (Courtesy Monterey Bay Aquarium.)

shatterproof "safety glass." Eventually, in 1932, Röhm produced the first "organic glass," which in 1936 was given the trade name of Plexiglas. Both the Röhm and Haas firm in Philadelphia and the factory in Darmstadt, Germany, continued work on the new plastic. In 1941 the American Röhm and Haas company sold $4.5 million worth of Plexiglas to the U.S. military aircraft industry for airplane canopies. Today the companies they founded continue to be major manufacturers of industrial chemicals, including acrylic plastic.

Meanwhile, the duPont Chemical Company patented its acrylic plastic as Lucite, which also served the World War II military aircraft market. In Japan, Mitsubishi Industries had learned of the technique through the Germans and was using acrylic plastic in its aircraft. Warplanes on all sides of the conflict during World War II incorporated acrylic plastics in windshields and canopies for weaponry platforms. The material was lighter than glass, had superior optical characteristics, and was almost shatterproof. After the war, in 1946, Plexiglas sales plummeted without the demands of the military.

But new uses would be found for the materials—including aquariums. As aquarium tanks increase in depth, the pressure on the tank walls increases. The deeper the tank, the thicker the window needs to be. Polished plate and tempered glass were traditionally used for aquarium windows, but these materials are extremely heavy. A tank 10 feet deep, for example, would need glass 3 inches thick. It would weigh many tons, and would be prohibitively expensive.

In 1960, at Marineland of Florida, the first American "organic glass," or acrylic polymer, windows were installed. Gradually, aquarists and architects came to realize the advantages of this relatively lightweight substance, which had far better optical qualities than glass. But, best of all, it promised larger viewing windows for their visitors.

Until the late 1960s, however, stock sizes of commercial acrylic were limited to less than an inch in thickness. Then, two companies—in very different ways—developed the capability of manufacturing the 4- to 24-inch-thick panels that make possible the huge expanses of viewing windows used in today's aquariums.

In Japan, Mitsubishi Rayon, producers of Shinkolite plastic, began to make large thick sheets from liquid acrylic by thermocasting—pouring liquid plastic into molds and then heating them until the plastic is cast into a rigid form. The resulting sheets are laminated together to build thickness. Although the laminations are clearly visible from the ends of the sheet, the view through the window is perfectly clear and without flaw, and the sheets are amazingly strong. During the construction of the Aquarium of the Americas in New Orleans, a 30-by-15-foot panel weighing more than 10 tons was accidentally dropped by the crane that was lowering the window into place when a lifting cable snapped. Almost miraculously, no one was injured as the plastic monolith shattered into thousands of pieces. None of the breaks occurred between lamination points! The window shattered as if it were a single plate.

The major American supplier, Reynolds Polymer Technology, chooses to increase thickness by using thicker casting molds rather than by laminating several sheets together. Its techniques of forming, which are accomplished in special molds within large curing ovens, are proprietary and are based in part on processes developed by an artist—California sculptor Bruce Beasley, who combined technology and art to bring the ocean inland. In 1967, the 27-year-old Beasley had already developed a worldwide reputation for his monumental metal sculptures—huge, abstract constructions of bronze and aluminum. Then he abruptly became interested in acrylic plastic. "I was thinking about transparency," Beasley explained. "I was having fantasies about sculpture where you could see the back side at the same time you could see the front."

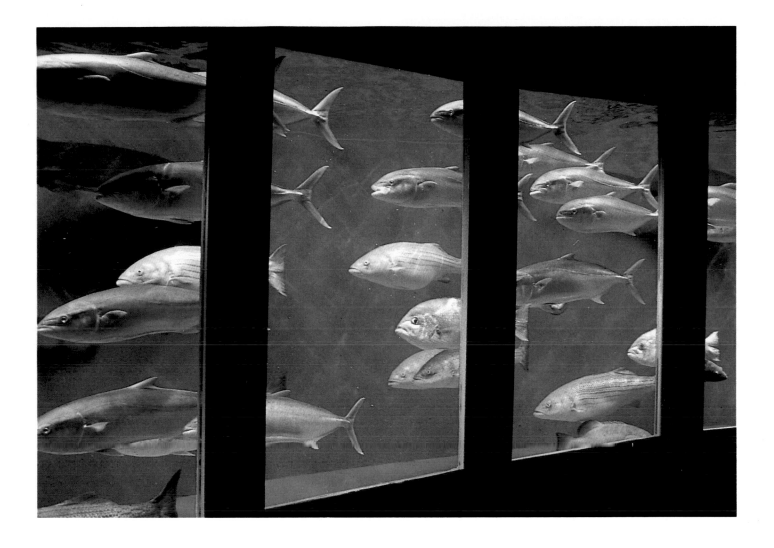

Glass, heavy, plastic only at high temperatures, and subject to shattering, was not a practical material. But acrylic plastic, with its fine transparency, practical durability, and relatively light weight, seemed the ideal material for clear sculpture. Beasley was faced with one problem: no one had managed to cast a piece of material more than a foot thick without introducing bubbles and other defects that spoiled the plastic's transparency.

Working methodically, casting various combinations of liquid plastic and melted acrylic pellets, Beasley experimented with mixtures in large ovens at temperatures reaching 350°F. Eventually he hit upon the satisfactory combination that solved many problems, including the primary challenging feature of acrylic, its tendency to shrink 15 to 20 percent during heat casting.

Using his newly developed and patented technique, Beasley sculpted and cast for the state of California the 13,000-pound free-form acrylic monument *Apolymon* that now stands before the state building in Sacramento. This beautiful abstract sculpture appears to be a huge ocean wave arrested in midcrest on the shore of the ancient lake bed of inland California. As one admirer in the dedication-day crowd in 1969 exclaimed, "They have brought the ocean to Sacramento."

This was an unwittingly prophetic remark because soon afterward, Beasley collaborated with the U.S. Navy to design submarine viewports, and also licensed Reynolds Polymer Technology to use his casting techniques commercially. The company has modified the artist's recipes to fit the commercial scale needed to produce major aquarium windows throughout the world. Today Reynolds advertises cast acrylic

Transparent tunnels fabricated of curved acrylic panels invite aquarium visitors to walk along the bottom of the sea surrounded by marine life, as shown here at the Niigata Aquarium, Japan. (Photo by Leighton Taylor.)

At the Oregon Coast Aquarium visitors enjoy the same view that a scuba diver would have in the adjacent harbor (although the water is probably clearer in the aquarium). (Photo by Chuck Forinash, Oregon Coast Aquarium.)

blocks up to 24 inches thick and panels as large as 26 by 10 feet by 15 inches thick. The edges of these single-cast sheets can be welded together using chemical glues and heat to form even larger clear expanses without the intrusion of metal or concrete beams, called *mullions*. Mullions support transparent panels whether they are in a house window or an aquarium. The number and placement of mullions are dictated by the material strength of the window. Relatively weak materials, like glass, need a lot of support. Strong, lightweight materials like acrylic can be bonded in ways that preclude the need for mullions.

The latitude afforded designers by these new techniques is vividly demonstrated by comparing the aquariums built within the span of just a few years. In 1979, when the Steinhart Roundabout opened in San Francisco's Golden Gate Park, large acrylic windows were not yet in common use. Hence, this first large-volume doughnut-shaped tank developed for fast-swimming fishes was constructed of 36 glass windows supported by concrete mullions. And when the Seattle Aquarium opened in 1979, a major exhibit feature was the AquaDome, designed to give the visitor a view of what it would be like to stand on the bottom of Puget Sound adjacent to the aquarium and be surrounded by native marine life. The architect-designer included the concrete window mullions of this novel tank as a strong design element.

Within a few short years of the opening of the Seattle Aquarium, designers were providing visitors with underwater pathways inside totally mullion-free transparent tunnels. In 1989, when the Tokyo Sea Life Park exhibit opened, acrylic fabrication had reached the point where the tank was completely circular and lacking mullions. Today's acrylic technology provides the next best thing to being wet. In the New York Aquarium's Discovery Cove, such clear acrylic panels are used to simulate the

experience of standing beneath a breaking wave. Children especially delight in crouching dry and secure beneath an overhead plastic panel, with hundreds of gallons of water rushing over their heads.

Behind the scenes, too, advances in plastic technology make possible today's large and naturalistic exhibits. Polyvinyl chloride (PVC) provides the circulatory system of every modern aquarium, replacing the piping that was once made from concrete, asbestos, and even cast iron. Corrosion of metallic materials is a major problem in aquariums, especially those with large saltwater exhibits. To walk behind the scenes of an unremodeled aquarium is to see a great spectacle of corrosion and rust. Few aquariums built in the last 10 years have any metal parts in evidence behind the scenes. Ladders and walkway grids are fabricated from plastic. Sturdy nylon nuts and bolts hold plastic structural beams together. Injection-molded polyethylene shades house powerful lights whose filaments admittedly still depend on metal parts as well as the electricity-conducting wire that serves them.

Even metal that is out of sight can do damage in an aquarium. The steel reinforcing bars used to give strength to cast-concrete tanks, walls, and floors are now

Two secrets to the success of the big central tank at the Osaka Ring of Fire Aquarium are plenty of light and easy access for aquarists. This behind-the-scenes view shows the surface of the open-ocean exhibit. (Photo by Leighton Taylor.)

covered with plastic and tied with special plastic wires before concrete is poured. Unshielded reinforcing bars, in common use in aquarium construction 20 years ago, are subject to corrosion even when embedded in concrete. Poorly cured concrete or (inevitably) cracked concrete admits saltwater to the unprotected surfaces of the steel bars. As the steel bars corrode and rust, they expand in diameter, and this in turn creates even larger cracks in the concrete and hastens corrosion. This process, called *spalling,* can literally crack an aquarium building apart.

The whole class of plastic products known as Fiberglas (actually plastic materials reinforced with various kinds of fibers) has also opened up a raft of improved exhibit techniques and structural methods. The simulated rocks and reef structures in many aquariums are crafted from Fiberglas-reinforced concrete (called FRC in the trade) by using latex molds taken from actual rock surfaces. This method permits extremely realistic exhibitry. The technique is not limited to rocks but can be used for trees, sand, or any natural surface. These lightweight, waterproof materials support the naturalism of exhibits while taking up little space and adding insubstantial weight to the floor loading of exhibit spaces.

If PVC pipes provide the arteries of aquariums' life-support systems, then pumps are the heart and filters are the kidneys. Large modern aquariums depend on electric pumps with noncorrosive impellers (the parts of the pump that force the water into a pipe) capable of moving huge quantities of water per time period. Any aquarium, small or large, hosting a substantial amount of living material (called *biomass* by aquarium biologists), must recirculate the water at least once every hour or hour and a half. In a small aquarium, say one that holds 200 gallons of water, this means having a pump that can move three gallons a minute. In an exhibit the size of the Aquarium of the Americas' Gulf of Mexico tank, which holds some 500,000 gallons, this means having a pump—or series of pumps—that can move 3,000 gallons of water a minute. Such pumps also require pipes 12 to 14 inches in diameter—large enough to require safety screening so that animals and aquarists are not sucked into them! Depending on the type of water system an aquarium uses, this water either leaves the aquarium and is replaced by new water or recirculates through mechanical filters. These are usually huge plastic-lined steel chambers or spun Fiberglas vessels containing sand, which remove particles of waste material and food.

Biological filtration of recirculated aquarium water can be provided in a number of ways, all of which require what aquarium biologists call *biological filters.* Biological filtration is a complex process, but briefly it is the organic removal of potentially toxic chemicals like nitrites and ammonia that result from the waste products of living animals. A variety of kinds of bacteria, considered "good" bacteria by aquarium biologists, are capable of removing these chemicals from the water system. Such bacteria live on the surface of sand or other large particles. Thus, biological filter beds might be located on the sandy floor of an aquarium or within a filter chamber. Aquarium designers provide large grids with screens so that the oxygen-loving bacteria can grow into huge colonies. The recirculating water comes from the mechanical filters and flows up through these biological filters. In very large tanks, aquarium designers might also provide separate chambers filled with small high-surface-area plastic nodules, often called *bioballs,* which provide surface area for the bacteria to live on.

Depending on where an aquarium is located, it might have one of three kinds of water systems—open, closed, or semiclosed. An open system, sometimes called a *pump and dump* system, requires a nearby source of high-quality water—usually seawater. Such a system is therefore limited to aquariums like the Monterey Bay Aquarium, the Waikiki Aquarium, the Oregon Coast Aquarium, and other institutions located adjacent to reliably clean water. Incoming seawater is filtered, flows through exhibit tanks, and is then returned—directly or indirectly, depending on the permitting agencies in the area—to the environment. After passing through the aquarium, the water is essentially indistinguishable from water containing the same animals in the natural environment.

Sometimes water quality is unreliable and aquariums design their systems so that an open system can be recirculated. The intake of water is shut off, and the water in the system is recirculated through filters, just as in a closed-system aquarium. This is often used and is called a semiclosed system. A major advantage of open and semi-closed systems is the access to "live seawater," that is, seawater that contains microscopic organisms, larvae, and food for filter-feeding animals on display. The disadvantage of living seawater is that these same organisms can settle on the interior walls of aquarium piping and create *biofouling* or "hardening of the arteries." Such biofouling clogs aquarium piping. To guard against this, most open-system aquariums have double supply lines. This permits periodic cleaning of one of the two lines while the other continues to provide water.

The Monterey Bay Aquarium, for example, regularly schedules cleaning of the aquarium pipes with an unusual tool called a "pig." This is a plastic projectile equal in size to the interior diameter of the pipe. The pipe to be cleaned must first sit dormant for a week or so, so that the biofouling will begin to loosen from its attachments. The projectiles are loaded into the pipe, just as a cartridge is loaded into a gun. The pipe is pressurized; the outside end of the pipe is then opened and the "pig" shoots through the pipe like a bullet down a rifle barrel, spinning and cleaning the inside surface of the pipe. It pops out on the ocean side of the pipe and is retrieved by aquarists in a boat. Biological material that flushes out of the pipe is harmless and becomes part of the organic cycle of the food chain.

Aquariums with totally closed systems are those far removed from the sea or from a source of good, clean seawater. Even harbor-side aquariums usually use closed systems because of the polluted nature of the adjacent water. Most closed systems now use artificial seawater made from filtered and dechlorinated city-system water added to blends of salt that simulate ocean water. Before it began to use artificial seawater, the Shedd Aquarium in Chicago, on the shores of salt-free Lake Michigan, relied on open-ocean seawater from the Florida coast. Once a year, barges filled with such water would be tugged up the Mississippi River to the Shedd Aquarium, where the fresh seawater would be added to the closed system and the year-old seawater flushed from the exhibit tanks.

Such a method of importation was used by Philip Henry Gosse, who wrote in 1854, "The purity of the seawater is of great importance. In London, seawater may be easily obtained by giving a trifling fee to the master or steward of any of the steamers that ply beyond the Thames, charging him to dip seawater from the clear open bed." Such a source was apparently not always satisfactory because Gosse was led to develop his own recipe for artificial seawater. But regardless of the source of water, no aquarium is totally closed, and every aquarium must periodically add "make-up water" to account for loss by evaporation, spillage, and the backwashing of filters.

Like many other species in the wrasse family, individuals of Coris gaimard *begin life as females. As an individual fish matures, she transforms into a functional male with the distinctive color pattern shown here. Ichthyologists first learned of such transformations by observing aquarium life.* (Photo by John E. Randall.)

3. Who Feeds the Fish?: Economic and Management Issues

"Yet the true measure of our success is not solely how many people come, but how many leave with a greater awareness of the wealth of life our oceans hold. For only through this awareness will the oceans rise to the forefront of world conservation efforts where they belong."

—Julie Packard, director, Monterey Bay Aquarium (1992)

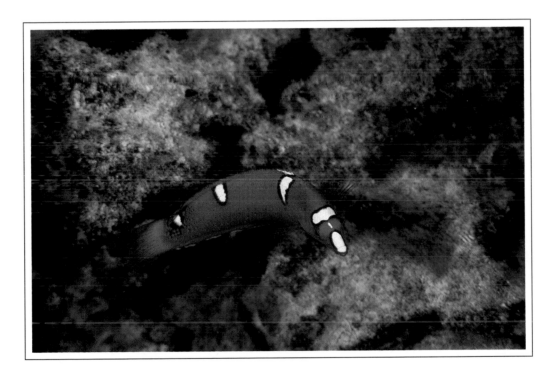

I n the United States, the range of organizational structures for aquariums covers a full scope of types of governance, from commercial, profit-making corporations to private, nonprofit, tax-exempt organizations. But there is a dominant trend for aquariums, which are, after all, institutions with significant social influence, to have at least a nominal dedication to educational goals. There also seems to be a strong positive correlation between success and commitment to an educational mission, which undergirds any entertainment value.

Sea World, Inc., for example, is now owned by a branch of the Anheuser Busch Company, which purchased the marine theme parks from the publishing firm of Harcourt Brace Jovanovich. Sea World's original corporate ownership (publicly traded as

Aquarium visitors unfamiliar with the diversity of life on a coral reef sometimes refuse to believe that this purple sea squirt is a real animal and not an artificial decoration. (Photo by Thomas Kelly, Waikiki Aquarium.)

As aquarium biology advances, more and more species of invertebrates (such as these feather duster worms) will be displayed and cultured. (Photo by Thomas Kelly, Waikiki Aquarium.)

Making eye contact with an octopus is only one of the many meaningful experiences offered by aquariums. (Photo by Thomas Kelly, Waikiki Aquarium.)

Sea World, Inc.) created the Hubbs-Sea World Research Foundation at the first site in San Diego, for scientific investigations on marine animals, and established a strong and active educational program. Under various owners, the park's educational mission has seemed to falter, but it now seems to be strengthening again.

In Hawaii the founders of commercially operated Sea Life Park recognized the value of a nonprofit alliance for research and education. The present owners still lease the land on which the aquarium-oceanarium is located from a research foundation established by the park's founders, Taylor A. Pryor and Karen Pryor. The original research arm is now the independent Oceanic Institute, an international center for aquacultural research.

City governments in the United States have traditionally operated the country's zoos. This practice has a few counterparts in aquariums. Probably the foremost example is the Seattle Aquarium, run by the parks department of the city of Seattle. There are also three American aquariums supported in part by state universities: the Waikiki Aquarium is a department of the University of Hawaii; the Scripps Aquarium is part of the University of California's Scripps Institution of Oceanography; and the Aquarium at the Hatfield Marine Science Center is associated with Oregon State University, and is also a cooperating institution with the neighboring nonprofit Oregon Coast Aquarium.

The usual form of governance for nonprofit aquariums is operation by a public-spirited yet private nonprofit corporation. Such organizations are sometimes called *501-C-3s,* after that section of the Internal Revenue Service's regulations that grants them tax-exempt status because of their educational goals and the restrictions on the use of any surplus revenue. They are administered by a volunteer board of directors (or governors, or trustees), who in turn hire a paid chief executive officer (usually called the executive director; sometimes called the president). This executive, in turn, is responsible for hiring and managing the rest of the paid staff and volunteers.

Over the last two decades, the trend for most cultural institutions in the United States has been to "earn their own way." Facilities that once offered unlimited free admission to the public now charge admission fees. These might be as low as an aggressively solicited "suggested donation" or as high as a substantial adult ticket price that far exceeds the cost of a first-run motion picture at the city's highest-priced theater. The high attendance at most aquariums suggests that people are willing to pay such prices for a satisfying aquarium visit that is both entertaining and educational.

Increased competition for public attention and decreased support from city, state, and federal governments have caused museums of all types, aquariums included, to be more aggressive in marketing and fund-raising. Modern aquariums actually advertise, an action unheard of and even frowned upon in nonprofit aquarium and museum circles less than 20 years ago. For example, a recent issue of *Sunset,* a popular national home and travel magazine, included a double-page color advertisement for the Monterey Bay Aquarium's special exhibit on jellyfish. These successful ads (as measured by increased attendance) also had significantly high educational content and even managed to state the mission of the aquarium: "to stimulate interest, increase knowledge, and promote the stewardship of Monterey Bay and the world's ocean environment through innovative exhibits, public education and scientific research."

A significant part of the operating budget of nonprofit aquariums now supports marketing departments and development departments (responsible for fund-raising and philanthropic prospecting), as well as travel programs that involve aquarium staff members who lead educational expeditions around the world. Once popular (but now considered ethically questionable by many professionals) were "collecting ex-peditions" on which amateur scuba divers joined aquarium biologists to collect spec-imens for shipment and display. Because such collecting requires skill and is likely to be environmentally sensitive, it is best left to trained collectors familiar with the biology of the sought-after animals and the local customs of the collecting area.

State and city governments have proven less adept at management of aquariums, and the granting of operating funds can vary markedly from year to year. This is understandably due to the multitude of concerns of government agencies, their shift-ing priorities, and the increasing demand to meet basic social needs in our cities. There is a demonstrated risk for a government to use a popular aquarium that pro-duces a surplus of revenues as a source of funds for other programs that lack earning power. While such a practice can temporarily lessen budget crises, it eventually results in the diminishment of an aquarium's quality and success, with consequent drops in attendance and admission revenues.

Admittedly, this robbing of Peter (the patron of fishes) to pay Paul (the patron of far-flung congregations) happens in corporate-owned facilities as well. When the highly popular aquariums of Sea World (in Ohio, Florida, Texas, and California) were owned by Harcourt Brace Jovanovich (HBJ), this extensive publishing corporation was ridden with debt from a successful defensive attempt to stave off a corporate takeover. Payments on the resulting heavy debt forced the corporation to redirect funds earned by the popular aquariums to meet debt service. HBJ eventually sold off the valuable aquarium park properties to Anheuser Busch, a leisure-oriented company with related management experience from operating Busch Gardens (formerly Cy-press Gardens) as a successful animal theme park. Under its present corporate own-ership, the parks have refocused on their mission of entertainment blended with marine education.

In contrast, cultural institutions in most European countries and Japan are the beneficiaries of strong and consistent support from public funds. For example, the Osaka Ring of Fire Aquarium and the Nagoya Aquarium are run by their cities' port authorities. Tokyo Sea Life Park is administered indirectly by the Tokyo metropolitan government through the Ueno Zoological Society. There is also a strong tradition of for-profit aquariums in Japan. For decades, railway companies have built and operated aquariums as a way to encourage holiday travel and determine the siting of destina-tion vacation resorts. Examples include the Niigata, Toba, and Hakone aquariums.

An unusual example of a commercially run Japanese aquarium is the Sunshine Aquarium, located in the Sunshine Metro Shopping Center, a complex of high-rise buildings hosting principally commercial and retail spaces. Here, on the tenth and eleventh floors of the complex, 85,000 square feet are devoted to the display of aquatic life. Exhibited species include sea otters, Commerson's dolphins, a variety of large sharks, bottlenose dolphins, and more than a thousand kinds of fish and inver-tebrates. Visitors sometimes marvel at the multi-story escalator ride necessary to reach the exhibitry in the aquariums designed by Cambridge Seven (including the National Aquarium in Baltimore and the Osaka Ring of Fire Aquarium), but at Sunshine Aquar-ium, a visitor must take a ten-story elevator trip to begin a tour.

Europe has a strong tradition of government support for cultural institutions, including aquariums, zoos, ballet companies, and art museums. In addition, there have long been successful privately funded and operated aquarium institutions in Europe. The early Brighton Aquarium, which opened in the English seaside resort in 1872 after three years of construction, was originally a private enterprise. It was de-veloped by a Mr. Edward Birch, an "English engineer of note," who organized a stock

One measure of an aquarium's strength is the ability to host successful reproduction. Green sea turtles like these (Chelonia mydas) mate at special spawning grounds in tropical seas. Female turtles journey long distances to lay their eggs at the same beaches where they once hatched. (Photo by George Balazs.)

Hundreds of sea turtles have been born over the past decade at Oahu's Sea Life Park. Research has shown that the temperatures at which eggs develop affect the sex ratio of the clutch, or group of eggs. (Photo by George Balazs.)

Hawaiian monk seals are among the rarest marine animals in the world. Biologists are working with male monk seals at the Waikiki Aquarium as part of a recovery program for the species under the Federal Endangered Species Act. (Photo by Thomas Kelly, Waikiki Aquarium.)

NOTICE TO THOSE WHO EAT TUNA

The tuna which we serve is not Yellowfin Tuna -- it is any of several other delicious kinds of tuna or albacore. Each year, thousands of dolphins die while Yellowfin Tuna are being caught in nets, a practice that we are strongly against and must be stopped.

When aquariums are dedicated to inspiring stewardship for nature, they must ensure that this commitment pervades every aspect of their enterprise, from the café to the classroom. (Photo by Leighton Taylor.)

These entry banners at Japan's Toba Aquarium use the popularity of sea otters to announce the aquarium's commitment to environmental awareness. (Photo by Leighton Taylor.)

company with a capital of $400,000. More recently, the Genoa (Italy) Aquarium, which opened in 1992, is operated by a joint venture of the American design firm Cambridge Seven Associates (operating through a related company named IDEA, for International Design for the Environment Associates) and an Italian investor group, with site-leasing contracts from the Genoa government and national funding. The Berlin Aquarium is now another excellent example of a government-supported institution, founded by a private company in 1869 and recently renovated with government funding.

In the United States there are numerous successful combinations of nonprofit management in various kinds of partnerships with governments, usually municipal. A good model of a private nonprofit management has been the New England Aquarium. This tax-exempt corporation was initially funded by the philanthropy of investors with financial interests in the adjacent harbor-front developments in the Haymarket and Fanueil Hall commercial areas. The tax-exempt New England Aquarium Corporation purchased its site and with additional philanthropic support built and staffed the facility.

The New England Aquarium's success in aiding the redevelopment of Boston's waterfront stimulated the city government of Baltimore to build a similar aquarium, planned in part to encourage commercial and recreational development of a decayed harbor side. Rather than operate it as a municipal institution, then-Mayor William Donald Schaefer encouraged the formation of the private nonprofit Baltimore Aquarium Society. This corporation owns and operates the aquarium under a formal agreement with the city. The model is being followed in Charleston for the South Carolina Aquarium, scheduled to open in 1996.

An interesting twist on the combination of philanthropy and government support is found at the Steinhart Aquarium, which opened in 1923, in San Francisco. In 1917 philanthropist Ignatz Steinhart agreed to underwrite the cost of the new aquarium as part of the existing California Academy of Sciences, a natural history museum in Golden Gate Park operated privately (with a public-service mission) on city parkland. Steinhart imposed a strong condition for his multimillion-dollar gift: he would underwrite the construction costs only if the city committed itself to perpetual support of the annual operating costs of the proposed aquarium. Steinhart was not satisfied with the promises of bureaucrats; he insisted on an addition to the city charter—he wanted it in writing. To this day the private, nonprofit California Academy of Sciences receives a significant annual operating contribution to the aquarium from the city's budget.

Like its counterparts in the United States, the Vancouver Aquarium, in British Columbia, Canada, is a private society with a public commitment. The aquarium is a tenant of the park board of the city of Vancouver. While it owns the aquarium buildings, exhibits, and support facilities, the society requires the approval of the city park board for any expansion or significant building changes, and even for adjustments in the admission price. Recent public concern and resulting political interest have caused the Vancouver Aquarium to adjust its policies in regard to marine mammals. This careful and studious preparation for aquarium policy is detailed in a very interesting 1992 document entitled *Values and Visions* (see bibliography).

Because of the commercial success of operations such as Marine World Africa USA and Sea World, and the economic (if tax-exempt) success of nonprofit aquariums, there is growing interest among developers in commercial aquariums. The West Edmonton Mall in Alberta, Canada, features a huge aquarium (2 million gallons) for the interest of shoppers. The new mega–shopping center planned for Minneapolis includes an aquarium. The Mirage Hotel and Gambling Casino in Las Vegas, Nevada, features bottlenose dolphins in what is advertised as an "educational context."

Based on the success of an eccentric but masterful commercial aquarium development in Auckland, New Zealand, two separate companies have begun to install "underwater worlds" in a variety of commercial centers. The first Underwater World in Auckland is a very successful tourist attraction in that charming city. The late Kelly Tarleton conceived a novel use for an abandoned (and full) set of settling tanks formerly used by the city sewage system. Tarleton set about mucking out the chambers, developed an innovative way to shape sheets of acrylic plastic, and installed an underwater tunnel on the floor of the empty sewage tanks. With the help of many colleagues (including John Rupp, now curator at the Point Defiance Zoo and Aquarium in Tacoma, Washington, and John Hewitt, now the director of the Aquarium of the Americas in New Orleans), Tarleton developed a water circulation system and stocked the new aquarium with New Zealand marine life. It has proven to be a great tourist attraction since its opening in 1980.

In the United States, commercial facilities based on this concept have been announced for Pier 39 in San Francisco, Santa Monica Pier, and a variety of shopping centers throughout the country. From an aquarium professional's point of view, there is a litmus test for the quality of these attractions: Is their purpose (the intent that justifies their holding of animals in artificial circumstances) to educate visitors and to learn from the organisms they host, or is their motive principally economic, tantamount to investment in such tourist attractions as auto museums and multiplex theaters?

Whether commercial or nonprofit, aquariums are expensive enterprises to operate. Even a relatively small aquarium (in terms of its annual attendance of 350,000 people) like the Waikiki Aquarium has an annual operating budget of almost $2 million, or an expenditure of approximately $5.75 per visitor. At the larger Monterey Bay Aquarium (with an annual attendance of about 1.79 million people), the annual operating budget is almost $26 million.

While visitors might be considered the most important people to walk through the doors of an aquarium, many a salaried staff member would suggest that the *second* most important group consists of the volunteer members of the staff. Volunteers are vital to the operation of nonprofit aquariums. If all of the people who donate their time to American aquariums were added up, they would number in the thousands. The Monterey Bay Aquarium alone, for example, has more than 300 people on its volunteer rolls.

The most enlightened aquarium managers consider volunteers as "staff members paid in some currency other than money." Such currency can take several forms: the advantages of training, appreciation and recognition, job satisfaction, and the opportunity to be involved in special activities, from shark collecting to dolphin rescues to helping a blind child hold a sea urchin. Just about every salaried job in an aquarium has its unsalaried counterpart, including accountants, fish feeders, and surrogate mothers for sea otters.

Interestingly, one of the more sought-after volunteer jobs at large aquariums seems to be washing windows. But these are special windows—washed from inside the aquarium exhibit while using scuba gear, perhaps with a shark looking over your shoulder. To keep the exhibit views crystal clear, divers must rub every inch of the great acrylic windows clean of algal scum. Such volunteers must be experienced, certified scuba divers. There is a waiting list at Monterey Bay Aquarium to join the 70-person roster of underwater window washers. In Japan, where there is no tradition of volunteerism (as there is in America, dating all the way back to the early nineteenth

At the Toba Aquarium a submarine robot cleans the aquarium windows using rotating white cleaning pads. The shark is apparently indifferent to its mechanical housekeeper. (Photo by Leighton Taylor.)

century, when de Tocqueville wrote of what he deemed our "national characteristic of helping one another"), large windows are cleaned by robots.

The annual dollar value to an aquarium of the time donated by volunteers (even calculated at the minimum wage per hour) can easily exceed $100,000. Thus, to replace volunteers with salaried staff, aquariums would have to increase their operating budgets significantly. Of course, there are costs associated with volunteers. These include the same kind of personnel and record-keeping costs entailed by salaried employees, including the time salaried staff must spend in training and supervising their willing helpers. They may also include the costs of covering volunteers with workers' compensation insurance, a practice increasingly followed by aquariums. Special costs for volunteers cover recognition parties, plaques, uniforms, and tuition for special-classes, as well as outlays for one or more volunteer coordinators, who serve as recruiters, coaches, and personnel officers for volunteers. Volunteers are not free, but they are worth every penny ten times over.

Volunteer service offers many benefits to the individuals who volunteer, including training, the opportunity to try out a job before committing oneself to a career, on-the-job experience, good references for job applications, and access to career openings within the profession even before they are advertised. In fact, a significant number of senior personnel in the aquarium profession began as volunteers.

Most aquariums have special programs for young people—from junior high school through university level—as well as for adult volunteers. If there is an aquarium in your community, you have a wonderful opportunity for an exciting and rewarding experience. Call them up and ask for the volunteer office. You may be teaching kindergartners about jellyfish or hand-feeding sharks within the month.

An extremely important budget element in every aquarium managed by a non-profit organization is income from membership. Not only is the money vital for operational support, but the involvement of community members in the aquarium's programs provides essential social endorsement. In a way, members are the "stockholders" in their aquariums. True, they receive tangible benefits for their contributions: free or reduced admission, newsletters, discounts in the retail shop, special tuition for classes, and first choice for special-event tickets and field trips. Surveys have shown, however, that most members feel they also receive a significant *intangible* member benefit. Members get considerable satisfaction in helping to support a successful institution that is devoted to serving the community and conserving the environment. Such programs can be of significant size. For example, the Monterey Bay Aquarium hosts a membership of 30,000 households, or approximately 90,000 members.

The management of the modern aquarium and the operating budget required are complex. Personnel include biologists with Ph.D. degrees, laboratory technicians, water engineers, gift-shop managers, educational curriculum specialists, librarians, veterinarians, aquarium biologists, security guards, janitors, clerical staff, financial officers, marketing specialists, volunteer coordinators, and all manner of supporting personnel. In addition, budgets include large categories for animal food and care, big electrical bills for lighting and pump operations, and reserve funds for exhibit improvement and research.

The leader of such an institution, usually called the executive director, sometimes the president, must bring a variety of skills to the job. Her or his knowledge must range from plumbing and biology to double-entry bookkeeping and critical-path planning. The director must have the diplomacy and savoir-faire to raise money from wealthy widows, bank presidents, and governmental granting agencies. The leader of an aquarium must be as at home with sharks as with lawyers and politicians. The television news camera and the scuba tank are both tools of the trade for a successful aquarium director.

Such a person is a blend of excellent manager, committed biologist, and educator. With such a combination and diversity of talents being called for, it is not surprising that no two aquarium directors are alike. It might be instructive to meet some examples.

Bill Flynn, the president of the Tennessee Aquarium, is an example of the kind of director who has come up through the practical ranks of the aquarium field back in the days when aquarists were male, wore blue collars, and called themselves "keepers" and "husbandrymen." In an interview held shortly before the opening of the Tennessee Aquarium in April 1992, Bill reviewed his career: "I have been in the aquarium field for quite a long time, beginning back in the 1950s, when I helped build the New York Aquarium in Coney Island. And when I say build, I mean that literally—I was an electrician. After it was finished, I stayed on at the aquarium as a troubleshooter. One day I would work on the pumps and filtration system, and the next I would be called in to look at sick animals. I became fascinated with aquariums and aquatic life. I have been involved with them ever since—at the AquaZoo in Pittsburgh, Sea World in San Diego, and then as deputy executive director of the

National Aquarium in Baltimore, where I oversaw the planning, construction, and stocking of the exhibits. I was there when I was approached to head the new Tennessee Aquarium.

"Here in Chattanooga I have a large interdisciplinary staff working for me. It is important to remember that the aquarium contains more than just fish; it is really a 'life center' that houses all sorts of animals and plant life. There are aquarists, zoologists, biologists, and horticulturists at the aquarium, all working to present the total ecosystem of the Tennessee River accurately.

"The aquarium's aquarists have numerous responsibilities. They help collect the fish that appear in the collection and see that their transition from the natural environment to an artificial one is smooth. They also care for the animals, monitoring water chemistry and diet to ensure that the fish are healthy. The aquarists also help make changes in the exhibits, experimenting with such things as the light admitted to tanks in order to get fish to behave as they would in nature.

"We also have a curator of forests, who is responsible for the day-to-day management of the Appalachian Cove Forest and Mississippi Delta environments. Under him are horticulturists to take care of the plants and herpetologists to look after the reptiles and amphibians. It really is a major undertaking to oversee such complex environments.

"I am convinced that the greatest impact of the Tennessee Aquarium will be in the area of public education. I firmly believe that education offers the best long-term solution to our environmental problems. Everyone who visits the Tennessee Aquarium will leave it having learned something new, and, I feel safe to say, with a new awareness of and reverence for the natural world."

Bruce Carlson, of the Waikiki Aquarium, is an example of an aquarium director formally trained as a marine biologist. Carlson is a scientist who knows the biology of the organisms he exhibits. He is also an accomplished manager and fund-raiser. An older generation of directors like Bill Flynn of Tennessee and Bill Braker of Shedd started in blue collars and moved to their three-piece suits. Carlson started in a wet suit and added a tie. His job requires him to risk shark attack while on a 100-foot dive off the Palau barrier reef and to risk indigestion while promoting his institution as the speaker at a Rotary Club luncheon.

"I started working in museums when I was an undergraduate at the University of Michigan," explains Carlson. "During the school year I worked at the Museum of Zoology, and in the summer at the American Museum of Natural History in New York. After graduation, I spent three years in the Peace Corps in Fiji, helping the University of the South Pacific establish study collections of fish and corals. That's where I really got hooked on the tropics.

"When I came to the University of Hawaii to start my doctoral work on coral-reef biology, I got a part-time job as an aquarist here at Waikiki Aquarium. Part of the 'pay' was a free room—actually more like a crew cabin on a submarine. Maybe that's a bad analogy. I went to sleep every night to the sound of the running water in the tanks; submariners probably wouldn't sleep with that kind of noise. The cabin was partially suspended over a set of the display tanks, and I had to climb a ladder to get to it. There's nothing like sleeping with your fish and shrimp to get to know them.

"At the time, the aquarium was under a long-term program of improvement. The University of Hawaii, of which the aquarium is a department, encouraged graduate students like me to work here. Gradually, some of us moved from student-helper positions to professional appointments. Today at least four of us on the senior staff are former students. This place has been a real training ground. Many of our staff who began as student-helpers have moved on to work at big aquariums on the mainland."

Carlson exemplifies the increasing number of executive directors with scientific backgrounds. Dr. Murray Newman, director of the Vancouver Aquarium, was a pioneer in combining academic training with the business skills of planning, management, fund-raising, public relations, and governmental lobbying. His institution has also benefited from his charisma and visionary leadership. In 1955, when Newman came to Vancouver, after earning degrees at U.C.L.A. and getting his hands wet at Steinhart Aquarium and Marineland of the Pacific, the aquarium was a modest array of fish tanks in Stanley Park. When he retired in 1992, the Vancouver Aquarium was recognized as a premier attraction in Canada, with a distinguished research program (which ranges from sculpins to narwhals, the Amazon to the Arctic) and a treasured program of public education.

As these examples prove, the leadership of a public aquarium of excellence requires a special combination of skills. At least 10 new aquariums will open in North America between 1992 and 2002. It will be a challenge to those institutions to recruit the staff—especially the leaders, the directors—they need to ensure their success. An aquarium director must have more than management skills, although these are essential. Somehow she or he must also have gained a deep and lasting commitment to the real purpose of an aquarium—inspiring its visitors to know and care about the natural world. Often such a commitment begins in graduate school; sometimes through a hobby; sometimes through a related profession like teaching. Wherever it is gained, it is essential.

As Paul van den Sande, curator of the aquarium at the Antwerp, Belgium, zoo and secretary of the European Curators' Union, has said, "Some aquariums are small and local in their audience. They are the chapels teaching the gospel of nature. Others are the grand cathedrals of the region, inspiring congregations to wonder at nature's splendor. We need more chapels, more great cathedrals. Most of all we need people with the call to minister them."

Aquarium biologists have recently researched and refined techniques to maintain and breed pelagic medusae. Jellyfish have become beautiful and popular display animals that support efforts to interpret the challenges of life in the open sea. (Courtesy Monterey Bay Aquarium.)

4. Nature under Glass: Profiles of Special Animals

"The successful maintenance of a seawater aquarium is mostly
witchcraft mixed with a little science. In this book I have
attempted to describe the science, but with the realization that
understanding the witchcraft might be more useful."

—Stephen Spotte in *Seawater Aquariums* (1979)

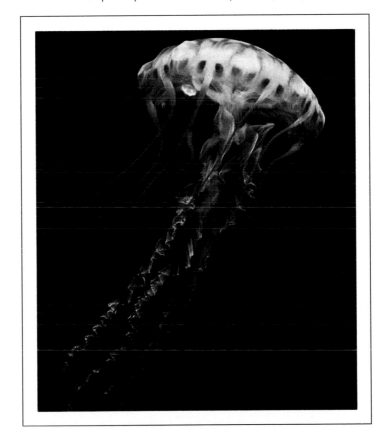

No matter how well designed an aquarium building may be, or how complex the exhibits, or how excellent the quality of any other feature, the vital factor for the success of an aquarium is the standard of care for the plants and animals for which it is responsible. There is no substitute for conscientious and enlightened husbandry—the collection, maintenance, and display of living organisms in a state as close to their natural habitat as possible. In this chapter we will examine some of the practices that excellent aquariums follow, and we will consider a selection of some of the wonderful organisms to which aquariums can be host. Our diverse list ranges from chambered nautiluses and reef corals to sea otters and sharks.

First, it will probably be useful to review some aspects of what people for years have called *animal husbandry*. Although *husbandry* is a well-established term in the aquarium profession, I wish it were not. It connotes activities tantamount to farming and sounds like an exclusively male activity. The women and men who are professional aquarists, who study plants and animals in their natural habitats and continue to study them while they care for them within the aquarium, are serious biologists. I suggest we abandon *husbandry* for the better term *aquarium biology*.

The standards of aquarium biology have increased markedly in recent decades under two major influences: the information learned practically and formally over the years and possessed by the highly educated and trained biologists now working as aquarists; and the external demands of a public with a growing environmental ethic.

In the early days of aquariums, the mere display of an animal was considered success. There is a big difference, however, between the survival of an animal and its truly thriving. P. T. Barnum displayed fish from the Florida keys shipped to his museum in New York by rail. They arrived early in the spring and were usually dead by the first heat wave or the first frost. In his autobiography, Barnum reveals much about his attitudes toward the mission of his "museum" and his standards of animal care, as well as giving us an idea of the variety of his exhibits, way back in the 1860s:

> *I not only procured living sharks, porpoises, sea horses, and many rare fish from the sea in the vicinity of New York, but in the summer of 1861 I dispatched a fishing smack and crew to the Island of Bermuda and its neighborhood, whence they brought scores of specimens of the beautiful "angel fish," and numerous other tropical fish of brilliant colors and unique forms.*
>
> *But as cold weather approached, these tropical fish began to die, and before the following spring they were all gone. I, therefore, replenished this portion of my aquaria during the summer, and for several summers in succession, by sending a special vessel to the Gulf for specimens. These operations were very expensive, but I really did not care for the cost, if I could only secure valuable attractions.*

Reading Barnum's admission now, with an additional century and more of aquarium experience, one is tempted to scold the old showman for his practices. Perhaps they were due in part to his commercial intent, but we must also credit his pioneering persistence in bringing a new view of the natural world to urban New Yorkers.

It is likely that the people directly charged with the care of animals have always taken their responsibilities seriously, even if they were sometimes ill equipped to do so. By 1900 a few of Barnum's former customers may have joined a younger generation in visiting the New York Aquarium, where (as a contemporary observer, Charles Bristol, wrote in *The Century* magazine) dedicated aquarists held "many an anxious consultation over fishes that refuse to eat or that develop some disease and lose their vigor. This one needs a salve for some wound, that one is suffering from some fungous growth."

Already, aquariums were attempting to duplicate natural conditions for their animals. The New York Aquarium, wrote Bristol, was "furnished with a refrigerating-apparatus on the one hand, and a warming apparatus on the other, so that salmon from the icy waters of Maine may feel at home, while the tropical fishes are comfortable in the neighboring tanks."

Nonetheless, emergencies were a part of an aquarist's life. Bristol reported a dedicated response in Manhattan before the turn of the century:

During one winter a heavy snow-storm set in on a Friday, when the stock of coal is usually replenished. The dealer waited for the storm to pass by, but Saturday found the streets impassable and the cold intense. With the utmost economy the coal-supply gave out at midnight on Saturday. To stop the pumps meant death to the whole population [of aquarium animals and plants], and all hands began to collect old lumber and boxes to keep the fires going [in the boilers that provided steam to drive the pumps and other equipment]. Soon after daybreak on Sunday the wood-supply gave out; but fortunately, at this juncture a small load of coal was dragged to the door, and disaster was averted.

One is tempted to think that if the delivery of coal had not come, the aquarists would not have hesitated to throw the director's desk on the boiler fire. Even today, with dependable utilities and well-engineered equipment, the dedication of aquarists is sometimes taxed. At the New England Aquarium in 1978, when a crippling winter storm shut down the city of Boston, the aquarium staff—the director, librarians, secretaries, biologists, and all—stayed overnight to operate emergency equipment and to care for the animals. Obviously, in the Boston, Tokyo, Chicago, or San Francisco of today, as in the New York of the 1890s, aquarium biology is sometimes an around-the-clock job.

Today's responsible aquarists acknowledge that success demands the obligation to provide conditions that guarantee that their multitudes of animals and plants will flourish—and live at least as long as they would in their natural habitat. Measures of such thriving are color, growth, feeding, inter- and intraspecies behaviors, and—best of all—completion of the entire life cycle, from courtship and reproduction to the maturation of aquarium-born young. As our knowledge of natural systems and species biology increases, the aquarium profession achieves more and more successes in maintaining healthy animals and plants and in sustaining communities in the aquarium setting.

Such accomplishments are formally recognized by professional organizations. In North America the American Association of Zoological Parks and Aquariums (AAZPA) annually awards zoos and aquariums with the "Bean Award." In Japan, similar acknowledgment is made by the Japanese Association of Zoological Gardens and Aquariums (JAZGA). (See the accompanying panel.)

This growing success is due to a number of factors. The observation, study, and collection of plants and animals in the wild by the same people who care for them in aquariums is now common owing to the ubiquity of jet air travel and the widespread use of scuba diving for specimen collection. Increased use of artificial seawater permits inland aquariums to keep a much greater variety of animals in higher-quality conditions. (Recall that even in Gosse's day, aquarists used artificial seawater, for which Gosse published a recipe in 1856.) But even today, there is great variation in the quality of this "imitation ocean." More attention needs to be paid to maintaining high standards in the mixing of artificial seawater. There really is no substitute for the real thing.

Early gains in the thriving of animals have understandably been achieved at aquariums near their natural habitats. Examples include the Noumea Aquarium in New Caledonia, the Waikiki Aquarium in Hawaii, the Naples Aquarium in Italy, and the Okinawa Aquarium in Japan. The success of these aquariums has also been due to the quality of the seawater available. Such aquariums use open systems in which fresh seawater is copiously available and waste seawater can be easily disposed. Such aquariums have been historically successful with animals that were easily available.

American Association of Zoological Parks and Aquariums The Edward H. Bean Awards

The Edward H. Bean Award is the highest distinction given to an institution by the American Association of Zoological Parks and Aquariums. It is presented in recognition of efforts by zoological institutions in the management and husbandry of various animal species. The award acclaims the most significant birth or hatching of a full species and/or subspecies or a significant propagation program involving one or more species and/or subspecies.

The AAZPA established the Edward H. Bean Awards in September 1956. Robert Bean, then-director of Chicago's Brookfield Zoo, offered the service of his society in sponsoring the initial award. The awards were named in honor of Edward H. Bean, the first director of the Brookfield Zoo, and are a fitting tribute to this great man. The first award was presented at the AAZPA Annual Conference in 1957 for the birth of "Colo," the world-famous gorilla born at the Columbus Zoological Gardens the previous year.

During the early stages of the Bean Awards, a single award was given, but now the association has expanded the concept of the award to include achievements in several classes of animal life, thereby recognizing the steadily increasing efforts at propagation and the major achievements of our institutions in that regard. The following list is a summary of awards relating to aquarium species.

YEAR OF BIRTH	AQUARIUM	BIRTH/HATCHING OF
1966	New York Zoological Park	Adélie penguin
	Hanna-Barbera Marineland (Marineland of the Pacific)	Bat ray
1970	New York Zoological Park	Tufted puffin
	New York Aquarium	Black piranha
1971	Shark-Quarium, Florida	Bonnethead shark
1973	New England Aquarium	Chain dogfish
1974	New York Zoological Park	North Pacific murre
1975	Belle Isle Aquarium	Freshwater stingray

1978	Hanna-Barbera Marineland (Marineland of the Pacific)	Pacific walrus
	Vancouver Public Aquarium	Wolf eel
1979	Seattle Aquarium	Pacific spiny lumpsucker
	Sea World, Inc. (San Diego)	Penguin propagation program
1980	Vancouver Public Aquarium	Cockscomb prickleback
	Sea World, Inc. (San Diego)	Emperor penguin
1982	Seattle Aquarium	Coho salmon breeding program
	Vancouver Public Aquarium	Marine fishes breeding program
1983	Seattle Aquarium	Giant Pacific octopus
	Sea World, Inc. (San Diego)	King and emperor penguins propagation program
1984	Belle Isle Zoo and Aquarium	Checkerboard stingray propagation program
1985	Sea World of Florida	Killer whale
1986	Sea Life Park	False killer whale
1989	Tulsa Zoological Park	Atlantic spadefish
1990	Waikiki Aquarium	Breeding program for chambered nautiluses

One of the best examples of a Japanese aquarium that has been successful in supporting the reproduction of marine animals in its care is the Okinawa Expo Aquarium. This accomplished institution, which opened in 1975, has received awards from the Japanese Association of Zoological Gardens and Aquariums for reproduction in aquariums of eagle rays, cat sharks, sandbar sharks, whitetip sharks, two species of anemone fish, squid, cuttlefish, and manatees.

Through careful research in both the wild and at aquariums, biologists support the reproduction and rearing of killer whales such as this nursing calf at Sea World of Texas. (Courtesy Sea World of California.)

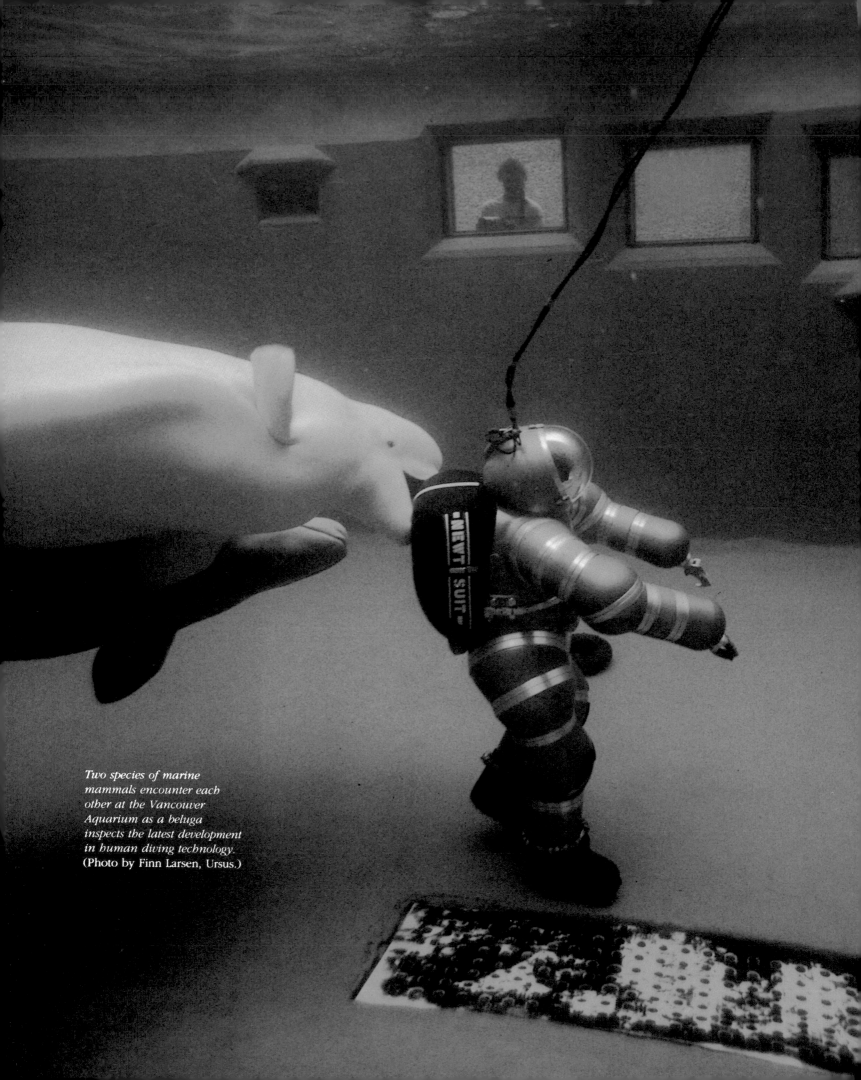

Two species of marine mammals encounter each other at the Vancouver Aquarium as a beluga inspects the latest development in human diving technology. (Photo by Finn Larsen, Ursus.)

Before the Marine Mammal Protection Act was passed in 1973, the collection of such animals was unrestricted. This baby Amazonian manatee (Trichechus inunguis), *held by longtime director of the Steinhart Aquarium, Earl Herald, was rescued by a tourist from a food market in Brazil. After recovering from the fisherman's harpoon wound, "Butterball" lived for 20 years at the San Francisco aquarium.* (Courtesy Steinhart Aquarium–California Academy of Sciences.)

True success was achieved only when conscientious aquarists began to treat all of their animals as if they had been collected at great distance. They now realize that even local animals, although easily replaceable, cannot be considered to be expendable. Each individual animal deserves the best in care and quality of environment. The list of animals that have thrived in aquariums is happily growing and includes some "difficult to keep" species.

Hard lessons about keeping animals healthy and in solving the technical problems of aquarium biology, from pumps to recipes for artificial seawater, have often been solved initially by amateur hobbyists working with a passionate interest. The intensity of this absorption and the sophistication and breadth of knowledge of these individuals are evident in journals and magazines.

American aquarists, professional and amateur, rely, for example, on the monthly magazine *Freshwater and Marine Aquarium*. In fact, colleagues and I have even (formally and academically) described new species of fish in the pages of this widely circulated journal. It has its counterparts in Europe, Japan, and other countries where aquarium biologists want to stay informed about advances in practical biology and new equipment. The pages of such magazines contain everything from ads for freeze-dried antarctic krill to scientific descriptions of new species of reef fishes.

Ironically, there is fear in some circles that such widespread obvious interest will harm the natural environment from which marine animals destined for home aquariums are collected. It is true that the aquarium hobby worldwide is of major importance. In the United States alone, millions of dollars are spent every year on the maintenance of fresh- and saltwater aquariums by hobbyists. Most of this money is spent on freshwater fish, the overwhelming majority the product of fish farms from Asia and South America.

The organisms maintained by home saltwater aquarists, and by some public aquariums that do not collect their own specimens, are collected in the wild using techniques that are sometimes questionable and even irresponsible. The worst offenses are the use of chemicals as collecting aids. The most notorious is potassium cyanide, which results in the immediate death of numbers of fish and invertebrates at the collecting site and the postponed death of captive fish whose livers are irrevers-

Many smaller species of damselfish, like these one-spot damsels (Dascyllus albisella), *congregate over shelter. Some choose coral heads, others sea urchins. Such fish do well in aquariums, especially when fed diets that simulate the tiny planktonic animals they pluck from the water above their refuge.* (Photo by John E. Randall.)

Many species of tropical reef fishes, like these convict surgeonfish (Acanthurus triostegus), *graze on algae from the surface of coral rocks. Such plant-eating species provide important cleaning functions in aquariums.* (Photo by John E. Randall.)

ibly damaged. As long as these surviving fish are not fed, they continue to live. As soon as the fish reach the aquarium and are fed by the eager aquarist, the damaged livers fail to function and the fish die.

Responsible collectors are meticulous in their collection of specimens, using techniques that include hand-netting, barbless hooks, net-covered box traps, and a variety of soft nets. But even specimens that are hand-collected by net-wielding scuba divers can be the victims of environmentally damaging techniques. Impatient and irresponsible collector-divers, for example, may catch fish by breaking up the reef and the coral shelter in which fish try to hide.

Perhaps the most worrisome practice is the wholesale removal of live rocks and coral colonies from natural reef areas. Live coral colonies are removed from the reef, bleached, and sold as aquarium decor. Happily, this practice is becoming far less common now that the manufacture of simulated corals from synthetic materials such as PVC and Fiberglas-reinforced plastic has been achieved. "Live rocks" also enjoy a thriving market because these reef substrates provide diverse micro-communities of algae, invertebrates, and minerals, which are vital to a healthy reef community. Careful management of "live rock" harvesting is essential for reef conservation.

Some people are concerned that the harvest of living specimens for display in aquariums might have deleterious effects that outweigh the value of public education. As in any fishery, proper, enlightened controls are necessary to protect the resource. Certainly the mechanical damage to reefs and the removal of coral colonies and "live rocks," when widespread, can have significant effects. However, the mere harvesting or removal of juvenile or adult reef fish and most invertebrates is unlikely to have a lasting effect if properly managed.

Studies on Hawaiian reefs, initiated because of concern of overfishing by aquarium collectors, have demonstrated that controlled harvesting has very little lasting effect on the standing crop of reef communities. The reproductive potential of a typical individual reef fish, such as a butterflyfish, angelfish, or surgeonfish, numbers in the millions of young. What is limiting on the reef is habitat space—a housing shortage. The removal of adult fish results in the vacancy of habitat space for juveniles.

Conscientious aquarists strive to bring a piece of the natural world to an interested audience. Their ultimate goal is to maintain thriving plants and animals that exhibit health and behavior similar to that found in their natural habitats. Achieving such success takes time, effort, and research, and is reached in stages.

The first stage is the successful collection, transport, and survival in captivity; the second, the ability to provide the highest standards of nutrition, water quality, health care, and living conditions. Growth and healthy appearance are two measures of success, but the best criterion, and the third stage, is successful reproduction. Mating results in the survival of young to adulthood and the subsequent reproduction of these captive-bred progeny. The rearing of mahimahi (a tropical open-ocean relative of the tunas) through 10 generations at the Waikiki Aquarium in Hawaii is a very promising example of such breeding successes. Vancouver Aquarium has also been successful in raising a variety of cold-water fishes.

The conditions under which P. T. Barnum kept his marine animals and their consequent premature deaths would not be tolerated today, either by aquarium professionals or aquarium visitors. Even in institutions such as the Waikiki Aquarium and the Oregon Coast Aquarium, which are located immediately adjacent to rich collecting areas, each local animal is treated with the same care afforded to exotic species imported at significant expense.

In his classic treatise, *The Aquarium: An Unveiling of the Wonders of the Deep Sea,* which is surprisingly modern in its outlook and techniques, Philip Henry Gosse describes in detail the techniques of intertidal and offshore collecting. His quaint prose carries an undertone of the same excitement expressed by today's collectors, who are not hampered in their writing by the elaborate Victorian style of Gosse's time. In considering the title of Gosse's book, note that mid-nineteenth-century biologists considered the "deep sea" to be any depth greater than wading. And despite Gosse's regular use of the masculine pronoun, in his day many young women were avid intertidal collectors. Consider Gosse's advice—and remember it was given 140 years ago:

The time of lowest water on any particular day can be readily ascertained from the local tide-tables; and the young collector, in choosing the locality of his operations, will pay attention to this point beforehand. . . .

I use a wicker basket with a flat bottom and straight sides, divided into compartments. In two of these fit wide-mouthed jars, such, for example, as

Not all reef fishes are active in the daytime. Cardinal fish (Sphaeramia nematoptera) retire to crevices in the reef by day, coming out at night to feed. (Photo by John E. Randall.)

Though these Juvenile sweetlips (Plectorhinchus chaetodontoides) are beautiful, small, and delicately shaped, their specialized diet is difficult to simulate in an aquarium. Responsible aquarists will avoid displaying such species. (Photo by John E. Randall.)

are used for preserves: if made of glass they are the better, as admitting a more ready examination of their contents; but jars of white-ware or stone-ware will do. The larger objects procured are put into these; and I commonly carry also a wide-mouthed phial, such as the chemists keep quinine *in, fitted into a third compartment, to receive the minuter and more delicate things. Then there is a fourth division running the whole length of the basket, in which lie a hammer and chisel, and which may receive large shells, crabs, etc. that do not require constant immersion. A geologist's hammer with a cutting edge, as well as a striking face, is the most useful; and the chisel must not be such as carpenters use, but one made wholly of iron, tipped with steel, such as is used by smiths, and technically called a cold chisel.*

Sometimes, especially if the shore we are about to search be strewn with large stones or boulders, it will be well to secure the attendance of a man with a crow-bar, to turn over the stones; as on their under surface, and beneath their shadow, valuable specimens are often found. With the same instrument, inserted into the fissures, great pieces of loose slaty rock may be wrenched off, which are very productive. . . . Thus armed, we sally forth. . . .

One more means of obtaining animals remains to be mentioned—the surface-net. This may be made of stout muslin, in the form of a bag, two feet deep, sewed on a thick brass ring a foot in diameter, which is screwed at the end of a staff six feet long. The staff should be of tough wood, such as hickory or lance-wood. The net is held at the surface of the sea, the collector sitting in a boat rowed gently along. The afternoon and evening of a calm sunny day is most productive, especially in the latter part of summer and autumn, when the lovely Medusae . . . and many forms of freely swimming Annelida [segmented worms] and Crustacea [crabs, shrimp, copepods] occur in abundance.

The environmental damage caused by breaking up shoreline rocks would not be permitted now. Gosse was even criticized by his own son for encouraging amateurs to collect so assiduously. But the enthusiastic and professionally dedicated Gosse has his contemporary counterparts working in today's aquariums. One of them is certainly David Powell, now director of husbandry at the Monterey Bay Aquarium in California. Dave has been an influence on many major aquariums, either as a staff member or technical consultant. After graduate education, Dave worked as an aquarist at the innovative Marineland of the Pacific near Los Angeles in the 1950s. After years of pioneering work, he was recruited by the Steinhart Aquarium (part of the California Academy of Sciences) in San Francisco to help with the redesign of exhibits in 1963.

Dave's reputation as an aquarist and a collector grew, and he was lured back to southern California, to San Diego, to help design and build Sea World. With Sea World up and running, Dave returned to Steinhart in 1976 to help the young new director, John McCosker, open the Roundabout aquarium. This novel tank was designed as a circular home for large schooling fish and big sharks and was patterned after similar tanks in innovative Japanese aquariums.

But in 1980 Dave made the move that would cap his distinguished career and help give the world a great public aquarium. Philanthropist David Packard and his family enticed him to Monterey to help design and operate what some consider to be the West's foremost aquarium, the Monterey Bay Aquarium. He continues to serve as director of husbandry and now oversees design and construction of a major new

The males of many species of reef fishes are colored differently from the females. This male ribbon eel (Rhinomuraena quaesita) *is typical of most males in having brighter, more distinctive colors than its female counterparts.* (Photo by John E. Randall.)

addition, a building complex that will feature deep-sea and pelagic (open ocean) animals when it is finished in 1996. As one listens to Dave recount his past (and future) collecting trips, it is clear that he and P. H. Gosse would have had a lot of productive fun together:

"My first diving outfit was a surplus World War II rebreather unit used by submariners to escape sunken subs. There were real mechanical and physiological limitations on this gear. I still have the design documents for an improved breathing apparatus I developed. The water in southern California can get real cold, and wet suits weren't yet invented. Back in the fifties we were learning to dive and to grin and bear the floods of cold water that would leak into our misnamed 'dry suits.'

"My cousin and I had a boat which we would take to Catalina Island almost every weekend, when school and jobs would allow. Some of the first animals I collected were the brilliantly colored red and electric blue Catalina gobies (*Lythripnus dalli*). These small fish cling to algae-covered rock faces around the kelp beds. Because they are not free-swimming fish they are real candidates to be collected. Using a suction-tube device called a 'slurp gun,' which I built with the help of a friend, it still took real care and a knowledge of the animals' behavior to place this plastic tube around the resting animal and suck it up harmlessly into a collection chamber. After

Not all pufferfishes bear spines. The whole family known as tobies (Canthigasteridae) *are small and smooth-bodied, like this model toby* (Canthigaster valentini). (Photo by John E. Randall.)

Trumpet fish (Aulostomus chinensis) *may occur on a reef with different individual color patterns—some yellow, some gray, some almost black. These innocuous-looking fish are actually significant predators on small reef fishes and do well only in large community exhibits.* (Photo by John E. Randall.)

those early days of collecting, diving equipment greatly improved, and I've collected fish with nets, by hand, all over the world. But, ironically, it seems now that we are able to make very deep dives using the deep-diving submersibles of the Monterey Bay Aquarium Research Institute, we are back to using suction devices to collect animals from the sea floor at depths of 1,000 feet. I'm just glad I am in the submersible; the water is *really* cold that far down!"

Porcupinefish (Diodon holacanthus) *respond to threats by inflating themselves with water. The scientific name comes from their large, fused teeth, with which they bite coral branches.* (Photo by John E. Randall.)

Among many professional aquarists on the West Coast and the tropical Pacific, another diver, Robert Kiwala, is known as "the collectors' collector." Bob has worked as the scientific collector for the Scripps Institution of Oceanography, supporting the work of both research scientists and the public aquarium. He served on the staff of the Steinhart Aquarium and was the principal marine collector for the Monterey Bay Aquarium. He is now a consultant to a variety of aquariums and the fisheries department of the Cook Islands regarding matters of aquarium fish collection. In the course of his career, Bob has developed a variety of techniques for the collection of many kinds of marine animals:

"Whether you collect fish and invertebrates by net, trap, or my preferred method—by hand, with a hand net while diving or walking in a tide pool—each animal has to be treated personally and with sensitive care. A good example of this

Specimens must be collected carefully from the ocean depths. Here, an expert diver-biologist monitors the collection of chambered nautiluses, one of the most popular species at the Waikiki Aquarium. (Photo by Bruce Carlson, Waikiki Aquarium.)

are the rockfish of California. This diverse group lives among the kelp beds and on deep rocky bottoms down to 500 feet.

"When such deep-living specimens are brought to the reduced pressure at the surface, the gas bladders (which they use for buoyancy and to resonate sound) can 'blow up' and damage the fish. To catch the deeper-living species, I drop baited barbless hooks from the boat. Once I can feel there are fish on the line, I slowly pull the line up to a depth of about 150 feet, tie it off, and then go over the side with scuba. I drop down the fishing line to where the eight or ten hooked fish are slowly swimming around the line. I take each fish carefully in my gloved hand, because they are spiny and the water is cold, gently hold them, and insert a small but sharp hypodermic needle (selected from an array of sizes suited to each species) under a scale on the skin below the dorsal fin on the back, pierce the gas bladder, and allow the excess gas under pressure to escape out the needle.

"I pull on the fishing line and a colleague in the boat pulls the fish up to shallower water, where more gas escapes under pressure. Eventually, the fish have equalized the pressure to the shallower depth, the needle is removed, and they are brought aboard the boat into a holding tank. This procedure needs to be accomplished very carefully, but I've never lost a fish due to infection or trauma. They heal very quickly and show no aftereffects from the depressurization treatment. The fish collected carefully this way can survive far longer in captivity than they could in the wild. The

point to make is that each fish must be handled and considered a very special individual."

Marjorie Awai is an aquarist at the Waikiki Aquarium in Honolulu. After studying marine biology at Oregon State University, she decided to combine her interest in marine science with the practical work of collecting and maintaining marine animals at a public aquarium. In this way she helps people enjoy the same views that she sees in her work and study underwater on reefs throughout the tropical Pacific Ocean.

"Today's marine aquarium displays just would not be possible without the ability to scuba dive," says Awai. "Everyone I know who works in aquariums takes scuba diving for granted. It is a skill every fish collector should have—like reading or the ability to do math. But the real secret of collecting marine animals, particularly reef fish, is knowing as much as possible about their behavior and ecology. You don't catch reef fish by bullying them. You catch them by thinking like they do, knowing where they are going to swim next, what scares them, what makes them feel less threatened, and so forth. The worst thing you can do is frighten them into a net or scare them into a hole and then bash the coral head they are hiding in. That's not only irresponsible, it is bad biology.

"Of course, not all marine animals that we display occur in shallow water. A favorite animal of the visitors to the Waikiki Aquarium is the chambered nautilus. They live at the base of deep reef faces—from 300 to 1,000 feet. We catch them in chicken-wire traps, left on the bottom for 48 hours and then carefully raised to the boat. Unlike fish, chambered nautiluses have very little problem adjusting to pressure changes. But still—the secret to collecting them is knowing their biology and behavior. We have put a lot of time into research conducted both in the sea and in the laboratory. Some of our results have been published in scientific journals, and we have received a national award for breeding nautiluses in our aquariums.

"To be honest, there is a real personal responsibility in catching and maintaining marine animals. The more patient and conscientious we are, the better job we do."

The best way to understand the complexity of knowledge and skills and the dedication required to collect, display, interpret, and care for marine organisms is to review some of the successes of modern aquariums. Although the best institutions exhibit organisms as mixed communities of plants and animals—the way they are found in nature—the following discussion will focus on selected animals and plants that modern aquarists are studying and keeping with growing success.

Corals

Sea anemones are large, colorful, temperate-zone relatives of the reef corals of warm tropical islands. Abundant in coastal England, they were popular collectors' items for Victorian men and women interested in natural history, who often maintained parlor aquariums for their continued display.

Coral reefs are the most diverse communities in the sea. They present colorful and lively views of ocean communities. Warm, sunlit waters where reefs grow are the most welcoming places where humans can view the sea. It is no coincidence that the first underwater color photographs (published by *National Geographic* magazine in 1927) were of coral reefs.

The topography of these special places results from the combined actions of groups of animals and plants that possess a special ability to remove dissolved minerals from seawater and fix them into rocklike skeletons. The most common substance produced is $CaCO_3$—calcium carbonate, or limestone. The resulting materials form

Viewed close up, coral polyps resemble their relatives the sea anemones. (Photo by Thomas Kelly, Waikiki Aquarium.)

islands, white sand beaches, and the huge barrier reefs of Australia and Belize. These living structures—great landmarks of the planet—are visible from outer space and result from the combined efforts of myriads of minute organisms.

Reefs are places of special beauty, but they are also dynamic factories powered by solar energy, fixers of dissolved resources, and three-dimensional habitats for thousands of kinds of fish. Major contributors to the reef are the colonial animals called *reef-building corals*. Perhaps equal in importance but less flamboyant in their appearance are the coralline algae, which are essential contributors to reef development.

While reef-building corals are limited to warm, sunlit, tropical seas, their relatives are spread throughout the world's oceans. Corals belong to the phylum Cnidaria, which includes jellyfish, sea anemones, sea fans, soft corals, and non–reef-building corals, which are widespread in darker, colder waters (and some of which were maintained by the pioneering aquarist Anna Thynne in the 1840s).

Because of their biological consequence and aesthetic beauty, coral reefs have long been an essential part of any aquarium professing comprehensiveness. Corals were once considered "too difficult to keep," and their successful display was limited to institutions in areas near coral reefs such as the Bermuda Aquarium, the Waikiki Aquarium, and, most notably, the Noumea Aquarium in New Caledonia, whose early success has been documented by the former director, Rene Catala, in his 1961 book *Carnival of the Sea.* (Catala also illustrated an interesting side effect—the fluorescing of corals under ultraviolet light.) Although many aquariums can now maintain small tanks of living coral, most simulate coral reefs with well-made Fiberglas replicas among which swim genuine fish. The grand plan of some aquariums is to maintain a large section of living coral reef in tanks large enough to accommodate scuba divers.

Only recently have aquarists been successful in keeping reef-building corals and providing displays with any real relation to their natural counterparts. Ironically, they have done so by returning to the concept of the balanced aquarium discussed in such detail by Gosse, Taylor, and their Victorian colleagues. To keep living corals successfully, the aquarist must provide a balanced mix of plants and animals.

A major feature of reef-building corals is the symbiotic relationship of the plant cells (called *zooxanthellae*) living among the cells of the coral's (animal) tissue. To meet the complete needs of reef-building corals and their algal allies, aquarists must provide very high quality seawater (not stationary but flowing briskly over the coral), lots and lots of sunlight (or its artificial equivalent, usually metal halide lamps), and plenty of plant life. It is often necessary to install separate tanks of algae through which the recirculated water flows but which are not on view.

An entire aquarium, the Great Barrier Reef Aquarium in Townsville, Australia, has been constructed on the principle of equipping the water-circulation system with *algal scrubbers* to permit the display of a living reef. These large tanks, installed on the roof where there is plenty of sunlight to encourage plant growth, are filled with green algae that metabolically remove waste products generated by the coral animals. But coral reefs are open systems (not closed) so occasional water changes ensure success.

Tissue of both hard and soft corals is often brightly pigmented, adding rich colors to shallow reef waters where sunlight is bright. The red shades around the margin of this picture are coralline algae. (Photo by Thomas Kelly, Waikiki Aquarium.)

For years aquariums have furnished their fish displays with artificial coral or natural coral skeletons. In the last 20 years aquarists have successfully kept living corals in aquariums. At the Waikiki Aquarium some individual colonies (Euphyllia ancora) *have been maintained for more than 10 years and have reproduced in the exhibit tanks.* (Photo by Thomas Kelly, Waikiki Aquarium.)

Moon jellies (Aurelia aurita) *were the first species of jellyfish to be successfully displayed in aquariums.* (Courtesy Monterey Bay Aquarium.)

Jellyfish

In early 1992 the marketing director of the Monterey Bay Aquarium looked up from the advertising layout he was approving and remarked to a visitor, "If someone had told me three years ago that I would be advertising live jellyfish on billboards and in magazines, I would have said they were nuts! Sharks certainly, sea otters for sure, kelp maybe, but I never thought the public would go for jellyfish."

Until the last decade, no aquarium had the ability to display jellyfish with any degree of continuing success. These paradoxically simple yet complex animals are relatives of sea anemones and corals. Unlike their sessile relatives who must remain attached to fixed surfaces, jellyfish (also called *medusae,* after the Greek mythological gorgon, Medusa), for most of their lives are open-water animals.

Many kinds of jellyfish have two parts to their life cycle. In the polyp stage, they are attached to the ocean floor. Later in life, they are free-swimming, delicate space-ships of the open water. Inspired by some early, almost serendipitous, success in keeping small jellyfish, aquarists at the Monterey Bay Aquarium began to widen their efforts. They corresponded with Japanese aquarists successful in displaying moon jellies (*Aurelia aurita*). They consulted with marine biologists at the University of

In nature, most species of jellyfish, including sea nettles (Chrysaoara fuscescens), know no boundaries. An essential part of aquarium design for jellyfish is the provision of water-flow patterns that push the gently moving medusae away from aquarium walls. (Courtesy Monterey Bay Aquarium.)

California, Los Angeles, who were studying living plankton in the laboratory and the open ocean.

At Monterey, aquarists adapted various kinds of aquarium setups for jellyfish. They had the most success with a scientific apparatus used to study plankton. This circular tank with water current rotating within it had been playfully named a *kreisel,* the German word for carousel or merry-go-round. In their original form, kreisels were circular, horizontal aquariums with water flowing around the circumference. Aquarists adapted these to a vertical installation (for better viewing) and developed an aquarium in which the medusae slowly flow in a circle and thus never encounter an aquarium wall.

The story of the Monterey Bay Aquarium's major jellyfish exhibit, whimsically named "Planet of the Jellies," which opened in the spring of 1992, is a classic case study of the dedication of a modern aquarium to combining field research, laboratory investigation, and practical aquarium biology in order to present new views of and insights into ocean life.

In an interview prior to the opening of this pioneering exhibit, husbandry director Dave Powell of Monterey explained that "with any animal, learning to keep them outside the wild is a step-by-step process. First, you have to be able to collect them— you can't do anything until you solve that. Then you have to transport them back to the aquarium. You have to figure out a tank design that will meet their needs. And you have to be able to feed them. Finally, you have to get them to reproduce so that you're not dependent on finding animals in the wild."

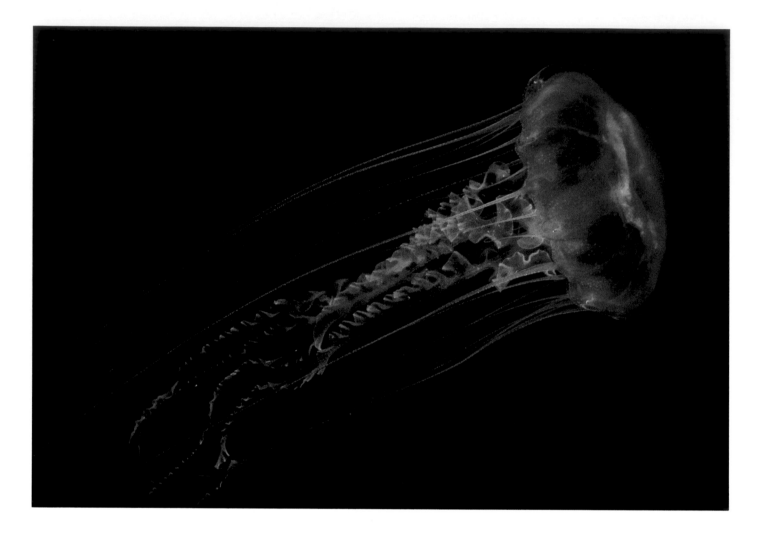

Solving such problems involves more than the practical work of aquarium biology. It requires the commitment and support of the institution's leadership. Dedication to such projects must clearly be a policy of the aquarium's management. Powell pointed out that "our executive director and trustees agreed to commit time and money just for research and development. That gave our aquarists the time to work on new things."

And jellies were certainly new. "No one had ever exhibited jellies in the United States before," explained Powell. "I wanted us to have them because of their beauty—and because of the challenge." Senior aquarist Freya Sommer helped lead the successful work with jellies. Interviewed with Powell, she admitted, "I'd never seen jellies in real life before I came here. And this was the first time I'd ever seen a moon-jelly polyp. They were just little specks." Success with the moon jellies piqued Freya's interest, and she spent her research time working with another species—the purple-striped jelly (*Pelagia colorata*). To her surprise, she discovered it had a polyp stage that no one knew existed. She successfully raised new generations of jellies, and the methods she developed have worked with other species, including umbrella jellies, sea nettles, and upside-down jellies, all of which are displayed at Monterey.

Following the proven example at Monterey, new aquariums are dedicating part of their operating budgets to research and development for new exhibits based on a thorough knowledge of biology.

Delicate and graceful medusae are not totally subject to the whims of currents but have surprisingly strong muscles in their bells. Pulsations move the jellyfish briskly and gracefully through the water. (Courtesy Monterey Bay Aquarium.)

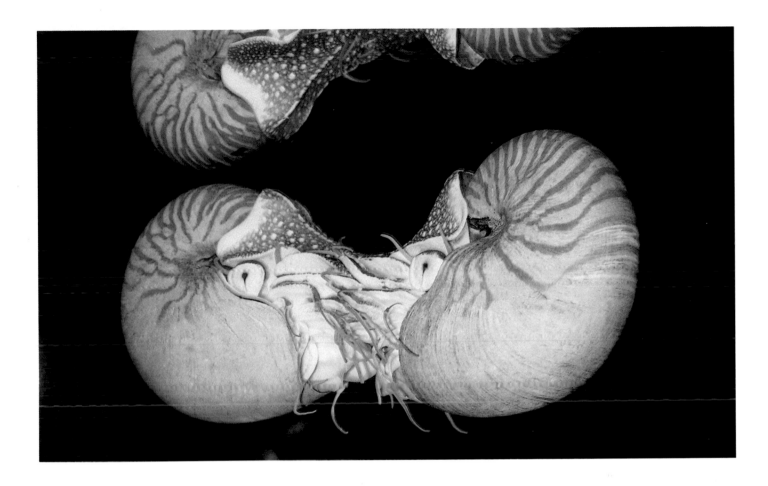

During copulation the male chambered nautilus passes a package of sperm to the female, who retains it until she attaches her eggs to the surfaces of rocks. (Photo by Thomas Kelly, Waikiki Aquarium.)

Chambered Nautiluses

The shell of the chambered nautilus has stimulated artists and writers, ranging from the poetic lines of Oliver Wendell Holmes's "build thee more stately mansions, oh my soul" to the work of mathematicians and baroque jewelers. The living animals have been far less familiar. In fact, living nautiluses have only been commonly seen for the last 20 years, when display in public aquariums has become increasingly widespread. Through these displays, millions of people have been able to view living chambered nautiluses and learn about the life history of this fascinating animal with such ancient origins.

Nautilus is the most primitive of cephalopod molluscs, a group that also includes squid and cuttlefish. The distinctive external shell, chambered and spiral-shaped, is an adaptation for buoyancy control. Because of this unique structure, it is possible to relate the five species of living nautiluses to fossils more than 500 million years old. Thousands of species of cephalopods with external shells once dominated the oceans, but all of them except for the single genus *Nautilus* are now extinct.

Living nautiluses are limited to the tropical Pacific oceans, where they live at the base of steep reef faces at depths ranging from 300 to 1,200 feet. This is well beyond the range of conventional scuba diving, so no one has observed a living nautilus firsthand in its natural habitat (although live specimens have been safely brought to shallower depths in traps, released, and observed by divers and snorkelers). Remote

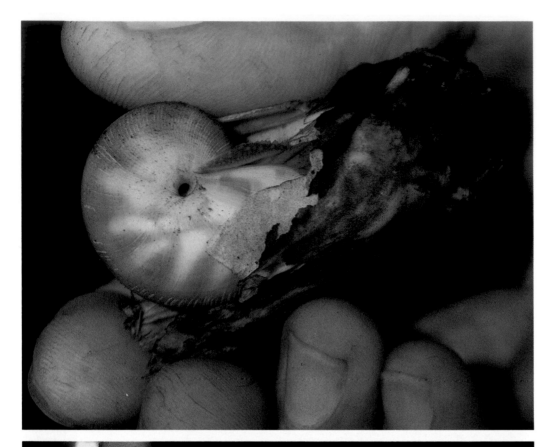

Held by the fingers of an aquarium director and marine biologist, the first chambered nautilus (Nautilus belauensis) *to hatch in an American aquarium ventures forth.* (Photo by Thomas Kelly, Waikiki Aquarium.)

One secret to the success of keeping nautiluses in an aquarium is high-quality natural food. At the Waikiki Aquarium the menu includes hand-fed shrimp. (Photo by Thomas Kelly, Waikiki Aquarium.)

movie cameras have given us secondhand views of the animals in natural deep conditions. There has long been fishing in the Philippine Islands for the nautilus shells, but the living animal has only recently been available for study by scientists and for viewing by the public.

Rene Catala at the Noumea Aquarium in New Caledonia first displayed living nautiluses in 1958, using specimens collected on nearby reefs. Attempts to ship nautiluses to other aquariums were mostly unsuccessful until 1976, when biologist Bruce Carlson of the Waikiki Aquarium in Honolulu collected and air-shipped living *Nautilus pompilius* from Fiji to Hawaii. Since that time aquariums throughout the United States, Japan, and Europe have routinely displayed nautiluses, using specimens initially provided by the Waikiki Aquarium and subsequently by commercial collectors who adapted the collecting and shipping techniques developed by Carlson at Waikiki.

Beginning with this initial success in 1976, staff and associates at the Waikiki Aquarium, led by Carlson, have been directed toward three objectives: to study and describe the nautilus in its natural environment; to apply this knowledge to improve husbandry techniques; and to breed the nautilus in captivity and describe its embryology. None of this research has been proprietary, and the scientific results, as well as specimens, have been shared by the Waikiki Aquarium with research colleagues at public aquariums throughout the world—a fine example of the collegiality of public aquariums.

Before Carlson's work, most references on the ecology and behavior of nautiluses described an inferred pattern of nocturnal activity, with a move from deep water into relatively shallow water (only a few hundred feet). This speculation can be traced to Arthur Willey, who conducted research in New Britain in the South Pacific in the late 1800s. Willey wrote that "the nautilus migrate in shoals nocturnally from deeper to shallower water in quest of food." He provided few details on which to base this conclusion, but his speculations have been accepted as fact in subsequent literature on nautiluses.

With the aim of successfully keeping nautiluses in captivity, staff of the Waikiki Aquarium conducted field trials in the Palau Islands beginning in 1978, working with scientists Peter Ward and Bruce Saunders. Having developed successful trapping techniques and finding that captured animals could be tagged, released, and recaptured, aquarium scientists developed a sonic transmitter that permitted tracking of free-swimming nautiluses in their natural environment.

By listening to depth-sensitive sonic signals transmitted from the free-swimming nautiluses, scientists in a stationary vessel equipped with hydrophones were able to track their migratory pattern. They found that Willey's early speculation was indeed true. The study animal was tracked from a depth of 1,100 feet to 275 feet in less than 4½ hours. In the tropics such a vertical migration results in an associated temperature change ranging from 45°F at the deepest to a warm 70°F at 275 feet.

Aquarium scientists found that by the next morning (before dawn), the animal had returned to a depth of 1,100 feet. These data conclusively confirmed Willey's belief that nautiluses migrate daily between deep and shallow water. More important, this provided essential information about the conditions experienced by nautiluses in their natural habitat.

Copulation and egg laying by nautiluses have been observed repeatedly in tanks at the Waikiki Aquarium since the first eggs were laid in 1976. None of the eggs was fertile, however. Seven of fourteen public aquariums in America, Europe, Japan, and New Caledonia surveyed by Carlson in 1985 reported eggs laid in captivity, but all were infertile. Japanese aquarists from Yomiyuriland Marine Aquarium near Tokyo had published details on the production of captive eggs that were also infertile. Because no nautilus eggs had ever been found in the wild, scientists had speculated that nautiluses probably laid eggs in very deep water. Failure to achieve fertility was blamed on the aquarists' inability to provide cold enough temperatures and high enough pressures.

The Waikiki Aquarium shared its field research results with other aquarists. As a consequence of these results, changes were made in aquarium tanks to simulate the resulting temperature changes related to daily migrations of nautiluses. The Shima Aquarium in Japan, using this information in concert with the Toba Aquarium, achieved the first hatching of nautiluses in captivity in December 1988. The hatchlings resembled miniature adults but survived only 33 days. Obviously, the information gathered in field studies and applied to captive biology was essential for breeding success. Subsequently, the Waikiki Aquarium has propagated 12 hatchlings from their breeding colony of 34 adults, with the first hatchings occurring in October 1990. A second group of 17 hatched in 1992.

This success story is an excellent example of a modern aquarium basing husbandry and culture techniques on careful observation and measurement of the natural biology of selected species. It was a special achievement, given the depth at which nautiluses live. In addition to providing information and specimens to the world, the Waikiki Aquarium cooperated in the co-production of a British Broadcasting Company/KHET Honolulu produced television documentary narrated by David Attenborough, which has been aired throughout the world and has increased appreciation for the species and its tropical-reef habitat.

Sharks

If there were a list of the ten most popular aquarium exhibits, sharks would be near the top, vying for space with dolphins, whales, sea otters, and (believe it or not) jellyfish. From the early public aquariums of Victorian England to today's large oceanariums such as Sea World and Okinawa Expo Aquarium, sharks have always been a major draw. Most people commonly relegate all sharks to a fearsome group of large, human-eating predators. Actually, they comprise a diverse group, whose habitats range from the deepest, darkest seas to the sheltering stems of kelp plants, from warm tropical reefs to the murky green waters off San Francisco and Long Island. Only a relative handful of shark species exceed 6 feet in length as adults; most species are less than half that length. In the world's oceans (and certain freshwater areas, such as Lake Nicaragua and the Ganges River) swim more than 350 kinds of sharks. Although this may seem like a lot, it is a relatively small vertebrate group compared to the 8,000 species of birds and more than 24,000 species of bony fish.

Sharks are considered a kind of fish because biologists define *fish* as animals with backbones that breathe by using gills. Biological relationships of these sharks place them into seven distinct taxonomic groups. But more pragmatic classifications usually divide sharks into two groups: dangerous and nondangerous, or, perhaps, large and small. The "dangerous" category includes fewer than a dozen species.

Sharks also fall into other practical subdivisions based on swimming habits and respiratory capability: active, open-water swimmers and sedentary bottom-dwellers. Active swimmers are also called *ram ventilators*. Such sharks swim constantly to force—or "ram"—seawater through their open mouths and over their gills in order

The graceful strength of rays and sharks is always fascinating. At the Ring of Fire Aquarium in Osaka, this visitor has a particularly expansive view of at least 12 species of sharks. (Photo by Peter Chermayeff.)

to extract sufficient dissolved oxygen. (Rare exceptions to this have been observed. Large, usually actively swimming, sharks appear periodically to enter a trancelike state and lie still on the bottom of reef caves. Biologists have called these *sleeping sharks*. Their rate of respiration drops markedly, and the amount of water passing over their gills is greatly reduced.)

Sedentary bottom-dwelling sharks, long popular with aquarists, possess well-developed gill muscles that actively pump water into their mouths and over their gills. These sharks normally divide their time between remaining quiet and stationary on the bottom and swimming actively through the water.

The first sharks to be successfully displayed in aquariums were representatives of smaller, sedentary, cold-water species. A guidebook for the Aquarium of the Zoological Station of Naples, published in 1913, describes three species of sharks commonly on display. Sharks from this group (including dogfish, cat sharks, and smooth

hounds) were among those first displayed in aquariums. Many of them are egg-laying species and are still commonly kept in aquariums around the world. Also included are horn sharks, common to California kelp beds, and their Japanese and Australian relatives. Because adults readily lay eggs that hatch in captivity, resulting in active young with interesting color patterns, sharks of the horn shark and cat shark families have been widely displayed in aquariums since the days of Victorian England and imperial Japan.

The most common shark in the world is the spiny dogfish *(Squalus acanthias)*. These 1- to 2-foot sharks are caught by the millions in the North Sea for fishmeal and fish and chips. They also provided early display specimens for the colder-water aquariums of Germany and England. As interesting and easy to keep as these small sharks may be, it is the large sharks that are of greatest interest to aquarium visitors.

Aquariums located closest to the source of supply were the first to successfully display large specimens of sand tiger shark *(Eugomphodus taurus)*. The New York

Bonnethead sharks have much narrower heads than other hammerheads. Biologists have speculatively suggested several functions for this unusual shape. The broad head may act as a forward wing, serving as a hydrodynamic plane to increase maneuverabilty. The wide separation of their eyes and the odor-sensitive nostrils may increase the shark's ability to locate prey. (Photo courtesy Sea World of California.)

Whale sharks (Rhiniodon typus) *are the largest known species of shark, reaching a length reportedly exceeding 35 feet. These docile plankton-feeding sharks are fed kilos of shrimp daily at the Osaka Aquarium.* (Photo by Noboru Hashimoto, Sygma Press; courtesy Cambridge Seven Associates.)

Aquarium successfully maintained 8- to 10-foot specimens at the turn of the century. Sand tigers do very well in aquariums and are commonly displayed.

They should not be confused with another large species, the tiger shark *(Galeocerdo cuvier)*. Although these tropical sharks are big (up to 18 feet) and dangerous (they sometimes mistake swimmers for their normal prey, sea turtles), they do not do especially well in captivity. Sometimes they even get upset stomachs in the aquarium. In April 1935, at the Coogee Aquarium in Sydney, Australia, a 13-foot tiger shark vomited up the tattooed arm of one James Smith, a man of unconventional life-style. Medical examiners found that the arm had in fact been neatly severed by a knifelike instrument, not by the bite of a shark. The tiger had scavenged the body of a murder victim dumped in Sydney Harbor and unwittingly helped solve the crime!

One of the early pioneers in catching, transporting, and maintaining large sharks was Count Ilia Tolstoy, grandson of the Russian novelist. In 1936 Tolstoy began a series of field experiments designed to test methods of catching and anesthetizing large Atlantic sharks ranging up to 8 feet in length. He, his partners, and his supporters, including millionaire naturalist Cornelius Vanderbilt Whitney, aimed to establish a novel ocean attraction in northeast Florida. They had to know whether they could stock it with large, lively sharks. Their enterprise opened in 1938 as Marine Studios, later renamed Marineland of Florida. Ahead of his time in many ways, Tolstoy suspected that sharks failed to survive capture because their frantic struggles on the fishing line or in the net unbalanced their blood chemistry. An excess of lactic acid in their bloodstream proved fatal. Today, biologists still experiment with adjustments to the blood chemistry of freshly caught sharks, basing their attempts on the results of medical research on human trauma victims.

Despite many attempts and continuing research, aquarium biologists do not yet know enough to maintain great white sharks in an aquarium. (Photo by Al Giddings, Images Unlimited.)

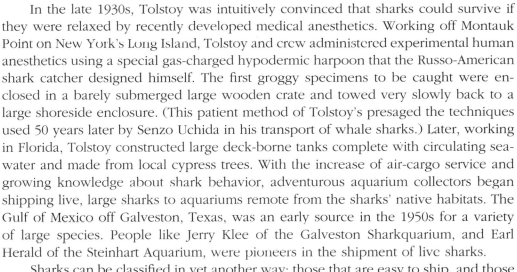

In the late 1930s, Tolstoy was intuitively convinced that sharks could survive if they were relaxed by recently developed medical anesthetics. Working off Montauk Point on New York's Long Island, Tolstoy and crew administered experimental human anesthetics using a special gas-charged hypodermic harpoon that the Russo-American shark catcher designed himself. The first groggy specimens to be caught were enclosed in a barely submerged large wooden crate and towed very slowly back to a large shoreside enclosure. (This patient method of Tolstoy's presaged the techniques used 50 years later by Senzo Uchida in his transport of whale sharks.) Later, working in Florida, Tolstoy constructed large deck-borne tanks complete with circulating seawater and made from local cypress trees. With the increase of air-cargo service and growing knowledge about shark behavior, adventurous aquarium collectors began shipping live, large sharks to aquariums remote from the sharks' native habitats. The Gulf of Mexico off Galveston, Texas, was an early source in the 1950s for a variety of large species. People like Jerry Klee of the Galveston Sharkquarium, and Earl Herald of the Steinhart Aquarium, were pioneers in the shipment of live sharks.

Sharks can be classified in yet another way: those that are easy to ship, and those that are very difficult to ship. The first group is much smaller than the second. Because most sharks are ram ventilators (and belong to the second, hard-to-ship, group), they need a high volume of oxygenated seawater over their gills when they are held stationary in a shipping container. Early shark shippers like Dave Powell and his Sea World colleagues built special shipping boxes with recirculating water pumps and custom mouthpieces. Also, it soon became evident that blood circulation of active sharks depends significantly on the sweeping movements of their tail fins. Shark "flight attendants" learned to move the tails by hand to ensure proper blood flow.

In the handling and shipping of sharks, aquarists discovered that some species (such as bull sharks) exhibit an interesting nervous reaction, called the *tonic reflex,* when turned upside down. A shark exhibiting the tonic reflex drops its metabolic rate and goes into a state of almost suspended animation. Shark aquarists quickly learned that this was a useful response, and some sharks are still shipped upside down.

Shipping a large shark is a complicated business and a lot of hard work. An 8-foot shark may weigh 600 pounds, yet the water necessary to fill the shipping container will weigh 8 pounds a gallon. An 8-foot shark needs at least 500 gallons or 2 tons of water to safely hold it to its destination. There are many tales in the aquarium trade about seawater being spilled aboard planes in flight and the interesting reactions of pilots to the sloshing of corrosive seawater in their cargo bays.

Obviously, it is much easier to ship small sharks, but they don't have the excitement and appeal that large specimens offer once they reach their display destination. In 1970, however, aquarists at the Waikiki Aquarium began to collect and ship what is now one of the most widespread tropical shark species displayed. Juvenile blacktip reef sharks *(Carcharhinus melanopterus)* are common in the shallow sandy bottoms of tropical islands. Adult females about 5 feet long enter these lagoons, give birth to 6 to 12 baby sharks each, and then return to the deeper reefs outside the lagoon. They leave the 12- to 16-inch pups to spend their early days in the protection of the lagoon. Waikiki Aquarium collectors found they could easily run down these small sharks in the shin-deep lagoons.

In fact, at one collecting area, Canton Island in the Phoenix group south of Hawaii, they found a collecting ally in "Blackie," a Labrador retriever. Blackie had converted his duck-retrieving skills to shark collecting! He would run through the shallows, herding a juvenile blacktip closer and closer to the beach. When it reached

the margin of sand and sea, he would thrust out a paw and catapult the shark to the dry sand, where it could be quickly picked up by a waiting aquarist.

Blacktip reef sharks are ideal aquarium display animals because they can be collected young and shipped in small boxes unaccompanied by an aquarist, just as coral-reef fishes are shipped in the commercial trade. Even when newly born, baby blacktips look like scale models of their large parents. Thus, even a small aquarium can display sharks that have the visual appeal of large specimens.

Biologists at the Waikiki Aquarium, working with colleagues throughout the world to whom they provided specimens, conducted a study that found the growth rate of blacktips could easily be controlled by food rations. Aquariums with small exhibit tanks could feed a minimum of food (still sufficient to maintain normal behavior) and slow the sharks' growth rate. Aquariums with large tanks could feed up to eight times that ration and more than double the growth rate. Thus, blacktips could be collected and shipped at a small size and quickly grown to a larger size in a large exhibit tank. In 1990, at Sea World of San Diego, an adult blacktip collected as a juvenile by the Waikiki Aquarium and grown to maturity in the Sea World exhibit bred with a male roommate. In September 1991 she gave birth to the first blacktip reef sharks born in an American aquarium.

The reproductive success of the blacktip reef shark in captivity is relatively recent, but the world record for such success, as well as for the variety of shark species kept, must be awarded to the Okinawa Expo Aquarium. Opened in 1975, this aquarium has displayed more than 40 species of sharks in 12 families, as well as 16 species of rays in 5 families. Seven species of sharks and seven species of rays have reproduced

Of the nine species of hammerhead sharks, aquarium biologists have been most successful in keeping and rearing bonnetheads (Sphyrna tiburo). The young shark in the picture was born in Sea World, San Diego, and shares the exhibit tank with its parents. Like many sharks, hammerheads give birth to a small litter of young annually. (Courtesy Sea World of California.)

in the display tank. (See the bibliography for a complete review by aquarium director and biologist, Senzo Uchida.)

The most remarkable achievement among many at Okinawa Expo Aquarium is the successful collection and display of specimens of the world's largest shark (indeed it is the world's largest fish), the whale shark *(Rhiniodon typus)*. This feat has since been duplicated at the Ring of Fire Aquarium in Osaka, where in 1992, two specimens, a male and a female, both over 20 feet long, were on display. Whale sharks are so named because of their large size (specimens have been reliably reported up to 40 feet long) and because they feed by straining small fish and invertebrates in a manner similar to that of baleen whales. Whale sharks are calm, docile, slow-swimming creatures that often permit divers to approach them.

The Izumito Sea Paradise Aquarium first displayed a whale shark in 1934. Okinawa Expo Aquarium displayed their first specimen in 1980. The collecting technique used by the aquarium exploits the facility's seaside location. Aquarists from Expo tow a special barge to the collecting area some miles offshore. The barge has sides and a bottom but is open at both ends. When a shark is sighted, the barge is submerged so that the tops of the sides barely crest the water's surface. Swimmers guide the whale shark into the barge, close the two ends, and very slowly tow the barge with the enclosed shark to the pier at Okinawa. A hammocklike sling is placed beneath the shark. Both shark and sling are hoisted with a heavy-duty crane into a flatbed truck carrying a very large tank full of water. The truck carefully but quickly transports the shark to the aquarium where it is lifted and placed into the tank.

The large exhibit tank at Expo where whale sharks and other species are housed is 88 feet long, 39 feet wide, and 11 feet deep and holds more than 290,000 gallons of water. It has held at least four specimens of whale sharks, one at a time, over the past two decades.

Whale sharks have done well in captivity. The main problem they present is their large size at initial collection. In the future, small whale sharks may be displayed in many aquariums once collectors discover where to find juvenile specimens. Although it is not known for certain, the reproductive mode of whale sharks is believed to be oviparity (egg laying). Only one whale shark egg case has ever been found. The shape and size of a rugby ball, it was dredged up from a depth of 250 feet from the bottom of the Gulf of Mexico. More than six juvenile specimens are preserved in scientific collections. All are less than 3 feet long and all bear an umbilical scar (shark belly button) between their pectoral fins. This scar disappears in adults but represents the attachment point of the pseudoumbilicus that connected the young to the yolk sac in the egg. All of these small free-swimming specimens were found in the central Pacific, near the surface but in water more than 10,000 feet deep. The fact that these juveniles were found in such deep water so far from shore suggests that perhaps the reproductive mode is what biologists term *ovoviviparous,* meaning that the female retains the egg case inside her body and the young shark hatches from the egg case inside the mother. She then gives live birth to the recently hatched shark. Thus, the egg case found in Mexico might have been prematurely released by a mother. In any case, it would be an aquarist's dream to obtain a live 2-foot-long whale shark, not only for its novelty and scientific importance but also for its ease of transport.

What does the future hold for sharks in captivity? Which species will we be likely to see in aquariums in the next decade? What new technological and biological methods do we have now to help us keep sharks that we lacked 10 years ago?

Limitations on the size of tanks in which to keep sharks no longer present problems. Life-support systems, window size, and concrete construction techniques all permit huge tanks. (The Living Seas Pavilion at Walt Disney's Epcot Center holds 6 million gallons of saltwater.) Increased knowledge about the behavior and biology of sharks gained over the past 20 years has greatly helped in displaying a variety of larger species. At first, aquarists thought that because large sharks were ram ventilators, they would need tank shapes that afforded very long swimming distances and enlarged areas for turning. Tanks shaped like large dumbbells—long chaseways connecting two large circular pools—were conceived.

Tanks of infinite length—that is, constructed in the shape of circles, in which sharks could swim constantly against a current provided by pumps—proved very successful. The "shark channel" at Miami Seaquarium successfully houses bonnethead, lemon, bull, and tiger sharks. This tank is also conveniently located adjacent to a natural body of seawater. Such convenience became disaster when Hurricane Andrew flooded it in 1992.

What about aquariums located away from the sea? The circular Roundabout constructed at the Steinhart Aquarium in San Francisco's Golden Gate Park, 3 miles from the beach, was built in 1979 especially to house large sharks and large schooling fish. Although the design was based on a similar tank built in Shima, Japan, in 1956, Steinhart's Roundabout was an innovation. Shaped like a water-filled doughnut, the 200,000-gallon, 35-foot-diameter tank is viewed from the large central area entered via stairs from a level below. The Roundabout uses a series of flat panels of thick acrylic plastic secured to steel mullions. If it were built today, the windows would instead be much wider, curved plates of thick acrylic installed against the concrete walls, buffered by plastic and rubber gaskets.

But there are more subtle differences that will affect the design and construction of shark aquariums of the future based on the shark's own biology. For 200 years, since the Italian anatomist Lorenzini first drew and named the ampullae of Lorenzini, biologists have tried to demonstrate the function of these jelly-filled, enclosed, special nerve endings on the snouts and cheeks of sharks. Experiments showed that the organs were sensitive to salinity differences and to other chemical changes, including pH. Adrianus Kalmijn, working with California leopard sharks, showed that the physical modality to which these ampullae responded is electrical current—and extremely low levels of current at that. The muscle cells of all animals give off small electrical signals. Sharks' sensitivity is apparently an adaptation to detect the presence of prey. Kalmijn's sharks were searching for buried flatfish. Biologists have suggested that large sharks like the great white use electrosensitivity to respond to the movements of prey such as seals or seal lions—or surfers. During very close approaches, when the laterally situated eyes of the shark no longer provide binocular vision (or when the eyes are rolled back to guard against scratching by the victim), this electrical sensitivity may aid the shark in detecting the movement of its prey. This may also explain why white sharks "attack" boat propellers, steel platforms, and aluminum shark cages. Metals react with seawater to emit small currents of electricity.

It is likely that the electrosensitivity of sharks, unlike the periodic use of echolocation by marine mammals, is always "on." Thus, captive sharks in an aquarium that is electrically active (because of metal window frames and reinforcing steel within concrete) probably detect electrical signals of varying strength constantly. Perhaps some kinds of sharks can tolerate such levels. For others, great whites for example, such constant ambiguous inputs may be sufficiently stressful, added to the initial physiological shock of capture, to be fatal. Architects, engineers, and aquarists are now working to design "electrically silent" tanks, in which large sensitive sharks may, perhaps, be kept successfully.

What else might the future hold? On April 1, 1989, a shark biologist known for his discovery of a new family of rare sharks—popularly called "megamouth" and known at that time from only two specimens each more than 14 feet long—stood before a national conference of shark specialists gathered in Los Angeles and made a startling announcement. At the end of an intermission between scheduled presentations of research papers, he stood, unannounced, to say that during the break he had called his office in Honolulu (where the first megamouth specimen was caught), only to be told that a fisherman had retrieved a lobster trap and found six live juvenile megamouths, each nearly 2 feet long. Two of the six sharks had survived and at that very moment were on display at the Waikiki Aquarium. The audience of usually reserved scientists burst into spontaneous applause, punctuated with joyful hoots and shouts. As the excitement eased, the biologist at the microphone added, "By the way, my colleagues in Hawaii also asked me to wish you a very happy April Fool's Day!" The prankster-biologist was properly chastised with friendly banter by the duped conferees. However, he had (seduced by the tradition of the date) put into words the fond wish of everyone at the conference: to see up close, to inspect and observe at leisure, a rare species never seen alive by any biologist.

Since their discovery in 1974, four more megamouth sharks have been caught. All were adult moribund males, longer than 14 feet. But Megamouth VI has suggested the most promise for aquarists. Caught in a gill net off Dana Point, California, Megamouth VI was towed, backward, still alive, by a rope tied around its huge tail into the harbor. He spent almost 24 hours on the bottom under a boat dock. After photography sessions and rigorous examination by biologists, he was again towed offshore, where two sonic transmitters were attached to his back with subdermal darts shot with harpoons. Megamouth VI was then released, and he swam calmly off to deeper water. Using the attached transmitters and hydrophones, biologists tracked him for more than 48 hours. His behavior followed earlier predictions. Megamouth VI seemed to follow the midwater community of small crustaceans and fishes that migrate to the surface at night and submerge during the day.

The survival of Megamouth VI after such rigorous treatment suggests that juveniles might do very well in large aquariums. Biologists now seek the capture of smaller specimens. Perhaps someday a true announcement of megamouths on display can be made.

Fishes

Of all the organisms displayed by aquariums, fishes are the ones most closely associated with classic exhibits. In American aquariums of the 1920s through the 1960s, many exhibits featured *only* fishes, and sometimes groups of just a single species. Yet, as we have seen, many kinds of invertebrates and plants are important members of the biological communities where fishes occur. Today aquariums strive to establish *ecosystem exhibits*. These are displays that in their best examples, like the Monterey Bay Aquarium's kelp forest exhibit, simulate the complexity of the natural world. (The kelp exhibit, for example, includes about 80 percent of the plant and animal species

Many species in the wrasse family (including this adult Coris gaimard) *have distinctively different color patterns from juveniles. Males and females also have distinctive colors. (Photo by John E. Randall.)*

found in a wild kelp forest. Because the exhibit is protected and food is provided for its tenants, the exhibit holds two to three times the biomass of the natural community.) Such *mixed aquariums* (a reference to the variety of species occurring together) are not a new idea, although the success at Monterey is novel.

In the early days of aquariums in nineteenth-century Europe and America, many aquarists wrote about the need for "balance" within an aquarium of animals and plants. When fishes began to be kept in large numbers in relatively large tanks (about 200 gallons and larger), aquarists noticed that they were often subject to parasites and disfiguring, sometimes fatal, diseases. Trial and error taught that such afflictions could be cured by adding to the water such chemicals as copper sulfate, formaldehyde, and vital dyes. If the fishes were removed from the display tank for treatment and returned after they healed, no damage was done to the balanced aquarium. As bigger aquarium tanks became standard, aquarists found that it was more efficient to maintain residual prophylactic doses of chemicals in the water to ensure apparent fish health. Such chemicals were also toxic to aquarium plants and invertebrates (snails, worms, and so forth). Eventually, it became commonplace for fishes to be maintained in what Gosse would have called an *unbalanced aquarium*—in other words, a tank containing only fishes. The standard practice of maintaining low levels of copper in fish tanks excluded all but the most hardy plant life, and artificial substitutes replaced them.

These same chemicals also kill invertebrates. Thus, it became necessary for aquariums to display fishes and invertebrates separately. In the last 10 to 20 years, stimulated by the work of practical marine biologists and amateur saltwater aquarists, the aquarium that mixes plants, invertebrates, and fishes has returned. Better hygiene and greater knowledge of both living systems and the technology of water treatment make this possible.

In early aquariums, fishes were often displayed by species. Today it is possible to exhibit fishes, and the plants and animals with which they live, from a specific habitat area, such as the Amazon, the Mississippi, the Great Barrier Reef, even the Antarctic seas. Aquarists can show a "snapshot" of the real world in their aquariums.

Typically, people have associated aquariums, both home and public, with "tropical fish." The term is vague but includes fishes from the warm fresh waters of tropical regions—African lakes and Asian and South American rivers. Such species are relatively easy to keep and breed, and the overwhelming percentage of freshwater fishes displayed in public aquariums have been raised in large commercial fish farms in Asia, Latin America, and the United States. Technically, coral-reef fishes are "tropical fish" too, but far fewer were displayed in aquariums until fairly recently, despite early attempts like Barnum's exhibits. Now, fishes of all sorts are displayed in public aquariums, and the fishes of coral reefs are among the most popular.

Biologists have described more than 24,000 species of fishes in the fresh waters and oceans of the world. Undoubtedly there are others yet to be discovered. Despite the growing skills and knowledge of aquarium biologists, many species may never be displayed. Within such a range of diversity, it is not surprising to find that some fishes are easy to acclimate to the aquarium, while others have so far proven impossible to keep.

Aquarium-breeding of nest-building reef fishes like this clownfish (Amphiprion chrysopterus.) *is far less difficult than rearing open-ocean species. Clownfish nestle among the sausage-shaped tentacles of carpet anemones. Immune to the tentacles' poison cells, the clownfish build their nests close to the anemone's protection. A female has laid the yellow eggs (left) for the male to fertilize and guard. Pink and green algae border the nest. (Photo by Thomas Kelly, Waikiki Aquarium.)*

This same diversity makes it both easy and difficult to rear fishes in an aquarium and have them reproduce. Some fishes, such as those that bear fully developed young—guppies, for example—are very easy to raise in hatcheries. Most fishes, including almost all marine species, are difficult to culture because they are *broadcast spawners*—they release (broadcast) their thousands upon thousands of eggs and sperm into open water, where fertilization occurs.

The juvenile imperial angelfish (Pomacanthus imperator) *has a distinctly different color pattern from the adult (see page xvii).* (Photo by John E. Randall.)

After a day or two, depending on the species and the temperature, a tiny, transparent, barely visible larva hatches from the free-floating egg. Larvae float in the open sea (or lake) for weeks as part of the plankton, feeding on even tinier creatures and being fed upon by fishes and invertebrates. Although fish larvae are active swimmers, their small size limits their mobility, and they are subject to the vagaries of currents. Finally, with the help of onshore currents, lucky larvae find a suitable place to settle and metamorphose into juveniles. (The unlucky ones—and there are millions—reenter the food chain through the mouths of thousands of kinds of predators.)

Because of this schizoid life-style—open-water planker and inshore or pelagic (open-ocean) swimmer—few marine species have been successfully raised in aquariums or hatcheries. A notable exception is the dolphinfish or mahimahi *(Coryphaena hippurus)*. Aquarium biologists at the Waikiki Aquarium have raised this species through 10 generations! Based on successful efforts like this, there is great promise for the successful culture of many more kinds of marine fishes.

Raising fish in the aquarium has several advantages. Although there is very little danger from aquarists of overcollection of broadcast-spawning species from the wild, there is a satisfaction in not having to harvest fish from natural populations for aquarium display. The successful rearing of fish is also a measure of the high standard of the aquarium's exhibit conditions, especially high water quality and proper nutrition.

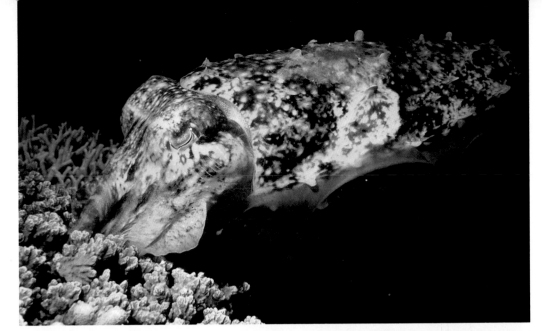

Although the European cuttlefish has been displayed at the Naples Aquarium for decades, this tropical species (Sepia latimanus) *was first exhibited in 1978 when aquarium-born specimens were on view at the Waikiki Aquarium. These hatchlings matured in eggs, which this adult female deposited on a western Pacific reef. She is shown here in the act of egg deposition.* (Photo by Bruce Carlson, Waikiki Aquarium.)

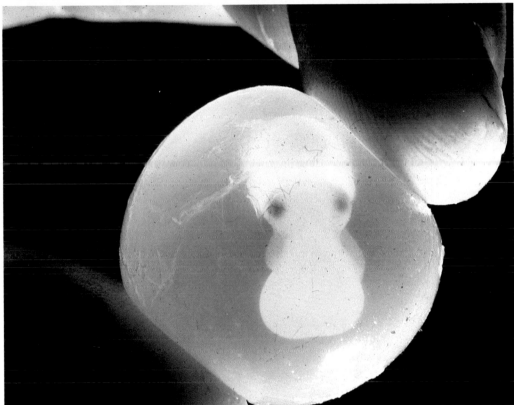

A cuttlefish embryo is sustained by nutrients from the large yolk seen just beneath the black eyes. After hatching it must fend for itself on the reef. (Photo by Bruce Carlson, Waikiki Aquarium.)

These baby cuttlefish (Sepia latimanus) *were hatched at the Waikiki Aquarium from eggs collected in the wild (above).* (Photo by Bruce Carlson, Waikiki Aquarium.)

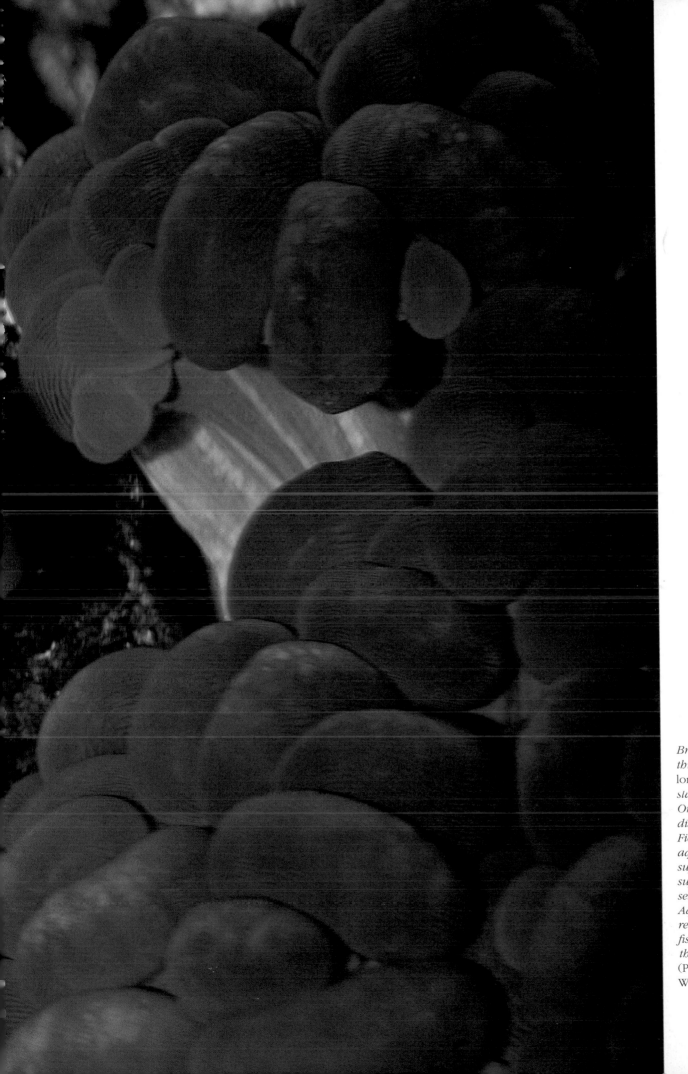

Brightly colored reef fish like this flame angel (Centropyge loriculus) *are the traditional stars of marine aquariums. Only recently have they been displayed in natural settings. Field research and applied aquarium biology have supplied the knowledge to support this multi-species "reef selection" at the Waikiki Aquarium. Here the complete reef community—corals, fishes, algae, invertebrates— thrive together in the exhibit.* (Photo by Thomas Kelly, Waikiki Aquarium.)

puffers bite off large chunks of coral branches from the reef. There are "ambushing guilds" like hawk fish, lizard fish, and eels, as well as "chasers" like barracuda, jacks, and sharks.

Of the thousands of shallow-water, tropical marine fishes of the dozens of guilds, let's select two kinds for a review. One works in the daytime, like the majority of reef fishes; the other works at night.

One of the most conspicuous and familiar kinds of fishes on a sunlit coral reef, whether in the Caribbean, the South Pacific, or the Red Sea, are butterflyfish (*Chaetodon* spp.), of which there are dozens of species. Like their terrestrial namesakes, butterflyfish are readily visible, flitting among the coral gardens, and are often colored with black, yellow, and white patterns. For the most part butterflyfish are coral pluckers. There are some exceptions, like the long-nosed butterflyfish (*Forcipiger* spp.), which select small worms and shrimps from cracks and crevices in the reef.

Few butterflyfish species are solitary. Some live in groups of six to a dozen. The great majority of species form pairs that patrol and defend a territory of the reef. This feeding territory is about the size of a small living room. Studies on butterflyfish indicate that a pair can survive and maintain such a territory for up to eight years on a stable reef. The lifetime of the same species exceeds ten years in captivity.

At night the coral reef becomes a different place. Day-active fish like butterflyfish retire to the protection of caves and cracks about sunset. After darkness falls, big-eyed fishes leave their shelter in the reef to feed on plankton and other reef creatures. But even on moonless nights, on some tropical reefs, it is not entirely dark. A sharp-eyed scuba diver can detect dozens of tiny headlights darting within the reef and along its walls. These are the lights of "flashlight fish" and are the shallow-water counterpart to bioluminescence, "the living light" that is usually associated with deep-sea creatures. Although aquarists have not yet been able to maintain deep-sea animals with much success (there are active research projects now underway in Japan and the United States), flashlight fish provide an elegant, easily kept example of the phenomenon of living light.

Flashlight fish have a large organ beneath each eye that is filled with bacteria capable of producing light by metabolic means. Some species of flashlight fish are able to "turn off" their lights using a sort of eyelid. Others shine their lights constantly. Research in aquariums has revealed that the fish (not unexpectedly) use their headlights to find food.

Mixing different fish guilds in an aquarium display with invertebrates, corals, and plants requires extensive and firsthand knowledge of their biology, excellent water systems, and, if aggressive larger fishes are to be included, a great deal of room. Each kind presents fascinating challenges to aquarists, although some are easier guests than others. Eaters of shrimp, crabs, and worms, like the wrasses, also have the interesting habit of burying themselves in the sand at night when their daytime activities cease. This means that the right kind of sand and bottom structure must be provided. It also means that the smaller rocks on the tank bottom will be disturbed regularly.

Properly maintaining fishes in an aquarium means satisfactorily supplying their every need: food, space, light, water quality, and a safe yet stimulating environment. It is impossible to totally duplicate natural conditions in an aquarium—it is even difficult to simulate them—but good aquarists can closely approach the balance of the natural world.

Many kinds of fishes seem to be able to shift their diet when moved to an aquarium without apparent effect, as long as their nutritional needs are met, although a few species, some butterflyfish for example, seem to be restricted in diet only to

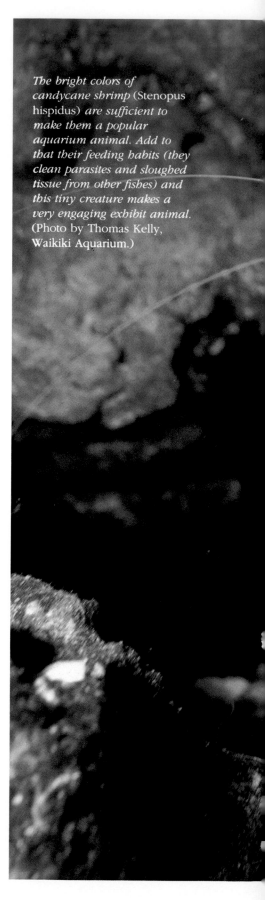

The bright colors of candycane shrimp (Stenopus hispidus) *are sufficient to make them a popular aquarium animal. Add to that their feeding habits (they clean parasites and sloughed tissue from other fishes) and this tiny creature makes a very engaging exhibit animal.* (Photo by Thomas Kelly, Waikiki Aquarium.)

live coral. Because they cannot adjust to life in the aquarium, they should not be collected. Others, such as wrasses, may search beneath small rocks and within the sand of their natural habitat for shrimp and worms but will readily take chopped fish and prepared food in an aquarium.

To duplicate the food value of the natural diets of many reef fishes, aquarists have developed special recipes. Such blends are prepared weekly or monthly and can be frozen. A typical formulation includes algae, chopped shrimp, carrots, perhaps commercial fish-food pellets, and certainly vitamins. All of the ingredients are chopped and blended in a food processor, stabilized in gelatin, and poured into a tray. Once the concoction jells, aquarists cut it into small squares (like tiny brownies) for feeding to reef fishes. Differing amounts of gelatin are used, depending on whether the fish prefer floating, sinking, or neutrally buoyant food to imitate their natural prey in the aquarium.

The delicate feather duster worm is a graceful member of the coral community. (Photo by Thomas Kelly, Waikiki Aquarium.)

This smaller lesser-known relative of the famous Maine lobster has a name almost as long as its tail: Enoplometopus occidentalis. *A native of the Hawaiian reefs, it is a popular animal with aquarium visitors.* (Photo by Thomas Kelly, Waikiki Aquarium.)

Tropical crustaceans like this Hawaiian lobster are often brightly colored and exhibit complex behaviors. These qualities make them appealing animals to aquarium visitors and thus introduce a new, positive perspective about invertebrates that might even help people feel more kindly toward the lobster's relatives— the roaches under their sinks. (Photo by Thomas Kelly, Waikiki Aquarium.)

Food preparation may be costly, but it is the provision of space that presents the most expensive challenge. Certainly no one would contrive to keep tunas in a 500-gallon aquarium. That much is intuitive. Today, when technology permits tanks of immense size, limited only by budget, how large must a tank be? Some, of course, like Osaka's central tank and Disney's Epcot Living Seas exhibit, are huge. But clever aquarists have managed to design tanks for schooling fishes that are infinitely long— they are circular. The first of these *aquatic doughnuts* (in geometry such a shape is termed a *torus*—aquarists call them *roundabouts*) was built in Japan at Aburatsubo Aquarium and Shima Marineland. The classic American roundabout is at the Steinhart Aquarium in San Francisco. This 77,000-gallon aquarium opened in 1979 and hosts yellowtail, striped bass, and other temperate-water schooling fishes. The aquarium has also attempted to keep such large sharks as threshers and great whites in it.

Perhaps the most difficult (to date) shallow-water fishes to keep are the open-ocean species. Although they live within 100 to 200 feet of the surface, they are not truly shallow-water fishes because they live in areas of the ocean over great depths. These include species like tunas, mahimahi, molamola, blue sharks, oceanic whitetip sharks, and whale sharks. Molamola, one of the most unusual looking of all open-ocean fishes, was kept successfully at Marineland of Florida in the 1950s and is a popular species in Japanese aquariums, though it is rarely displayed in America.

Tunas make an exciting aquarium display and have only recently been on view. The greatest success has been in Japan, at Tokyo Sea Life Park, where schools of four species have been maintained since the park opened in 1989. To collect and maintain such healthy schools has been a major accomplishment. Species include bluefin tuna *(Thunnus thynnus),* yellowfin tuna *(T. albacares),* Eastern little tuna *(Euthynnus affinis),* skipjack tuna *(E. pelamis),* and oriental bonito *(Sarda orientalis).*

The second phase of the Monterey Bay Aquarium, now in design and scheduled to open in 1996, will include a huge open-ocean tank of more than 1 million gallons (.5 "giant"). It will display many kinds of pelagic animals, including molamola and the world's first display of schooling albacore, one of the fastest-swimming kinds of tunas. Research and fishing expeditions in concert with Japanese colleagues have been underway for the past three years.

Aquatic Birds

Like most fishes, dragon eels (Enchelycore pardalis) *and their relatives, the morays, inhale water through their mouths and exhale out the gill openings. Thus, their open mouths and bared teeth indicate breathing and not necessarily aggression. The two pairs of nostrils of the dragon eel are highly sensitive and can be directional because of the long tubes on each nostril.* (Photo by Thomas Kelly, Waikiki Aquarium.)

Birds may not typically be associated with aquariums, although many species are definitely aquatic. Within the last decade, however, aquariums have been increasingly displaying sea- and shorebirds as essential parts of aquatic ecosystems. Aquarium biologists and visitors alike are learning much about the biology and behavior of birds from such exhibits. People get a new viewpoint when they see birds underwater. For example, we might have been taught early in school that penguins cannot fly. Yet anyone who sees a black-footed penguin jump from the shore and zoom along the bottom will argue with that. They certainly "fly underwater."

Visitors also gain a new perspective on birds in exhibits like the Steinhart Aquarium's trout stream exhibit, where water ouzels, which frequently nest behind waterfalls, dive to the rocky bottom of a trout stream, gain a purchase with their large feet,

and literally walk along the stream bottom, feeding on animals picked from among the rocks.

Although it is difficult to show wide-ranging seabirds like albatross, shearwaters, frigate birds, and boobies, Sea Life Park in Hawaii has managed to encourage wild individuals to build their nests within the park's seaside vegetation in an area near natural nesting grounds.

Perhaps the earliest attempt to display seabirds was at Marineland of Florida, where pelicans and cormorants formed a popular part of the exhibitry. But the real strides in exhibiting aquatic birds within a natural habitat, both on land and underwater, have been made relatively recently. One excellent example is the Shorebird exhibit at the Monterey Bay Aquarium. The visitor enters an aviary with a clear view of the shoreline and horizon of Monterey Bay. The exhibit itself is a cutaway of a sand dune with a beach that slopes to an aquarium tank about 5 feet deep. A hidden wave generator produces small surf that laps the beach. Shorebirds like curlews, avocets, and sandpipers feed along the sand and wade into the water, where stingrays, croakers, and other fish abound. Biologists at Monterey hand-raise the birds from eggs laid at the aquarium and also include in the exhibit birds rescued from injury in the wild.

Perhaps the most ambitious aquatic bird exhibit is at Sea World in San Diego. Called the Penguin Encounter, it also hosts other kinds of polar seabirds. The Penguin Encounter owes its success to field research conducted in the Antarctic, led by Frank S. Todd. In 1972 Todd and his Hubbs Sea World Institute associates began their work on polar penguins with the help of the National Science Foundation. Their goal was

to establish a colony of high antarctic penguins that could be used for year-round long-term research. During the Southern Hemisphere summers of 1975 and 1978, Todd and his colleagues collected 80 native pairs of Adélie penguins and 60 young emperor penguins, and also established colonies of king and Humboldt penguins.

Now more than 400 polar penguins of seven species are maintained at Sea World in San Diego. Hundreds of penguins and other polar birds have been hand-reared at Sea World, including Adélie, emperor, king, chinstrap, Humboldt, gentoo, rock hopper, macaroni, and Magellanic penguins, as well as southern giant petrels, brown skuas, southern kelp gulls, Antarctic terns, blue-eyed shags, and snowy sheathbills.

Preliminary work was accomplished in a large research freezer that covered an area of approximately 3,200 square feet at constantly maintained freezing temperatures, with two saltwater pools. Up to 10,000 pounds of snow and ice were provided daily, and day length was maintained on a Southern Hemisphere schedule. As a result of this experience with the research freezer, in 1981 Sea World designed its Penguin Encounter exhibit, which opened to the public in May 1983. The complex was built for both exhibition and research.

In addition to the antarctic bird and penguin display, there is a companion exhibit of birds from the Northern Hemisphere. More than 150 birds are maintained in this exhibit, including Atlantic puffins, horned puffins, tufted puffins, pigeon guillemots,

rhinoceros auklets, Cassin's auklets, common guillemots, razorbills, harlequin ducks, spectacled eiders, and smews.

Sea World biologists consider the Penguin Encounter to be one of the most popular exhibits ever conceived by Sea World. It has provided the means for millions of people to see colonies of penguins under simulated natural conditions. It also provides an important research center. All of the penguin species with sexually mature birds in the population breed regularly. Sea World contends that with its exhibits in Ohio, Florida, and Texas, more than 10 million people a year will be exposed to the fascinating world of penguins. Especially interested readers should review two important papers by Frank S. Todd, listed in the bibliography.

Such an exhibit, with its need for air-conditioning and daily production of snow and ice, consumes a lot of energy. In addition to the environmental issues related to energy consumption, Sea World is understandably cautious about expense. To help address both concerns, the design-engineers for the project, Enartec, developed a very efficient system of cogeneration. A complex electrical generating plant uses normally wasted heat to create more electricity for the cooling systems. The system is so efficient that at certain times of the night and colder times of the year, Sea World can supply energy to the local utility company.

Based on its success, the penguin exhibit has been duplicated at other Sea World parks and emulated at other aquariums, for example, in Nagoya and Shirohama.

Sea Otters

Furry animals with big brown eyes have traditionally been considered within the purview of zoos. But as we have seen, the boundaries between zoos and aquariums (and even aquariums and natural history museums) are becoming blurred. More and more aquariums are including animals within their ecosystem exhibits that are definitely not fishes. Traditionally, aquariums displayed fishes; zoos exhibited mammals. There were exceptions, of course. Some of the earliest aquariums, such as Woodward Gardens Aquarium in San Francisco, displayed sea lions in the 1870s. Today's aquariums continue to push the boundary of the early (and now invalid) distinction. Aquariums now display rain-forest sloths, morpho butterflies, aviaries of sea- and shorebirds, penguins on ice, and riverside exhibits with raccoons, river otters, and water snakes.

A special furry, big-eyed mammal unique to modern aquariums is the popular sea otter of the northern Pacific Ocean, *Enhydra lutris*. Historically widespread, sea otters once ranged across the arc of the Pacific from northern Japan, to coastal Russia, along rocky Alaskan shores, and southward down the Washington, Oregon, and California coasts to northern Baja California. Extensive harvesting for the rich, dense pelts began in the 1700s and continued largely unregulated until 1911, when hunting was prohibited by the North Pacific Fur Seal Convention, signed by the United States, Great Britain, Russia, and Japan. Such intensive hunting pushed sea otters to local extinction. Only small groups of sea otters survived in remote areas of the Soviet Union, Alaska, and central California. This last group may have numbered less than 50 individuals when hunting was stopped.

The state of California protected these survivors, and by the mid-1970s the population had increased to almost 1,800 otters. In 1977 the California population gained

Male Emperor penguins incubate eggs and brood their chicks on the top of their feet (with the help of mates) rather than maintaining a nest. At Sea World's Penguin Encounter in San Diego, exhibit conditions—temperature, ice, snow, and day length—duplicate the Antarctic ice fields. (Courtesy Sea World of California)

The all-time favorite animals in any aquarium are sea otters. Here, mother and pup bask upside down in the sun at the Monterey Bay Aquarium. The pup often reclines on the mother's stomach. (Photos by Doc White, Images Unlimited.)

Part of our fascination with otters is due to their dexterous forepaws. Whether floating on their backs and cracking molluscs on their chests, carrying rocks around the exhibit, or fastidiously grooming their thick fur, sea otters seem to be always busy doing interesting things. (Photo by Craig Racicot, Monterey Bay Aquarium.)

further protection under the federal Endangered Species Act of 1973 because of the threat of danger from oil contamination. All American populations are protected by the Marine Mammal Protection Act of 1972.

Sea otters have only recently been displayed in modern aquariums. The first sea otter exhibit was established at the Point Defiance Zoo and Aquarium in Tacoma, Washington, in 1967. A male named Gus came from the Alaska population. In 1968 he was joined by another male, John, but the two aggressive males did not get along well, so John moved to the Vancouver Aquarium in 1969. In 1972 Vancouver aquarists built a well-designed facility based on a thorough knowledge of the species' biology learned through field research. This sea otter haven was enlarged again in 1990.

In 1992 the following aquariums had sea otter displays approved by the Marine Mammal Commission and were active in breeding and rehabilitation:

Monterey Bay Aquarium, Monterey, California

New York Aquarium, Brooklyn, New York

Oregon Coast Aquarium, Newport, Oregon

Point Defiance Zoo and Aquarium, Tacoma, Washington

Sea World, San Diego, California

Seattle Aquarium, Seattle, Washington

John G. Shedd Aquarium, Chicago, Illinois

In addition, in 1992 there were 101 sea otters in 24 aquariums in Japan. Breeding has been accomplished at Tacoma, Vancouver, Seattle, and several Japanese aquariums.

Much of the essential knowledge about nurturing and rearing pups has been gained through rehabilitation programs that have rescued orphaned sea otter pups from the wild. Abandoned pups are found by beach walkers on the central California coast, along the beach or in the intertidal zone. Thomas D. Williams, the veterinarian of the Monterey Bay Aquarium, points out that the premature separation of the mother and the pup might occur because of severe storms or poor health in the mother, who thus abandons her pup. Usually, when a mother gives birth to twins, she may abandon one pup shortly after birth. In many cases, rescued otters have been released back to nature when they were big enough. Some have been retained as breeding stock and for educational display.

In a normal situation the mother cares for the juvenile for five to seven months, preparing it for survival in the harsh ocean environment. During the first 30 days the sea otter pup is nearly helpless. Its fur is different in structure from the adults' and makes it so buoyant that a pup cannot dive. It floats on its back, unable to turn. After about three months this juvenile fur is gradually lost. During the first few weeks of an otter's life, the mother spends up to a third of her time grooming it with her forepaws while holding it on her chest and stomach. The pup's nourishment is exclusively provided by the mother's milk during the first month. By the time it is four months old, it relies mainly on solid food gathered by the mother.

When they are about three to three and a half months old, most pups can swim independently and are capable divers. They groom their fur without help from their mother. By the time they are six months old, pups are able to break open hard-shelled food items like sea urchins and mollusks by pounding on them with rocks. When they become independent of the mother, at about six to eight months old, pups weigh between 22 and 40 pounds.

Found only in the northern Pacific Ocean, otters were hunted almost to extinction at the end of the nineteenth century. Now protected from hunting but still at risk from oil spills and shark attack, otters are occasionally rescued from such accidents in the wild. Important rehabilitation centers are maintained at several American aquariums. (Courtesy Monterey Bay Aquarium.)

Caring for rescued sea otter pups requires extensive labor—grooming, feeding, and socializing. Fortunately, volunteers provide loving care without financial cost to the host aquarium. (Courtesy Monterey Bay Aquarium.)

At the Monterey Bay Aquarium, from 1984 to 1991, Williams reports that 37 pups were brought to the program, 23 of which survived. As the knowledge of pup care has increased, the survival rate of abandoned pups since 1989 has also increased to 92 percent.

When a suspected orphan is reported, the aquarium sends observers to watch the pup for at least two hours to make certain the mother is indeed not in the area. The pup is then carefully transported to the aquarium. Care is exerted both for the animal's well-being and the handlers', because the pups are capable of severe biting. Williams stresses that capture and transport must be accomplished calmly, quietly, and rapidly.

After a medical examination and preventive treatment with antibiotics, the rescued pup is introduced to the nursery and bonded with a human caretaker. Such bonding makes the rearing of sea otter pups very labor intensive. Research is underway to develop surrogate caretakers to augment the human attention.

There is a certain California flavor to the sea otter nursery at Monterey. The pups are kept on 4-by-7-foot water-bed mattresses. A heated rectangular pad (clearly resembling the surfer's boogey board used on nearby beaches) is under development as a surrogate mother. The heated board, covered with soft material, has a hole for a nursing bottle. The young pup can recline on the board, much as it would rest on the chest of its mother while floating in a kelp bed. As they grow, pups are also introduced into a hot tub–size saltwater tank with a haul-out platform surrounded by screening to prevent falling, much like a playpen. When they are three to four months old, pups are placed in outdoor pools.

The milk of most marine mammals is high in fat. Sea otter milk is typically rich: 65 percent fat, 31 percent protein, and 2½ percent carbohydrate. An aquarium-reared pup is fed at least 25 to 35 percent of its body weight each day until it is three months old. Duplication of such an energy-packed milk is not an easy or inexpensive matter. Sea otter formula includes squid, manila clam meat, dextrose, multivitamins, cod liver

Surrogate mothers are not necessarily female. Monterey Bay Aquarium volunteer John Morgan mothers a rescued sea otter pup in the special nursery area the aquarium has dedicated to their program, led by veterinarian Tom Williams. (Courtesy Monterey Bay Aquarium.)

oil, calcium, phosphorus, and enriched cow's milk. The mixture is blended for two to three minutes, warmed to body temperature, and fed to the pups every three hours.

Solid food is introduced to captive pups at about one month and increased in volume up to 100 percent of feeding when the pup is three months old. Solid food at Monterey includes pieces of fish and clam. When the pup is three months old, all hand-feeding is stopped and food is placed in an outside pool for the otter to retrieve. When pups are three to four months old, they are fed half live prey (mussels, clams) and half prepared food.

Pup handlers (many of them experienced, trained volunteers) spend much time grooming the juvenile pups, just as the sea otter mothers would. The human volunteers use lightweight cotton towels, electric hair dryers, and a variety of brushes. Williams explains that "techniques for raising orphan sea otter pups have been perfected to the point that survival rates are higher than those that can be expected in the wild. Infant otters require intensive care and substantial time investment. Studies should be focused on maintaining survival rates while reducing human-pup interaction and dependency." Williams and his team communicate widely and constantly with colleagues throughout the world in the rescue and care of sea otters. Periodically they convene workshops with colleagues dedicated to the raising of other wild juveniles, including condors, sea lions, and polar bears.

Although sea otters are extremely popular with aquarium visitors, they sometimes try the patience of aquarists and handlers. Adapted to using rocks to break open the shells of their prey in the wild, sea otters in captivity become adept at breaking and scratching glass in their exhibit tanks as well as chewing pipes and generally being boisterous occupants of their expensive habitats. Sea otters in the wild charm scuba divers and naturalists. They float on their backs at the surface in kelp beds, resting between diving forays for a variety of food items. Some of these items are also important to fishermen, such as abalone. Some California abalone fishermen feel that sea otters are unfair competition and overexploit their resource. It is interesting to note, however, that south of Point Conception, where there are no otters but there is active commercial fishing, the abalone are as depleted as they are where otters occur.

Some of the aquarium-raised orphans stay in their safe home, but most are released back to the uncertainties of the wild. They cannot just be given a full meal and a fond farewell, however. They need a lengthy time of supervised reacquaintance with the wild habitat. The young otter who has spent its first months in the care of humans must learn about the real ocean. At the Monterey Bay Aquarium this is done carefully in the Great Tidepool, an area intermediate between protected life and the great outdoors of Monterey Bay. Human friends spend time swimming with the departing pup until it decides it is ready to seek its fortune on its own. Every released pup is equipped with an attached radio transmitter. The battery life of these small radios is up to 2½ years, and the animals are regularly tracked and located.

The research of biologists such as Williams and his colleagues at other aquariums, California and Alaska departments of wildlife, and federal biologists greatly increases our knowledge about how to help wild sea otters in times of environmental crisis, such as the Exxon *Valdez* disaster in Alaska, as well as in normal times.

Whales and Dolphins

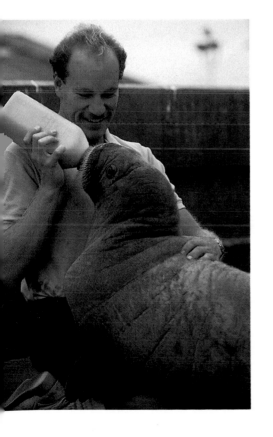

Baby walruses, although larger than their caregivers, still relate to them in social ways typical of many marine mammals. (Courtesy of Sea World of California.)

Among the most attractive group of animals to people interested in the sea are marine mammals. Included in this group are seals, sea lions, walruses, sea otters, whales, and dolphins (as well as polar bears and manatees). Perhaps their popularity lies in their complex behavior, perhaps in what seems to be their kindred interest in the world—and in us. Species of all of these groups have been kept in aquariums, some with great success. But their presence there is fraught with complexity.

The great majority of aquarium goers are enthralled by marine mammals and watch them eagerly. Biologists and animal behaviorists welcome the opportunity to learn from them and are understandably satisfied at their growing ability to raise new generations in the aquarium setting. Almost everyone is pleased when aquarium biologists can rescue and rehabilitate stranded and orphaned animals that would perish without help. Some, however, a vocal minority, feel that to remove animals from the wild is morally wrong. Others feel that the well-being of wild marine mammals depends in large part on public display, which enables people to develop a sensitivity to the natural populations of these animals and the need to protect their habitats.

We have ample evidence that marine mammals have developed this sensitivity in people. Attitudes have certainly changed toward such animals in the 30 to 40 years that they have been widely accessible to the public in aquariums. Federal laws and international conventions now protect the animals that many once—even recently— considered threats to human life and economy. Consumer boycotts have influenced fishing practices and regulations.

Some say this changed attitude is due to films, television, and direct-mail campaigns. But there is no disputing the powerful connection between living creatures— the child who sees a living dolphin will forevermore be changed by that experience. Recently the thought has been expressed that, while it may be true that aquarium animals have influenced the present appreciation and protection of marine mammals, we have learned our lesson and it is no longer necessary to display them. Sadly, we

have much evidence that the lessons learned by one generation are not always passed to the next. Close connections with animals in aquariums are essential to ensure the well-being of wild populations and habitats.

A growing number of people, including many biologists, are urging that we restrict the number of animals taken from the wild and rely on the progeny of animals born and maintained in aquariums (or rescued from the wild after being injured or orphaned). There is good reason to believe that aquarium biologists can successfully maintain self-sufficient populations through breeding programs. Particular attention is directed at several species: orca, beluga, bottlenose dolphins, harbor seals, sea lions, manatees, and sea otters.

More than 35 species of marine animals have been displayed in aquariums. These have included the cetaceans—Amazon dolphin, rough-toothed dolphin, spotted dolphin, spinner dolphin, common dolphin, bottlenose dolphin, Pacific white-sided dolphin, melon-headed whale, Commerson's dolphin, false killer whale, killer whale, pilot whale, harbor porpoise, and beluga; the pinnipeds—Steller sea lion, California sea lion, southern sea lion, South American seal, South African fur seal, northern fur seal, gray seal, harbor seal, Baikal seal, harp seal, hooded seal, Mediterranean monk seal, Hawaiian monk seal, leopard seal, northern elephant seal; the sirenian Amazon manatee and West Indian manatee; and walruses.

The whales and dolphins displayed in aquariums belong to the large group biologists call *toothed whales*. Only one specimen of baleen whale (those that filter

The first scientific attempts to understand wild cetaceans began with acoustic studies at sea in the 1940s and were later continued at aquariums. Here, a well-adjusted beluga swims upside down, a typical natural posture, in the Arctic Canada exhibit at the Vancouver Aquarium. (Photo by Leighton Taylor.)

Although California sea lions have been displayed for more than a century in American aquariums, they are now provided with natural living conditions both by the choice of enlightened aquarium biologists and the requirements of federal law. (Photo by Leighton Taylor.)

Seals, like other marine mammals, are highly social. This group at Point Defiance Zoo and Aquarium includes a nursing mother and her pup. (Photo by James Reuter, Jr.)

This pair of walrus were abandoned as young. They were rescued and reared at the Point Defiance Zoo and Aquarium, where they can be viewed through underwater windows and heard making their distinctive bell-tone vocalizations. (Photo by James Reuter, Jr.)

plankton using extensions of their palates called *baleen*) has ever been kept in an aquarium—Gigi, a juvenile gray whale collected in Mexico in 1971 by scientists and aquarists at Sea World of San Diego. She spent a year at Sea World as a beloved and very well studied guest. During her stay she grew from a length of 18 feet to 26½ feet. Gigi was returned to the ocean in 1972, equipped with a radio transmitter. She has been sighted and subsequently identified by unique bumps and markings, including a distinctive brand on her side. One sighting indicated that she was mothering a calf and hence had successfully readapted to the wild population. The battery and the radio have long since worn out. She has been sighted off San Diego in the annual gray-whale migration from Alaska to Mexico as recently as 1991.

The great majority of cetaceans in aquariums today are bottlenose dolphins (various subspecies of *Tursiops truncatus*). The American Association of Zoological Parks and Aquariums helps to maintain a studbook for this group of animals (as they do for many species) to ensure genetic mixing as aquariums continue to breed them. Many of these were born in aquariums.

The history of keeping marine animals in aquariums is variously long, depending on the species. Orca—killer whales—were first taken for public display from coastal waters of British Columbia and Puget Sound between 1962 and 1976. The U.S. gov-

The display of beluga whales has progressed far from P. T. Barnum's 19th-century exhibits. Aquarium biologists at the New York Aquarium, not far from Barnum's early venue, have joined colleagues in an international breeding program for beluga. (Photo by Laine Wilser.)

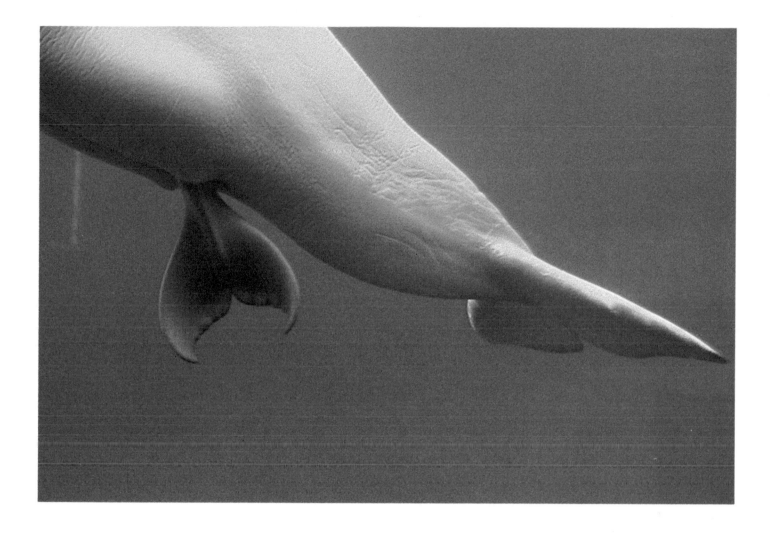

Cetaceans, like this baby beluga, born in the New York Aquarium in 1991, are usually born tail first so that they continue to receive oxygen from the mother's bloodstream until birth is almost complete. (Photo by Laine Wilser.)

ernment issued a permit to take killer whales from Alaskan waters for public display in 1983, but it was ruled invalid in 1985 in response to a lawsuit based on the National Environmental Policy Act. Since the mid-1970s, most animals destined for public display have been taken from waters off Iceland. Aquariums have dedicated their institutions to the breeding and rearing of these animals and are close to the point of stopping their collection from wild populations. Although P. T. Barnum kept beluga under less-than-optimal conditions in his New York attraction in 1861, they now thrive in aquariums designed to provide excellent conditions for reproduction and nurturing young.

Until the latter half of this century, aquariums traditionally limited their holdings to fishes, invertebrates, and perhaps seals and sea lions. When dolphins were displayed it was usually in zoos. As the Marine Mammal Protection Act (passed in 1973) articulates in human law, cetaceans (dolphins, porpoises, and whales) need ample room to thrive. Federal regulations specify minimum dimensions and water-quality standards for cetacean enclosures for research and educational displays. These are the only purposes for which permits to maintain cetaceans are granted.

Until 1938, when Marine Studios (later Marineland of Florida) was founded, no institution that displayed dolphins afforded them ample room to do more than stare back at visitors (although the porpoises in the Brighton aquarium's big tank were reported to "swim lively and answer to a whistle"). Marine Studios was not conceived as an aquarium; its founders wanted to build a huge underwater set for filming feature movies. But, as cetacean researcher Kenneth Norris has said in his excellent review of the history of research on dolphins (see bibliography), it inadvertently was to

Beluga whale mothers, like Kathi at the New York Aquarium, stay in close physical contact with their calves, often using sounds. Sonic communication in marine mammals is of great interest to scientists. (Photos by Rick Miller and Louis E. Garibaldi.)

spur an entire lineage of scientific endeavor. Without any visions of the trained shows we see today, they sent their collection crew to bring in some of the locally available bottlenose dolphins. Soon they accumulated a little society of dolphins caught in the inland channelways in back of the vast tank complex. There was no show routine at first. The dolphins were simply regarded as exhibits, like fish. The dolphins, however, regarded themselves as a society and began to do many of the things that they had done at sea. They courted, mated, and gave birth, helped each other, caught fish, quarreled, and generally behaved like the good mammals they were.

As the complex and exciting natural behavior of the bottlenose dolphins became obvious to Studios' owners, it also became increasingly clear to them that people were very interested in and willing to pay to see marine animals, particularly porpoises. Douglas Burden, cofounder of Marineland, expressed his belief that "if seals and sea lions, pigeons and rats could be trained, so could porpoises." (R. N. Hill provides a fascinating history of these pioneering days in his book *Window in the Sea*.) He decided to hire an experienced animal trainer, Adolph Frohn, whom we might credit as the first dolphin trainer in an aquarium setting. Frohn was born into a family of animal trainers in a circus wagon in Germany in 1904. He married a high-wire artist and toured the United States in an American circus with his own animal act. He worked with Frank Buck's big cat show. When Burden hired him to come to Marine Studios, he was with Barnum and Bailey, Ringling Brothers Circus.

In 1949 Burden proposed that Frohn be hired to attempt to train Flippy, one of the young bottlenose dolphins. If Frohn's trials were successful, the owners were prepared to build a large stadium in which Flippy could perform. Frohn began work with Flippy with no idea as to what the outcome would be. As an experienced trainer, he knew about the practicalities of shaping natural behavior, just as a Scottish shepherd knows how to convince his border collie to drive sheep on command. Hill writes of Frohn's successful attempts to train the bottlenose dolphin: "Training Flippy to Frohn's satisfaction required three years at the cost of $1000 a month, but it was well worth it to Marine Studios to be able to present the world's first educated porpoise in the new seashore stadium just north of the aquarium." Frohn later moved to the Miami Seaquarium, where porpoise training became increasingly popularized and where the "Flipper" television series was developed.

Serendipity at Marine Studios was not limited to dolphin behavior. The aquarium's first curator (fortunately for the profession) was a curious, collegial, and practical young biologist, Arthur McBride. He recognized the golden opportunities he had to observe new behaviors and adaptations of animals, and he did so in a systematic, even scientific, way, anticipating the importance of seizing the opportunities for research that an aquarium presents. McBride's work and his willingness to cooperate with other investigators spurred a long series of studies of bottlenose dolphins at Marineland of Florida.

Thus we can see the early development of the dichotomy in the way aquariums looked upon cetaceans in the early days, which still has strong repercussions today. On the one hand, they were considered circus performers to be exploited for the entertainment of avid crowds; on the other, they were recognized as highly complex marine animals whose behavioral adaptations tell us much about life in the sea.

In 1954 Marineland of the Pacific was built in Los Angeles. In exchange for stock, the Florida enterprise lent its name and its technical knowledge. The West Coast developers felt it was vital to have trained porpoises to ensure an entertaining visit to the new attraction, which was marvelously sited on the bluffs above the sea but was inconveniently distant from most of Los Angeles. Since the Californians didn't have any jumping porpoises, Marine Studios agreed to fly out two trained jumpers. Ken Norris, now widely recognized as the dean of cetacean researchers, was beginning his career at the new Marineland. Although Norris and his colleagues were able to catch Pacific bottlenose dolphins in the open ocean off southern California, many trainers still prefer to train animals from the coastal estuaries of the southwest Atlantic coast.

Craig Phillips relates an incident in his book *The Captive Sea* that gives us a look at the developing sensitivity to marine mammal collection. Early in 1961 the Miami Seaquarium began attempts to capture a local unusual white bottlenose dolphin—an albino—spotted by fishing boats from Beaufort, South Carolina. Nicknamed Carolina Snowball, this sought-after animal became the subject of local interest and concern. Phillips reported that "the local residents of the Beaufort area who had previously regarded the white dolphin as little more than a curiosity began to have second thoughts that Snowball would soon be taken to an aquarium in a different state" (the Miami Seaquarium), where she would have considerable value as an attraction. Legislative pressure was brought to bear, resulting in a law prohibiting the capture of "[any] porpoise by any means whatever in the waters of Beaufort County." The law did not apply to adjacent counties, and Seaquarium collectors continued their efforts outside Beaufort's territorial waters.

There is growing discord over the practice of collecting animals from the wild and displaying them in aquariums. The conflict is particularly marked with marine mammals. Some people have expressed the extreme view that no animal—fish, mammal, or invertebrate—should be removed from its wild habitat. Others suggest that it is their very display and the resulting personal contact with the aquarium visitor that are responsible for the new and growing "ocean ethic." Thirty years ago fishermen shot dolphins for stealing fish. Today, thanks to changing public attitudes, marine mammals are protected by federal law. Such stewardship is stimulated in large part by public contact with cetaceans in aquariums. It is unlikely that we would have wide public support for controls on commercial fishing practices in which dolphins are incidentally caught without such personal interactions between dolphin and aquarium visitor. Strident calls to action may be necessary, but they go unacknowledged if the listeners lack the personal interest that can come only from a firsthand encounter with an active, healthy animal.

Given the protection of various international, federal, and state regulations and the growing activism of Americans, sea otters may once again expand their range to include coastal Oregon. (Photo by Michael Durham, Oregon Coast Aquarium.)

5. A Traveler's Guide to the Aquariums of North America and Beyond

G iven a year, a very large travel budget, and great stamina, an avid aquarium fan could travel the world, visiting a different institution every day. Some would be small; some would be big; some old and some new. Please realize that the following guide, with profiles of a few of these many aquariums, cannot be comprehensive within the limited space of these pages. In selecting them, I also fear the wrath of my colleagues whose aquariums are not covered in detail: my apologies. Bearing in mind that a good aquarium does not have to be a big aquarium, and that novelty demands our attention, I have tried to present a representative and varied selection of significant aquariums. This list is incomplete—and new aquariums are being planned as I write.

I know North American and Japanese aquariums best, so I have probably over-emphasized these. Europe has added at least three fine institutions in the first half of the 1990s. I hope there will be more to come. I am especially (and regrettably) unfamiliar with the aquariums of Africa and Latin America. I invite correspondents to educate me.

Many fine aquariums are included within zoos, where they are frequently sub-

sumed as a department. Less commonly they share equal billing, as at the Point Defiance Zoo and Aquarium in Tacoma, Washington. I wish we did not have to distinguish between zoos and aquariums. After all, they share the same ideal of displaying and interpreting complete ecosystems to ensure the survival of the natural world and its creatures. Michael Robinson, director of the National Zoo, Smithsonian Institution, has suggested a new term for modern zoos—*bioparks*. Perhaps because of its lack of euphony and mixed etymological parentage, it has not caught on. I have limited these profiles to institutions that name themselves (sometimes using other words) as *aquariums,* or whose exhibitry is primarily aquatic. In the appended Directory, any zoo that claims more than 50 species of fishes has been included.

As discussed earlier, there are many ways to express the size of an aquarium. Yet the criteria for judging the *quality* of an aquarium are not necessarily the same. In the following profiles I have listed some standard kinds of statistics (such as annual attendance). I give these only as relative measures. Figures should not be considered precise. Although they have been provided by the aquariums either directly or indirectly (in professional directories and journals), attendance and admission fees are subject to change, and such measures as "area of public space" are usually approximated (sometimes exaggerated) by an aquarium's marketing department.

I hope you will be stimulated by the brief descriptions here to plan your own trip by using the Directory of World Aquariums (see Appendix). I have relied on the following sources; I welcome additions, corrections, and comments.

1. *Directory of the American Association of Zoological Parks and Aquariums*

2. *International Zoo Yearbook*

3. Roster of the Japanese Association of Zoological Parks and Aquariums

4. Membership list of the European Union of Aquarium Curators

5. *Reference Guide to Marine Parks and Aquaria* (Pacheco and Smith, 1989, published by Lyons & Burford, New York)

North America

An American traveler who disliked flying could still see some of the world's great aquariums by driving the coastlines and interior of the continent by car. Beginning in the upper left corner, in British Columbia, the **Vancouver Aquarium** makes a good starting point.

The Vancouver Aquarium
VANCOUVER, BRITISH COLUMBIA, CANADA

YEAR OPENED: 1956

APPROXIMATE ANNUAL ATTENDANCE: 950,000 +

AREA (IN SQUARE FEET): 78,000

TOTAL VOLUME OF TANKS (IN GALLONS): 2,000,000 +

Operated by: Vancouver Public Aquarium Association (private, nonprofit); *Architect:* various and staff; *Exhibit Designer:* various and staff; *Funded by:* gifts, grants, and revenue

The Vancouver Aquarium bridges the gap between the old and the new, providing an excellent example of a successful institution under continual renewal and improvement. Widely admired and abundantly successful with visitors and patrons, this distinguished aquarium may be underappreciated for its contributions to the present state of the art in aquarium education, management, exhibitry, and research.

The Vancouver Aquarium has quietly, effectively, and consistently improved and influenced the aquarium profession over the past three decades. In large part such contributions are due to the consistency and commitment of a visionary yet practical executive director, who has led the institution since 1956.

As a doctoral candidate at the University of British Columbia, Murray Newman worked closely with researchers and educators when he began to develop the modest new aquarium. In the fall of 1956 the aquarium was the first to display spawning salmon. In the 1990s Vancouver is committed to enhancing the breeding of killer whales in aquariums. Its killer whale exhibit is perhaps the world's finest and most naturalistic interpretation of killer whale habitat and biology.

Unlike most new aquariums, the Vancouver Aquarium did not appear full-blown like Botticelli's *Venus of the Waves.* She has grown beautiful and mature over time, regularly adding new attractions. These now include a large gallery devoted to tropical marine life, an impressive simulation of the Amazon rain forest, the Marine Mammal Center, with its backdrop of sandstone cliffs and British Columbian forest trees, and an entire gallery devoted to the northern Pacific, home of migrating salmon.

In 1990 the major exhibit complex Arctic Canada opened to the public. It successfully combines an immense (635,000-gallon) outdoor pool for beluga, habitats for harbor seals and sea otters, and an adjacent interpretive center and museum. Arctic Canada was conceived to provide habitats for arctic marine mammals and fishes and comprehensively interpret the Canadian Arctic.

The success of this exhibit is largely based on research investigations conducted by the aquarium. For the rain forest exhibit, staff visited the Amazon. For Arctic Canada, led by Newman and research director John Ford, they ventured many times to Lancaster Sound—the Northwest Passage—off northern Baffin Island. Although curators deeply wished to display living narwhals, their preliminary work suggested that the animals would not thrive in an aquarium, so the idea was rejected. Beluga whales do thrive—and reproduce—in the kind of excellent exhibit built at Vancouver. Sea otters and harbor seals share the attention of visitors in adjacent display areas.

The 5,000-square-foot Arctic Gallery features finely crafted museum displays and interactive exhibits about life in the Arctic and refrigerated aquariums containing arctic fishes and invertebrates. One entire wall is devoted to acrylic viewing windows into the beluga pool. Two windows extend from floor to ceiling, giving visitors an expansive sense of walking into the tank. The larger window measures 24 feet long by 8 feet high; it is 8 inches thick and weighs more than 10,000 pounds.

Vancouver's next exhibit complex will be devoted to the kelp-rich coasts of British Columbia's Queen Charlotte Islands and the great diversity of marine organisms living there.

Proceeding south along the Pacific Coast, the first stop in the United States is the **Seattle Aquarium,** with its pioneering salmon ladder, sea otters, Puget Sound exhibits, and Pacific coral-reef tank.

Polar bears, also under the protection of the Marine Mammal Protection Act, require well-designed enclosures and aquariums to ensure their safety and well-being, as well as that of aquarium biologists and visitors.

Just to the south, in Tacoma, is the **Point Defiance Zoo and Aquarium.** Important advances in animal care and exhibit design are being made here. The senior staff are widely respected for their skill in collecting and transporting sharks, for their sensitivity to marine mammal issues, and for their steady hand with elephants—an all-around group of "bioparkers." Of special interest here are the Coral Reef exhibit complex, the Rocky Shores exhibit, and the underwater views of adult polar bears.

The new **Oregon Coast Aquarium at Newport** is worth a special look.

Oregon Coast Aquarium
NEWPORT, OREGON

YEAR OPENED: 1992

APPROXIMATE ANNUAL ATTENDANCE: 600,000

AREA (IN SQUARE FEET): 56,000

TOTAL VOLUME OF TANKS (IN GALLONS): 1,000,000 +

Operated by: Oregon Coast Aquarium, Inc. (private, nonprofit); *Architect:* SRG Architects, Portland, Oregon; *Exhibit Designer:* Jim Peterson of Bios; and Fulton Gale Architects, both of Seattle, Washington; *Funded by:* state bonds, gifts, and grants

Excellent aquariums don't happen overnight. When the Oregon Coast Aquarium opened in May 1992, at least

15 years of planning, negotiating, and fund-raising had come before the celebration party. It is surprising that it took as long as it did. There has been strong support for the aquarium throughout the state and certainly in the coastal community of Newport. The site is well located on a large estuary that is part natural area, part charming fishing harbor and resort. The next-door neighbor is **Hatfield Marine Science Center,** a teaching and research branch of Oregon State University. Expertise and experience gained at Hatfield's small popular aquarium were shared with the planners of the new aquarium.

In its design the Oregon Coast Aquarium reflects a sensitivity to nature for which Oregonians are well-known. It is a comfortable, practical building with an exciting set of outdoor exhibits that invite discovery and exploration in full view of the bay, sky, and forests. Sometimes it is raining—this is Oregon, after all—but that's exactly the idea: to see Oregon in its natural state.

Wonderful exhibit complexes entice visitors outside: a seabird aviary, a rocky coast rookery of seals and sea lions, a natural grotto of local giant Pacific octopus, and a marvelously natural sea otter habitat. Sea otters, now locally extinct in Oregon, are reminders of what we can lose, and what, with care, we can rescue and regain.

Soon there will be more outdoor exhibits, including beaver pools, river otter lairs, and wild shorebird ponds, all joined by marshland walkways. A large open-ocean pool is also on the drawing boards.

This is the kind of aquarium that blends its exhibits with the natural world. Take your binoculars, comfortable shoes, and maybe a rain slicker.

On the north shore of San Francisco Bay (and accessible by ferry from the city) is **Marine World Africa USA**. This commercial 160-acre "animal theme park" features an ark of animals, from camels to butterflies to lobsters. In 1992 an excellent 300,000-gallon shark exhibit opened, adjoining a killer whale and dolphin stadium and a new aquarium building.

In San Francisco is one of America's oldest large aquariums, the venerable **Steinhart Aquarium,** part of the California Academy of Sciences, the natural history museum in Golden Gate Park. Two of the newly installed exhibit halls, Life Through Time and Wild California, include excellent aquarium exhibits as well as the latest techniques of combining museum exhibitry with living organisms. Not to be missed are the dioramas of

Although the Oregon Coast Aquarium displays animals found in Oregon's coastal ecosystems, it also displays sea otters. These animals, once abundant along the Oregon coast, are now considered locally extinct because of heavy hunting for their beautiful furs prior to 1911. The aquarium hopes that seeing these charming animals here will encourage visitors to be protective stewards of the environment—and to guard against taking the presence of common animals for granted. (Photo by Michael Durham, Oregon Coast Aquarium.)

ocean life displaying crab and fish larvae sculpted into models 200 times their normal size. Steinhart's traditional galleries include white-sided dolphins, penguins, living corals, and marine life from around the world. The Roundabout aquarium (see page 90) is both an exciting contemporary exhibit and an important piece of aquarium history.

After a three-hour coastal drive from San Francisco, the aquarium traveler will arrive at the **Monterey Bay Aquarium.**

Jellyfish are a popular exhibit species at the Oregon Coast Aquarium. (Photo by Michael Durham, Oregon Coast Aquarium.)

Monterey Bay Aquarium
Monterey and Pacific Grove, California

YEAR OPENED: 1984; new addition in 1996

APPROXIMATE ANNUAL ATTENDANCE: 1,700,000

AREA (IN SQUARE FEET): 216,000 + 90,000

TOTAL VOLUME OF TANKS (IN GALLONS): 1,900,000+

Operated by: Monterey Bay Aquarium Foundation; *Architect:* Esherick, Homsey, Dodge, and Davis; *Exhibit Designer:* Ace Design, Bios, Inc., and aquarium staff; *Funded by:* private philanthropy and earned income

(To all its other attributes, the aquarium can add the unique condition that its building straddles the legal boundary between two coastal cities.)

From its opening in 1891, Stanford University has exerted a significant influence on marine biology. Stanford's first president, David Starr Jordan, was the premier ichthyologist in the United States during his career. His study of fishes ranged around the world.

Jordan's successors and colleagues at Stanford University founded the Hopkins Marine Station, located on the south shore of Monterey Bay near the west end of Cannery Row, the mile-long strip of sardine canneries that were active in the first half of this century. After the sardine populations reached very low levels, fishing ceased, the canneries shut down, and many of the buildings fell into disrepair. Some of them were adapted as cafés, bars, and shops to serve a modest but growing number of tourists drawn to an area that author John Steinbeck had vividly described in his novels.

Meanwhile, Stanford students and researchers at Hopkins and their colleagues continued to study the complex marine biology of Monterey Bay's rich ecosystems—its kelp beds and deep submarine canyon. Many of the West's leading researchers and teachers of marine biology spent fruitful hours in the tide pools and kelp beds near Hopkins and in the classrooms and library established here.

The influence of Stanford, its Hopkins Marine Station, and two nearby colleague institutions, the University of California at Santa Cruz and Moss Landing Marine Laboratories, indirectly led to the founding of an aquarium that many people believe to be one of the best in the world—the Monterey Bay Aquarium. In 1974, Stanford alumnus (and cofounder of Hewlett-Packard elec-

The Monterey Bay Aquarium on historic Cannery Row maintains the vernacular of the fishing harbor made famous by John Steinbeck's novels. The chimneys for the Cannery boilers are simulated by the Fiberglas replicas—but many local residents swear that they are the original stacks. The walls of the building are formed in part by the exhibit tanks. Totally modern in both construction and design, the building blends almost seamlessly with the historic wooden buildings of the old waterfront. (Courtesy Monterey Bay Aquarium.)

tronics company) David Packard and his family looked to the crumbling Cannery Row and purchased three lots on the western end to ensure that the Hopkins Marine Station would have a compatible neighbor.

Gradually, three young family members, daughters Julie and Nancy and Nancy's husband, Robin Burnett, all of whom had studied marine biology, began to discuss with their professor-friends Steve Webster and Chuck Baxter the possibility of establishing an aquarium on the site. The idea gradually grew and began to take the shape of an institution devoted to interpreting Monterey Bay. The focus would not be limited to fishes but would feature plants and invertebrate marine life of the area.

As this informal team began to test its ideas with colleagues, they were more often than not met with disbelief, expressed in remarks such as "How can you expect people to come all the way to Monterey, a resort area for older, wealthy golfers, to see an aquarium that features cold-water animals noted for their lack of color and dull behavior? It will never work."; and "People will never come here to see plastic kelp and brown rockfish."

The team persisted and wisely hired as curator the experienced David Powell, who had begun work at Marineland of the Pacific and contributed mightily to the success of the Steinhart Aquarium and Sea World in San Diego. Further tempering the academic enthusiasm and

theory of the group with practicality was David Packard, noted for his organizational and management savvy. The Packard family's philanthropy toward this institution is a hallmark of private support for cultural institutions in the 1980s. It hearkens back to the generosity of John G. Shedd, Cornelius Vanderbilt, and Ignatz Steinhart.

In the first seven years of its existence, the aquarium hosted more than 11 million people and earned annual surpluses from admission revenues, retail sales, and program fees. These retained earnings are financing a $60 million expansion of the aquarium, scheduled to open in 1996. The early naysayers about brown fish and plastic kelp have been proven wrong.

The Monterey Bay Aquarium has reported its three most popular permanent exhibits to be the kelp forest, sea otters, and moon jellyfish. Yet in 1991, when their featured seasonal exhibit displayed 12 species of sharks, attendance increased significantly.

Many visitors who view the kelp-forest exhibit at the Monterey Bay Aquarium assume that they are looking in through a window to the actual bay environment itself. This realism is a product of clever exhibitry and aquarium biology of the highest caliber. In a way the visitors are right. If they were in the bay with a scuba tank on, they would see exactly the same animals, but the viewing conditions would be less satisfactory. During winter, when storms roil the surface of the kelp beds, the surface vegetation is ripped apart. Meanwhile,

The puffins of the northern rocky coastlines are just as much marine animals as the fish they eat. Modern aquariums are increasingly including seabirds in their attempts to interpret marine ecosystems. (Photo by Michael Durham, Oregon Coast Aquarium.)

Sea World researchers conducted extensive field studies on wild penguins to ensure a successful design for the Penguin Encounter exhibit. As a result all the penguin species with sexually mature birds in the population breed regularly. (Courtesy Sea World of California.)

in the aquarium, the growth rate of the exhibit kelp forest exceeds that in nature.

To achieve this degree of realism required careful planning. Three years before the opening of the exhibit, director of husbandry David Powell and his staff —all scuba divers—took the fabricated, realistic-looking, Fiberglas-reinforced concrete rocks offshore, lowered them to the bottom from their boat, fastened them to real rocks, and left them there for three years so that naturally occurring plants and animals would attach themselves to the rocks. When the exhibit tank was completed they retrieved the rocks with their diverse communities of plants and animals attached, brought them back to the aquarium, and installed them. They did not bring back as many rocks as they took out, however. The rocks were so realistic looking and became so much a part of the natural environment that several could not be relocated, despite the fact that divers swam through the area trying to detect the real from the simulated.

The entire building complex of the Monterey Bay Aquarium is a realistic analog of these naturalized rocks. Rather than create an architectural icon, architect Charles Davis (of Esherick, Homsey, Dodge, and Davis) chose to create a building that matched the vernacular architecture of Cannery Row. As a final touch, he installed replicas of the smokestacks that vented the boilers of the old Hoven Cannery, which once occupied the site.

On opening day of the aquarium, in October 1984, longtime residents of the area and former cannery workers grew nostalgic upon hearing once again the early-morning blast of the cannery whistle which had long fallen silent, perhaps voicing the aquarium's opening day motto: "The fish are back at Cannery Row."

Continuing southward, a visit to the Santa Barbara Museum of Natural History's **Stearns Wharf,** on the harbor front, will present a modest but enjoyable look at the marine life of the offshore, easily visible California Channel Islands, now the center of a National Marine Sanctuary.

Just before turning off the Los Angeles freeways for the **Cabrillo Marine Museum** in San Pedro (with a small but enjoyable blend of aquarium tanks and natural history exhibits about south coastal California), the aquarium fan should pause for 30 seconds of respectful silence for the former **Marineland of the Pacific.** Founded in 1955 and the site of several aquarium "firsts," as well as the training ground for many aquarium professionals, Marineland closed in 1988. The land and animal collections were bought by Sea World and the animals moved to various Sea World locations. The beautiful ocean-bluff site in Palos Verdes will be privately developed.

Continuing toward the California-Mexico border, the aquarium visitor has two more important stops: Scripps Aquarium (formally called the **Steven Birch Aquarium Museum**) and **Sea World** of San Diego.

Stephen Birch Aquarium Museum
(on the campus of Scripps Institution of Oceanography)
La Jolla, California

YEAR OPENED: 1992

APPROXIMATE ANNUAL ATTENDANCE: 500,000

AREA (IN SQUARE FEET): 49,000

TOTAL VOLUME OF TANKS (IN GALLONS): 112,000

Operated by: University of California; *Architect:* Wheeler Wimer Blackman and Associates; *Exhibit Designer:* staff; *Funded by:* gifts and grants, on state land

The new Stephen Birch Aquarium Museum traces its origins almost to the turn of the century. This handsome hillside structure and its grounds replaced the T. Wayland Vaughan Aquarium Museum which opened on the beachside campus of the Scripps Institution of Oceanography (SIO) in 1950. (Although patrons like Vaughan and Birch are honored with their names carved over the door, visitors usually simplify the title of a popular attraction. For years, people have considered this "the Scripps Aquarium," and it will likely continue to be known as that.)

In the summer of 1903, William E. Ritter, a professor of biology at the University of California (at the time with only a single campus, at Berkeley, near San Francisco), visited La Jolla. He settled in for a long summer field trip with a group of students. They were attracted by the variety and accessibility of marine life, the calm sea conditions, and the quiet community. Their visit was so successful that Ritter returned summer after summer. Eventually the university formalized a campus at La Jolla, benefiting from gifts of land from Ellen Browning Scripps, the beloved half-sister of wealthy newspaper publisher E. W. Scripps. (SIO is now part of the adjacent University of California, San Diego campus.)

From the beginning, Ritter and his students would set up small aquariums and demonstrations for the interest and enjoyment of summer visitors from the resort town. The curiosity of many a beachcombing youngster was undoubtedly encouraged by the visiting scholars and their impromptu displays. Such "exhibits" became so popular, and the kibitzing with the scientists so distracting, that a small aquarium was established, both to meet popular demand and to protect the researchers from interruption.

Scripps Institution grew markedly during the 1940s, when scientists had to meet the wartime need for information about the ocean. The value of such research for peacetime interests was also recognized, and Scripps is well established as an international center for research and teaching.

In 1950 the institution built a substantial aquarium at the foot of the campus pier, and its popularity swelled. Over half a million visitors a year began to share the campus with researchers. In the 1980s it became clear that the building needed replacement. It would be convenient for everyone if the new site was away from the main campus. A nearby hillside location was selected that affords a wonderful view of the campus, La Jolla Cove, and the Pacific Ocean. The aquarium's Tidepool Plaza is a fine vantage point from which to view migrating gray whales.

True to its origins, the new aquarium combines museum exhibits with living displays and offers extensive educational programs. The National Science Foundation considered the exhibits important enough to contribute $500,000 to their construction; Exploring the Blue Planet, as the museum complex is named, is a combination of permanent and changing interactive exhibits interpreting every aspect of the ocean and the ways we learn about it. Research conducted at Scripps is featured. The 33 exhibits in the adjacent aquarium section focus on marine life of the Pacific Ocean, from the cold waters of the Pacific Northwest and the temperate waters of California to the tropical areas of Mexico and the Indo-Pacific. Highlights include a 50,000-gallon kelp-forest aquarium and an outdoor re-creation of a La Jolla tide pool.

Sea World
San Diego, California
Aurora, Ohio
Orlando, Florida
San Antonio, Texas

San Diego

YEAR OPENED: 1964

APPROXIMATE ANNUAL ATTENDANCE: 3,700,000

AREA: 135 acres

TOTAL VOLUME OF TANKS (IN GALLONS): 6,000,000+

Operated by: Busch Entertainment Corporation; *Architect:* staff; *Exhibit Designer:* staff; *Funded by:* investment and revenues

AURORA

YEAR OPENED: 1970

APPROXIMATE ANNUAL ATTENDANCE: 1,300,000

AREA: 80 acres

TOTAL VOLUME OF TANKS (IN GALLONS): 3,000,000+

Operated by: Busch Entertainment Corporation; *Architect:* staff; *Exhibit Designer:* staff; *Funded by:* investment and revenues

ORLANDO

YEAR OPENED: 1973

APPROXIMATE ANNUAL ATTENDANCE: 4,000,000

AREA: 135 acres

TOTAL VOLUME OF TANKS (IN GALLONS): 6,000,000+

Operated by: Busch Entertainment Corporation; *Architect:* staff; *Exhibit Designer:* staff; *Funded by:* investment and revenues

SAN ANTONIO

YEAR OPENED: 1988

APPROXIMATE ANNUAL ATTENDANCE: 2,500,000

AREA: 250 acres

TOTAL VOLUME OF TANKS (IN GALLONS): 4,000,000+

Operated by: Busch Entertainment Corporation; *Architect:* staff; *Exhibit Designer:* staff; *Funded by:* investment and revenues

Public curiosity and interest in marine life can be big business. Most of the aquariums that exhibit and interpret the life of the waters are nonprofit, public-service institutions. However, the most successful organization dedicated to exhibiting marine life—if success is defined by the numbers of people served—is profit-making Sea World, Inc. Almost 12 million visitors attend the four parks (combined) every year.

Sea World began in San Diego in the 1960s as the brainchild of several California businessmen with an interest in the sea and extensive experience in the tourist industry. With the advice and counsel of biologists, including professors from nearby Scripps Institution, they refined their ideas and obtained a fine site in the marshlands of Mission Bay, north of the city of San Diego. Sea World, Inc. was formed and financed by private investment and stock offerings.

Their scientist-advisors convinced the developers that research and a commitment to responsible, wise use of resources were vital to the success of any enterprise concerned with living animals. An allied nonprofit research foundation was created, and biologists and veterinarians with extensive research and practical experience were made key members of the staff.

Today, Sea World (now owned by Busch Entertainment, Inc., a subsidiary of Anheuser Busch) leads the increasingly successful effort to breed and rear killer whales in aquariums, both their own and other, nonprofit facilities. This commitment to exhibit research has also paid off with such successful results as the Penguin Encounter (see pages 106-107) and the Shark Experience. Proud of their breeding results and aware of public interest, the parks now have tour programs called "Small Wonders," centering on these breeding successes.

But killer whales—orca—are the animals most closely associated with Sea World. The parks host more than 30 whales, the largest assemblage outside of an ocean. The company has registered the name *Shamu* for its key orca performers. Thus, like the popular dogs that played Lassie in movies and on television, the Shamu of the Florida park is not the same whale as the Shamu in San Diego. The experience of seeing these great animals firsthand (no matter what human name some feel the need to give them) creates an awe and appreciation in visitors that is vital for the survival of the species.

A visit to Sea World reveals some of the most exciting and important species living in the ocean—penguins, sharks, whales, and fishes. Such enterprises have the opportunity and the responsibility to help their visitors appreciate and protect the natural populations and habitats from which their displayed animals serve as ambassadors.

An especially avid visitor would continue to within eight miles of the Mexican border, to visit the **Chula Vista Interpretive Center,** a small but elegant nature center focused on the aquatic life of coastal estuaries. Surrounded by such an estuary, the center has some fine small aquariums and natural history exhibits and excellent education programs.

It is a long drive from Sea World in San Diego to the next aquarium stop in Texas. An aquarium fan with a historical bent might stop in Tucson, Arizona, to visit the **Arizona-Sonora Museum.** Although not an aquarium, this excellent exhibition of desert ecology was directed for many years by Merv Larson, who perfected the technique for fabricating artificial rocks and trees. His methods are widely used in aquarium displays around the world. This museum—really a nature center—also helped pioneer the idea of ecologically based exhibits.

Soon, across the border, there may be new aquariums to visit in Vera Cruz and Acapulco. But it's dry in the desert—let's drive on to the artificial oceans of south central Texas. We could take an alternate route north to Denver to visit the **Denver Zoo**'s new tropical complex, with its exhibits of coral seas. We could then approach Texas from Oklahoma City, where the **Oklahoma Zoo** maintains an excellent collection of aquatic displays of tropical communities and sharks and dolphins.

In San Antonio, **Sea World of Texas** opened as the fourth Sea World park in 1988. The elaborate and excellent exhibits pioneered in San Diego featuring sharks, polar birds, and marine mammals are duplicated here. The historic **Dallas Aquarium,** founded in 1936, is typical of older civic aquariums—a modest and dedicated facility that has helped generations of Texans learn about the aquatic life of the world's waters. When we reach the ocean coast at Corpus Christi, the **Texas State Aquarium** awaits.

Texas State Aquarium
CORPUS CHRISTI, TEXAS

YEAR OPENED: 1990

APPROXIMATE ANNUAL ATTENDANCE: 600,000+

AREA (IN SQUARE FEET): 43,000 on 7 acres

TOTAL VOLUME OF TANKS (IN GALLONS): 350,000+

Operated by: Texas State Aquarium Association (private, nonprofit); *Architect:* Phelps, Bomberger, and Garza; *Exhibit Designer:* J.A. Wetzel Associates, Boston; *Funded by:* city funds; gifts and grants

After 21 years of planning, much of it occupied with finding the right site, the Texas State Aquarium opened in the summer of 1990. And people were definitely eager to see it. Projected attendance for the first year was 600,000. More than 730,000 visitors came, an increase of 20 percent over the projection. The aquarium is dedicated to fostering a deeper public understanding and appreciation of the Gulf of Mexico and the Caribbean Sea through education, recreation, and research programs.

A grand outdoor entry, the Gulf of Mexico Plaza, features colorful mosaics of sea creatures, including manta rays and sharks, which lead the visitor into the building to their living counterparts, as well as groupers and the smaller, sometimes more fascinating, invertebrates and fish.

Based on its early success, the Texas State Aquarium plans a $5 million addition of a 300-seat auditorium, classroom, and research facility. Phase III will include a $20 million Caribbean wing.

Continuing eastward along the Texan coast of the Gulf of Mexico, the aquarium aficionado who is especially interested in sharks will give a respectful wave to Galveston, home of the former **Sea-Arama Marineworld** (yet another synonym for *aquarium*), where many of the techniques for collecting and shipping living sharks to aquariums throughout the world were developed.

In New Orleans, on the west side of the great Mississippi River, we will visit the **Aquarium of the Americas,** a recent addition to the riverfront and a very popular tourist attraction.

Aquarium of the Americas
NEW ORLEANS, LOUISIANA

YEAR OPENED: 1990

APPROXIMATE ANNUAL ATTENDANCE: 2,000,000+

AREA (IN SQUARE FEET): 108,000

TOTAL VOLUME OF TANKS (IN GALLONS): 1,190,000

Operated by: Audubon Institute; *Architect:* The Bienville Group, A Joint Venture; *Exhibit Designer:* Bios, Inc.; *Funded by:* city funds; gifts and grants

Aquarium professionals marvel at this facility for at least two reasons. First, it was conceived, designed, and built in the abnormally short time of less than four years. Everyone involved in the project agrees that, as one architect has expressed it, "The hot schedule for this project wasn't a pressure-cooker; it was a microwave oven!" Second, regardless of the cooking method, the result is already savory to millions of visitors. Planners expected 1.5 million people to visit during the first year. Their estimate was wrong; more than 2.36 million visitors enjoyed the Aquarium of the Americas in its first 12 months. Gracefully situated in a 16-acre park on the Mississippi riverfront, at the foot of Canal Street and adjacent to New Orleans's French Quarter, the aquarium seems to attract visitors magnetically.

The aquarium's name reveals its exhibition theme—the Americas. Visitors pass through a lofty entry gallery and step into a transparent acrylic tunnel where

When the Aquarium of the Americas opened in New Orleans, it immediately become a favorite landmark for residents and visitors alike. (Photo by Leighton Taylor.)

132,000 gallons of water—filled with the fish and marine life of a Caribbean coral reef—surround them. From this tropical American sea, the path leads to the brightly sky-lit Amazonian rain forest of South America, with birds, fish, plants, and invertebrates. Traveling north (literally and figuratively) from the Amazon area, visitors enter an exhibit complex of life on (and in) the Mississippi River, complete with trapper's cabin, banjo music, catfish, and crayfish. The largest aquarium is the Gulf of Mexico tank, with 500,000 gallons of seawater, sharks, tarpon, groupers, and the base of an oil rig, covered with marine life. Special galleries feature penguins related to those from South America, and diverse adaptations of fishes to aquatic life. Video programs fill the interpretive galleries.

The success of the Aquarium of the Americas has prompted the city and the aquarium's operators to accelerate their second-phase expansion. An IMAX theater and a large changing exhibit gallery will open in 1995. A huge open ocean tank, with room for whale sharks, is planned for phase 3.

The Tennessee Aquarium
CHATTANOOGA, TENNESSEE

YEAR OPENED: 1992

APPROXIMATE ANNUAL ATTENDANCE: 850,000

AREA (IN SQUARE FEET): 70,000 +

TOTAL VOLUME OF TANKS (IN GALLONS): 600,000

Operated by: Tennessee Aquarium Corporation; *Architect:* Cambridge Seven Associates; *Exhibit Designer:* Lyons/Zaremba

The city of Chattanooga now has both a distinguished civic landmark and a rich educational and recreational center in the Tennessee Aquarium. Architect Peter Chermayeff's design is widely heralded as an important new building. Heartened by the success of the Monterey Bay Aquarium's regional emphasis, the creators of the world's first large all-freshwater aquarium chose to highlight a unique part of America: the Tennessee River watershed. The streams, hardwood forests, and mountains of this area abound with diverse forms of life found on land and water, including vegetation, frogs, fishes, and birds. Together, the exhibits illustrate the "life story" of a drop of rain from the point where it falls into the headwaters of the Tennessee River in the Great Smoky

Aquariums are not just for fishes. They may also be home to seals, whales, dolphins, and manatees, like these at the rehabilitation center at the Lowry Park Zoo in Tampa, Florida. (Courtesy Lowry Park Zoo.)

Mountains until it flows out of the mouth of the Mississippi and into the Gulf of Mexico.

Along the Mississippi coast we'll find the commercial **Marine Life Aquarium** in Gulfport, which, until Chicago's Shedd Aquarium opened its marine mammal addition in 1991, advertised the "world's largest covered oceanarium." At Ocean Springs, near Biloxi, the Gulf Coast Research Laboratory maintains the **J. L. Scott Marine Education Center and Aquarium,** the only southern aquarium devoted to animals of Mississippi waters.

Florida offers a perspective on both the history and the future of aquariums, as well as examples of the present state of the art. At Orlando, **Sea World** operates its largest park, featuring the popular exhibits developed both here and in San Diego.

At Epcot Center, **Disney's Living Seas** holds the world's largest volume of artificial seawater—6 million gallons. Although the symbol of the Disney enterprises is an imaginary animal, the Orlando parks—Disney World and Epcot Center—feature a variety of aquatic life—waterbirds, fishes, and marine mammals. The Living Seas Pavilion at Epcot includes many engineering advances and stagecraft techniques likely to be used in the next generation of public aquariums.

Near St. Augustine, **Marineland of Florida** presents the aquarium pilgrim with an important historic site as well as a present-day opportunity to watch Florida marine life. Here, in the 1940s, a pioneering bottlenose dolphin taught its trainer to blow a whistle on cue and the *Creature from the Black Lagoon* made heroes of some snorkeling actors (see page 15). Today the park continues to display marine life and conduct research. Without the innovative work done here from the 1930s through the 1960s on sharks, marine mammals, and

water systems and tank designs, today's aquariums would be very different places.

The future **Florida Aquarium** is underway at Tampa on the harbor front. Codesigned by architects Chuck Davis (Monterey Bay Aquarium) and Gyo Obata (Smithsonian Air and Space Museum), this new institution will "tell the story of Florida's waters" in 90,000 square feet of public space when it opens in 1996.

Miami offers both history and contemporary experiences at the **Miami Seaquarium.** Founded in 1955, this aquarium, with its extensive grounds, was home to Flipper, the bottlenose dolphin, and the popular and influential television show of the same name was filmed here. Much early work was accomplished here on dolphin training and on maintaining large lemon sharks and young bonnethead sharks.

South of Miami, well into the keys at Islamorada, the commercial **Theater of the Sea** offers visitors the opportunity to swim with dolphins. Such programs are federally regulated under the Marine Mammal Protection Act, and the Marine Mammal Commission considers them to be experimental.

It is tempting to continue south into the Caribbean Sea, the real world of coral reefs and tropical oceans that aquariums try to simulate. Tourists to Cuba will surely want to visit the **National Aquarium** in Havana, which features the marine animals of the Cuban coast. The best of both worlds—rich reef and excellent aquarium—meet in the coral-rich Caribbean at the **Guadeloupe Aquarium** on that beautiful island in the French Virgin Islands, but we will save the Caribbean for another visit. Now, we will stop at the tip of Florida and turn northward to continue our tour of North American aquariums.

At Charleston, on the Cooper riverfront, the **South Carolina Aquarium** (scheduled to open in 1996) will interpret the rich maritime environment and human culture of this state and of the southern Atlantic seaboard. The champion of this new institution, Joseph P. Riley, Jr., who served as Charleston's mayor for five terms, has ensured that the institution is guided by a strong mission of education and interpretation. Wild and free dolphins and river otters swim in the river, in full view of the handsome building designed by Allen Eskew, codesigner of the Aquarium of the Americas.

In neighboring North Carolina, the state operates a network of three excellent aquariums, designed to serve as centers for public information, marine education, and research. The **North Carolina Aquariums** at Roanoke Island, Fort Fisher, and Pine Knoll Shores all offer special exhibits on the ecology of maritime and aquatic North Carolina. All three aquariums feature full schedules of programs and activities.

Just offshore, in the Gulf Stream, the **Bermuda Aquarium** in Hamilton offers excellent exhibits of warm-Atlantic marine life.

Back on the continent, at Virginia Beach, the **Virginia Marine Science Museum** (by some definitions, it is an aquarium) presents nearly 100,000 gallons of aquatic exhibits, including a 50,000-gallon Chesapeake Bay tank, where visitors meet firsthand the animals that live in the largest embayment of the eastern United States.

Although it is tempting to proceed directly to Baltimore by boat up the Chesapeake, we need to visit Washington, D.C., along the way. Here, in the lower floor of the Commerce Building, is the country's **National Aquarium.** Once operated by the U.S. Fish and Wildlife Service, then assigned to the Department of Commerce, the aquarium is now operated under a private contract to the federal government (the National Oceanic and Atmospheric Administration; NOAA). Although modestly sized, the National Aquarium has a long and distinguished history. It has enjoyed a variety of locations but can claim to be the nation's oldest non-commercial aquarium, with origins in Woods Hole, Massachusetts, in 1873. The National Aquarium later joined the National Zoo when it was founded on the grounds of the present Washington Monument. In the early 1960s the renowned designer Charles Eames was commissioned to design a major new home for the National Aquarium near the Mall. Sadly, support for the project failed. Eames produced a fine film on his distinguished design, but the National Aquarium remains in the basement of a federal office building.

National Aquarium in Baltimore
BALTIMORE, MARYLAND

YEAR OPENED: 1981; marine mammal building added in 1991

APPROXIMATE ANNUAL ATTENDANCE: 1,500,000

AREA (IN SQUARE FEET): 115,000 + 90,000

TOTAL VOLUME OF TANKS (IN GALLONS): 1,500,000

Operated by: National Aquarium in Baltimore, Inc. (private, nonprofit); *Architect:* Cambridge Seven Associates; *Exhibit Designer:* Cambridge Seven Associates; *Funded by:* city bonds; gifts and grants

In Maryland, proud residents fondly refer to the "Baltimore Aquarium," but officially the big buildings on the inner harbor front are known collectively as the **National Aquarium in Baltimore.** The sobriquet *national* was added as an amendment to federal legislation by a proud Maryland legislator, who reminded his colleagues that they had agreed to build an aquarium "within a 50-mile radius of the Mall" (Eames's project). Thus, with no expenditure of federal money, Congress managed to create another national aquarium. Critics were told that there could be other such "national aquariums" in a city of one's choice, but to date, our nation officially recognizes only the National Aquarium in Washington and the National Aquarium in Baltimore. Certainly the quality of Baltimore's aquarium justifies such recognition.

Although the National Aquarium in Baltimore opened in 1981, it has links to a long tradition of the appreciation of aquatic life in the region of the Chesapeake Bay and the port of Baltimore. In the early part of the century, a group of avid amateur aquarists established the Baltimore Fish Culturists Society and operated the Municipal Aquarium of Baltimore on City parkland. In the mid-seventies, Mayor William Donald Schaefer, well aware of the success of Boston's aquarium, forthrightly announced that the long-needed renewal of the Inner Harbor would begin with a world-class aquarium.

Community support was strong. Voters approved a bond measure, and contributions came in from many sources. Most donors sent money, but among the encouraging gifts was the donation of a Baltimore amateur aquarist, who gave his entire collection of animals and equipment. His aquarium experience dated from the Municipal Aquarium days.

While the city government championed the design

The National Aquarium in Baltimore provides a fine example of the many benefits public aquariums can offer a city. This institution provided Baltimore with an essential element to its harbor-front redevelopment, a handsome architectural addition to the city, and a popular and valued education and recreation center for citizens and visitors alike. (Courtesy Cambridge Seven Associates.)

and building of the aquarium, it wisely contracted its management to the National Aquarium in Baltimore, Inc. The original building opened in 1981, including a 75,000-cubic-foot rain forest and 220,000-gallon shark exhibit. Seminatural planting in the rain-forest exhibit provides open habitats for birds, reptiles, amphibians, mammals, and insects. Twelve thousand gallons of water circulate among pools, waterfalls, and a stream, providing homes for fish, turtles, and aquatic birds.

Below the rain forest, the Atlantic Coral Reef and Open Ocean exhibits are viewed through 13-foot-high acrylic windows. Other exhibits interpret Maryland's aquatic habitats, from the mountains to the sea. North Atlantic to the Pacific portrays the ecology of four distinct coastal environments.

In 1991 the National Aquarium opened its Marine Mammal Pavilion in a new building on an adjacent pier. The complex houses almost 90,000 square feet of space, including a 1.3-million-gallon marine mammal pool with bottlenose dolphins. There is seating for 1,350 people to watch scheduled performances of dolphin behavior. Aquarium officials clearly distinguish these educational demonstrations of cetacean biology from "dolphin shows."

The pavilion also includes an expansive display area filled with interactive exhibits about marine mammals. A full-size realistic model of a breaching humpback whale fills the airy space beneath the skylight.

Named "Scylla" after a well-known whale that regularly migrates along the Atlantic Coast, the humpback is the centerpiece for educational activities and demonstrations.

The aquarium is well known for its successful marketing programs. The resulting high attendance earns revenues for community educational programs and well-researched and effective exhibits.

In Camden, across the Delaware River from Philadelphia, the **Thomas H. Kean New Jersey State Aquarium** opened in 1992.

Thomas H. Kean New Jersey State Aquarium
CAMDEN, NEW JERSEY

YEAR OPENED: 1992

APPROXIMATE ANNUAL ATTENDANCE: 1,000,000

AREA (IN SQUARE FEET): 120,000 + 40,000

TOTAL VOLUME OF TANKS (IN GALLONS): 1,000,000 +

Operated by: New Jersey Academy for Aquatic Sciences; *Architect:* The Hillier Group; *Exhibit Designer:* Joseph A. Wetzel Associates; *Funded by:* state appropriation (through the Sports and Exposition Authority)

Named for the governor of New Jersey under whose administration it was founded, the Thomas H. Kean New Jersey State Aquarium is a major effort in a complex attempt to revitalize Camden's diminished riverfront. Such optimism is well founded: Boston and Baltimore now have active, pleasant, inner harbor fronts crowded with tourists and well stocked with retail enterprises, offices, and hotels. Both renascences began with first-class aquariums. The New Jersey Aquarium (as visitors are sure to call it) is definitely a commitment to first-rank status. The state's $52 million has financed excellent exhibits, a well-designed building, and landscaped grounds along the Delaware River.

Visitors can stroll through an acre of grounds that include woods around a rushing trout stream and a sandy beach surrounding a 170,000-gallon seal pool. The aquarium features the life of the Delaware River, from New Jersey's adjacent bays to its clear headwaters in the Catskills, as well as displaying fishes from around the world. Interactive exhibits give visitors a personal experience of the ways that fishes see, hear, smell, hunt, and hide. The highlight exhibit within the building is a huge (760,000-gallon) open-ocean aquarium, claimed to be the second largest in the United States, hosting sharks, fish, and rays. The major view into this tank is through a single window 18 by 24 feet, revealing the Edge of the Abyss. Divers equipped with underwater receivers and microphones answer questions from visitors.

Even distant passersby can learn something useful from the New Jersey Aquarium. Its huge dome, covering the central rotunda, is visible from nearby Philadelphia and main commuter routes and bridges. At night, an elaborate lighting system attached to a celestial clock and a computer transforms the dome into a colorful weather forecaster. A blue dome signifies blue skies; a white dome, overcast; red warns of approaching storms; and a flashing red dome says "stay home." New Jersey's weather forecaster is a novel example of the mission of the modern aquarium to reach out to its audience.

Next we are off to an aquarium on one of America's more renowned seashores—Coney Island—the third home of the **New York Aquarium.** Part of the New York Zoological Society and home of the Osborne Laboratories of Marine Sciences, the New York Aquarium has a rich history, an important present, and a promising future.

New York Aquarium
CONEY ISLAND, BROOKLYN, NEW YORK

YEAR OPENED: 1896

APPROXIMATE ANNUAL ATTENDANCE: 750,000

AREA (IN SQUARE FEET): 150,000 on 14 acres

TOTAL VOLUME OF TANKS (IN GALLONS): 1,800,000

Operated by: New York Zoological Society; *Architect:* various; *Exhibit Designer:* various and staff; *Funded by:* gifts and grants

Of all the aquariums profiled here, the New York Aquarium has been continuously active the longest. It proved early on that aquariums can consistently draw large crowds, and it continues to do so. At its original location on the southwest tip of Manhattan, a total of 28.5 million people visited its exhibits between 1897 and 1910, an average of 2 million visitors a year. Now, with its more remote location and contemporary competition from a great variety of other pastimes, the New York Aquarium draws more than 750,000 people annually. And it is guaranteed that, as satisfied as turn-of-the-century crowds may have been with their visit, today's families and schoolchildren have a much richer and more meaningful experience.

The aquarium has recently added two major new exhibits, both based on extensive research in educational techniques as well as on the biology of the displayed animals. The 20,000-square-foot Discovery Cove opened in summer 1989. Emphasizing enjoyable education for visitors of all ages, the complex is filled with interactive exhibits. A big crowd-pleaser is the wave crash—visitors stand, safe and dry, beneath a special acrylic window over which regularly breaks a large (400-gallon) ocean wave. Other exhibits include a walk-through New England fishing village complete with fishing boat and blaring bridge radio, touch pools (where visitors, young and old, can touch living sea creatures, perhaps for the first time), a walk-in diorama of a salt marsh, and 12,000-gallon tanks of corals and reef fish.

In 1991 the aquarium also hosted the successful delivery and rearing of two beluga babies, parented by the aquarium's prized adults. As part of the conservation-oriented New York Zoological Society, the New York Aquarium is dedicated to the reproduction of animals at the aquarium. It is also actively involved in research through its subsidiary, Osborne Laboratories of Marine Sciences, and active participation in field research.

In 1993 Sea Cliffs opened with an ambitious and extensive indoor-outdoor exhibit of walruses, harbor seals, northern fur seals, sea otters, and penguins, as well as fish and invertebrates.

On the nearby northern shore of Long Island, the **Cold Spring Harbor Fish Hatchery and Aquarium** is worth a visit. Although this book does not review the many fish hatcheries in the United States with demonstration aquariums, this institution has a very specific educational mandate similar to those of other, larger, public aquariums. In 1883 the first brown trout imported to the United States came to this hatchery from Germany. This quiet event changed the recreational fishing habits of Americans. For years, the Cold Spring Harbor hatchery provided brown trout for stocking lakes and streams. In 1979 public outcry at the state's plan to shut down the historic hatchery stimulated a move to convert it into an aquarium and environmental education center.

Connecticut tempts the aquarium goer with two attractions. The **Mystic Marinelife Aquarium** offers diverse and excellent exhibits on the aquatic communities of New England, the tropics, and the Pacific Coast. Mystic also enjoys an important place in the recent history and development of aquariums. It was founded by the principals of a commercial firm that first supplied bulk mixes for artificial seawater. A cofounded sister institution at Niagara Falls, New York, the **Aquarium of Niagara Falls,** opened in 1965 and helped pioneer the practices now used by many inland aquariums that have limited or no access to natural seawater.

Mystic features demonstrations of marine mammal behavior and maintains Seal Island, a unique 2½-acre refuge where seals and sea lions from the Atlantic and Pacific oceans live in simulations of their native habitats. The aquarium hosts the only adult colony of northern fur seals in the United States. Offering a wide range of education programs, the aquarium also involves the public in the rescue, rehabilitation, and release of stranded marine mammals. The aquarium has long been a center of applied research on aquarium systems, led by Dr. Stephen Spotte.

Also in Connecticut is the **Maritime Center in Norwalk,** opened in 1982 as part of the redevelopment effort of South Norwalk. The center combines aquariums highlighting the sea life of coastal Connecticut, with interactive museum exhibits that interpret human interactions with coastal waters. Like many revenue-conscious museums, the center includes an IMAX theater.

In Massachusetts, near the renowned Woods Hole Oceanographic Institute, is the **Woods Hole Aquarium.** This modest aquarium, with origins in the nineteenth century, is associated with the National Marine Fisheries Service. Exhibits feature economically important fishes and shellfishes of the western North Atlantic.

Northward, in Boston Harbor, is the institution that has served as a successful stimulating model for the great aquariums built in the 25 years following its opening (in 1969), in cities as varied as Baltimore, Monterey, and Osaka. The **New England Aquarium** served as a catalyst for redevelopment of Boston's harbor front and also initiated many successful techniques in aquarium display, engineering, and nonprofit management.

New England Aquarium
BOSTON, MASSACHUSETTS

YEAR OPENED: 1969

APPROXIMATE ANNUAL ATTENDANCE: 1.3 million

AREA (IN SQUARE FEET): 75,000

TOTAL VOLUME OF TANKS (IN GALLONS): 1,000,000

Operated by: New England Aquarium Corporation (private, nonprofit); *Architect:* Cambridge Seven Associates; *Exhibit Designer:* Cambridge Seven Associates; *Funded by:* gifts, grants and revenues

The New England Aquarium has long proclaimed its mission "to make known the world of water." In many ways this institution is the link between the classic aquariums of the early twentieth century and the new institutions to be built at the turn of the twenty-first century.

When it opened in 1969, the New England Aquarium combined the best of traditional ideas of display with new technology, new commitments to community and individual education, and a strong conviction about the importance of research. It was (and of course continues to be) sensibly businesslike and well managed. Even though it is a nonprofit corporation, the aquarium earns a surplus of revenues over expenses and invites the "investment" of the community through gifts and grants.

Some would call the New England Aquarium the first modern public aquarium. Its civic success in sparking the renewal of Boston Harbor encouraged the founding of the National Aquarium in Baltimore and, one can assert, has even influenced the founding of aquariums in Seattle, Monterey, Osaka, New Orleans, Tampa, Cleveland, and Charleston.

The New England Aquarium stimulated the redevelopment of Boston Harbor when it opened in 1969. It is the first in a successful series of aquariums designed by Cambridge Seven Associates. (Courtesy Cambridge Seven Associates.)

The exciting and inviting atmosphere found in today's aquariums, such as the New England Aquarium, contrasts sharply with the almost academic galleries of their turn-of-the-century predecessors. (Courtesy Cambridge Seven Associates.)

The staff and designers of the New England Aquarium successfully fulfilled their goal of simulating the underwater world. By using light, color, and motion, principally in the exhibits, they create the effect of the hidden aquatic world. The aquarium includes a 130,000-gallon open pool that houses penguins. Rising above it is a four-story, cylindrical, 187,000-gallon ocean tank with a simulated coral reef and a diversity of reef fishes and invertebrates. Adjacent galleries include a changing exhibit space and four permanent galleries that display a variety of aquatic life.

Limited space on the waterfront has restricted the building's size. Its popularity was underestimated, and it bulges with happy visitors on summer holidays. To provide more room for exhibits and visitors, the barge *Discovery* is moored to the adjacent dockside. Marine mammal demonstrations are held on the *Discovery* four to six times a day.

The growing popularity of the New England Aquarium justifies its expansion. Plans to relocate the facility to a neighboring decommissioned naval yard were considered, but it is likely that the present site will be enlarged by building new piers.

Marine life of the rocky shores and sandy bottoms of the Gulf of Maine (including the state's most famous animal, the Maine lobster) is exhibited at the **Mount Desert Oceanarium** and **Oceans East** in Boothbay Harbor. Plans for the opening of a major aquarium in Portland, Maine, in 1993 have been postponed. A new facility is being planned to replace the **West Boothbay Harbor Aquarium,** where biologists of the Maine Department of Marine Resources laboratory shared research results and enthusiastic interest in the marine ecology of the Gulf of Maine with visitors. Opening is projected for 1995.

The coastlines of the Great Lakes and the St. Lawrence Seaway offer several aquariums. In eastern Canada we find in Sainte-Foy the **Aquarium du Québec.** The former, modest Montreal Aquarium has been incorporated into the elaborate Biodome housed in the former Olympic bicycle racing arena. There are excellent

Dolphins and seals are not the only aquatic mammals. Hippopotamuses spend as much time in the water as they do on land. This aquarium-style underwater view of a hippo was taken at Toledo Zoo's Hippoquarium. (Courtesy Nestor Ramos, Enartec, Inc.)

aquatic exhibits at the **Metro Toronto Zoo.** The commercial **Marineland of Canada** in Niagara Falls is also located in Ontario.

In Ohio, where the Cuyahoga River enters Lake Erie, Cleveland is planning a superb aquarium, scheduled to open in 1997. The **Aquarium of the Great Waters** will feature Lake Erie and the African Rift lakes, the Great Barrier Reef, and the Nile River. Chuck Davis (Monterey Bay Aquarium) and Allen Eskew (Aquarium of the Americas) have been selected as architects. Meanwhile, the fish and spirit of the former Cleveland Aquarium live on within the **Cleveland Metroparks Zoo.**

At the nearby **Toledo Zoo,** every aquarium fan should see one of the few "aquariums" with hippopotamuses. This excellent exhibit displays the riverine habitat that is the real home of these aquatic beasts. Anyone familiar with aquarium water treatment will admire the filtration system that cleans up after swimming hippos!

In Aurora, Ohio, **Sea World** has operated a marine park since 1970. Initially, whales and porpoises commuted here from San Diego via airplane. Now they are

full-time residents even though the park is open only from May through September.

In the northern suburbs of Detroit, aquarium fans can visit the "oldest aquarium" (doing business in the same location since first opening) in the continental United States, the **Belle Isle Zoo and Aquarium.** Opened in 1904, this aquarium is the same age as the Waikiki Aquarium, which opened in Hawaii (then a territory of the United States) in the same year. Also in Michigan, at the western tip of Lake Superior, plans are underway for the **Lake Superior Center.** This facility plans to include a research and education center as well as aquarium and museum exhibits. The center has already established formal relationships with other facilities, focused on another great, deep lake, Lake Baikal in Siberia.

If, as Paul van den Sande has suggested, some aquariums are chapels and others are cathedrals, the Notre Dame of the Midwest is surely the **John G. Shedd Aquarium** in Chicago.

The new oceanarium at the John G. Shedd Aquarium in Chicago provides a simulated view of the Pacific Northwest, with native marine mammals on display, as well as expansive views of Lake Michigan. (Architect Lohan Associates. Photo by Hedrich Blessing.)

John G. Shedd Aquarium
CHICAGO, ILLINOIS

YEAR OPENED: 1930; major addition in 1991

APPROXIMATE ANNUAL ATTENDANCE: 1,250,000

AREA (IN SQUARE FEET): 225,000 + 170,000

TOTAL VOLUME OF TANKS (IN GALLONS): 3,000,000

Operated by: Shedd Aquarium Society (private, nonprofit); *Architect:* original building: Graham, Anderson, Probst, and White; marine mammal pavilion: Lohan, Associates; *Exhibit Designer:* staff; *Funded by:* gifts, grants, and revenues

The generosity of John Graves Shedd, a Chicago retailer and philanthropist, made possible North America's largest indoor aquarium. Shortly before his death in 1926, Shedd presented $3 million (equivalent to about $50 million in today's dollars) to the people of Chicago to build an aquarium. He had expressed the belief that "an aquarium would provide instructive entertainment for a larger number of people than any other type of institution."

He encouraged the organization by a group of representative businessmen of the Shedd Aquarium Society.

After Shedd's death, his family and the society carried on his plans to build the largest aquarium in the world. From 1924 to 1927, advisors visited foremost aquariums around the world, and their best features were incorporated.

The Chicago architectural firm of Graham, Anderson, Probst, and White designed the aquarium in classic style to complement the neighboring Field Museum of Natural History. The floor plan was also designed to be very formal. Six rectangular galleries surrounded a 40-foot-wide sunken pool in a skylit rotunda. This elegant "swamp" featured tropical plants, reptiles, and fish. In 1971 it was replaced with a 90,000-gallon coral-reef tank with artificial corals providing habitats for hundreds of coral-reef fishes from the Caribbean. In the early days Shedd used its own specially outfitted railcar to transport live specimens. Shedd has now long maintained its own collecting vessel in Florida for expeditions to Caribbean reefs and the Gulf Stream. The carefully collected plants and animals are air-shipped back to the aquarium.

Twenty years ago the use of acrylic windows was uncommon. The Shedd Coral Reef exhibit incorporated 2½-inch-thick triple-laminated glass.

Fulfilling its founder's global vision, the aquarium exhibits aquatic life from around the world. Many smaller exhibits in the galleries are devoted to tropical fresh and saltwater, cold fresh and saltwater, and temperate fresh and saltwater habitats. Shedd continues the tradition of the classic aquariums of displaying a great assortment of aquatic life.

When the aquarium formally opened on May 30, 1930, it was far from fully stocked. By June 1931, with the completion of the Balanced Aquarium Room (Gosse would have been pleased), Shedd housed the greatest variety of sea life under one roof.

Public response was positive, beyond even John G. Shedd's foresightful optimism. More than 4 million visitors attended in the first full year of operation, an attendance figure unequaled until 1990 at the Osaka Ring of Fire Aquarium. Despite its size and classic beauty, the Shedd Aquarium building has always seemed to turn its back to the marvelous view of the lake that laps at its back door. In April 1991 this was remedied when the exquisite Oceanarium opened. This multilevel marine mammal pavilion stands on almost 2 acres of landfill and was built at a cost of $45 million. Its expansive windows offer full views of Lake Michigan over the enclosed 2 million-gallon Whale Harbor, home to white-sided dolphins.

This is no circus arena, however. The design simulates a protected cove in the coastline of the Pacific Northwest, and the animals display naturally adaptive behavior. The addition includes a 1,000-seat amphitheater, special exhibit galleries, a 227-seat auditorium, a reference library, a members' lounge, and restaurants.

After this circumnavigation of North American aquariums by auto and an occasional ferry, the intrepid traveler must now board an airplane (ships would take too long) and head east or west for the next leg of the tour. New York Aquarium is not the only aquarium on an "island." While Coney Island has its appeal, I suggest we fly west from Chicago to Hawaii and continue westward to Japan and Asia.

Hawaii

On Oahu, in Honolulu, the University of Hawaii and the associated Friends of the Waikiki Aquarium operate the modest but internationally respected **Waikiki Aquarium,** a center for research and public education.

Waikiki Aquarium
HONOLULU, HAWAII

YEAR OPENED: 1904

APPROXIMATE ANNUAL ATTENDANCE: 350,000

AREA (IN SQUARE FEET): 35,000 on 3 acres

TOTAL VOLUME OF TANKS (IN GALLONS): 200,000

Operated by: University of Hawaii; *Architect:* Hart Wood; Ossipoff, Snyder, and Rowland; *Exhibit Designer:* staff, Kevin O'Farrell, and Bios, Inc.; *Funded by:* earned revenues, gifts and state grants

Each colorful marine species of Hawaii's reefs has its own distinctive and fascinating biology. In addition, almost every plant and animal is also a cultural object. The Hawaiian people have a long history and a complex culture. They view the life of the sea as an essential element in their own lives. Thus, the Waikiki Aquarium has a special task and opportunity—to learn about and to tell the stories of the Hawaiian ocean. It seems appropriate that this aquarium is part of an institution of higher learning and public service, the University of Hawaii.

The original aquarium (then known as the Honolulu Aquarium) was established in 1904 as a commercial enterprise by businessmen who wished to "show the world the riches of Hawaii's reefs." They also owned the city's trolley company. They built the aquarium at the far end of the streetcar line in Kapiolani Park (in the shadow of the landmark sea bluff called Diamond Head) to encourage ridership from downtown Honolulu.

In 1919 the University of Hawaii assumed the management of the aquarium and established an adjacent marine laboratory. The original building was replaced in 1950. The present one will be extensively rebuilt in 1993–94.

The Waikiki Aquarium is best known for its superb exhibits that duplicate life in tropical seas. Each aquarium displays a "piece of the real world." Fishes, coral, and invertebrates live together just as they do on the adjacent reefs.

The focus of the aquarium is on tropical Pacific marine life—chambered nautiluses, giant clams, reef sharks, sea snakes, Hawaiian monk seals, and mahimahi. The Sea Vision Theater continuously shows excellent documentaries about ocean life, several of them made for Public Television and the British Broadcasting Corporation by former staff members. Several exhibits

have research components. Some animals, such as mahi-mahi, chambered nautiluses, and Hawaiian monk seals, have been the subject of research articles published in international journals.

The secret to the Waikiki Aquarium's successful exhibits and research is its location. The living ocean that almost laps at its doorstep provides excellent-quality seawater. The nearby university attracts dedicated and highly trained staff members and curious students willing to work hard.

The essence of this Hawaiian aquarium is on view daily at the outdoor Edge of the Reef exhibit. To stand here, in view of the blue-green ocean, with trade winds rustling the native shoreside plants, and watch a wondering youngster of Hawaii stand eye to eye with a *humuhumunukunukuapua'a* is to know the bond between our life on the land and in the sea.

To the east of Honolulu, near Waimanalo, **Sea Life Park** may be the world's most beautifully sited aquarium. Backed by sheer volcanic cliffs covered with green plants, and fronted by aquamarine waters overlying

After years of research, aquarium biologists are finally achieving success in the reproduction of corals. This female green mushroom coral (Sandalolitha robusta) *expells eggs adjacent to a male colony in a display tank at the Waikiki Aquarium. The female colony was collected in Palau in 1983 and was first observed to spawn in 1992. This is one of three species the Waikiki Aquarium has been successful in spawning.* (Photo by Bruce Carlson, Waikiki Aquarium.)

coral reefs and white sand, the park looks out to small rocky islands that host seabird rookeries. Sea Life Park is famous for its success in keeping and training a diversity of marine mammals. In its first years of operation, beginning in 1964, cofounder Karen Pryor and her colleagues developed many training techniques for eliciting the cooperation and talents of bottlenose and spinner dolphins. The park featured many innovations: a large outdoor/indoor coral-reef exhibit; the assisted breeding and rearing of Hawaiian green sea turtles; and, in its early years, an active partnership with a cofounded research center, the Oceanic Institute. Although a commercial enterprise, Sea Life Park still professes a strong commitment to public education. The park is assisting the U.S. Fish and Wildlife Service in the rehabilitation of Hawaiian monk seals and has popular shark exhibits featuring some of the few scalloped hammerheads to be seen in aquariums.

A variety of plans are under discussion for aquariums on other Hawaiian islands, especially Hawaii and Maui, but Oahu is our only stop on this trip.

On the way to Japan, an adventurous aquarium fan might stop at the island of Guam to get a glimpse of what might be a future trend in aquariums. The government of Guam and its excellent University and Marine Laboratory are planning to open a public facility sometime after 1996. In the meantime, the **Swim-through Aquarium at the Pacific Islands Club** in Tumon Bay is open for an active aquarium experience. Club guests don masks, snorkels, and fins to tour the 250,000-gallon marine aquarium. The outdoor pool simulates the nearby reef in safe, controlled conditions. Although most of the coral is artificial, the fish are real and abundant. Less venturesome visitors can watch both fish and their daring friends through large viewing windows. Adjoining the reef tank is a deeper (20-foot) pool for scuba instruction. To provide healthy conditions for both fish and people, the Swim-through Aquarium is equipped with well-engineered water systems that circulate the entire pool volume once an hour and disinfect it with ozone.

Japan

Japan is indeed a country rich in aquariums. The 1992 roster of the Japanese Association of Zoological Gardens and Aquariums (JAZGA) lists 62 aquariums and 15 "zoos with aquariums."

Although there is a long tradition of keeping fish in Japan, public aquariums date only from the late nineteenth century. According to Hiromasa Yoshida of Suma Aqualife Park, the first public aquarium in Japan was established in Tokyo in 1882, at what is now known as the Ueno Zoological Gardens. This was reportedly "primitive," and the first "true" aquarium was constructed at the Second National Marine Fair, held in Kobe in 1897. The Port of Nagoya Public Aquarium (opened October 1992) will increase the still-growing list.

Japan's aquariums, like those of North America, are diverse. They range from small to large, commercial to municipal, serious and educational to slick and superficial. Aquariums abound throughout the country and are especially popular in seaside locations served by railways. Our overview can include only a small sample of these riches. Really serious travelers to Japanese aquariums should consult the appended Directory when planning their trips.

Here we will focus on the three largest and newest institutions: Tokyo Sea Life Park, the Osaka Ring of Fire Aquarium, and the Port of Nagoya Public Aquarium.

Tokyo Sea Life Park
TOKYO, JAPAN

YEAR OPENED: 1989

APPROXIMATE ANNUAL ATTENDANCE: 4,000,000

AREA (IN SQUARE FEET): 200,000 on 20 acres

TOTAL VOLUME OF TANKS (IN GALLONS): 1,100,000

Operated by: Ueno Park Zoo; *Architect:* Yoshio Taniguchi; *Exhibit Designer:* staff; *Funded by:* Tokyo metropolitan government

As an associated institution of Ueno Zoo, with support from the metropolitan government, Tokyo Sea Life Park traces its ancestry to the first aquarium in Japan, which opened in 1882 at the zoo. This evolved into a fine institution greatly expanded for the Tokyo Olympics in 1964. When even further improvement and expansion were needed, the aquarium moved to its present site— 20 acres within a 190-acre park, on the shores of Tokyo Harbor—and became Tokyo Sea Life Park.

In addition to its distinguished historical ties, Tokyo Sea Life Park has strong international connections. It is a sister aquarium to the Monterey Bay Aquarium and has colleague institutions in numerous countries, including Madagascar, New Zealand, Italy, and Spain.

Tokyo Sea Life Park is an elegant, handsome addition to Tokyo's harbor-front architecture, which also includes Cinderella's Magic Castle at Tokyo Disneyland. The park's silver dome mirrors the light of the bay. The surrounding reflecting pool seems to merge with the marine horizon. The canopies of the bay-level dining area look like sails on the harbor as a visitor approaches from the pine-forested park.

Within the grounds, some distance from the main building, is an apparently wild and natural stream, banked with the extraordinary rocks that seem endemic to Japan. A semicircular building faces the stream and provides an amphitheater for visitors to view the life of the water through acrylic windows. The same windows look out on the stream bank and forest. Occasionally, an aquarium visitor walks through the distant forest, and an interesting merging of the real world with the exhibit occurs.

This special area is a contemplative retreat from the main building. The central aquarium is filled with the excitement of fast-swimming schools of tunas, hammer-head sharks, Japanese schoolchildren, and active on-view research areas.

The biological highlight of Tokyo Sea Life Park is the presentation of active, healthy schools of five kinds of tunas, a rare achievement for an aquarium. Aquarium biologists began earnest research on tunas in 1987, when they were still based at Ueno Zoo. Their research and collecting experimentation took them to far fishing grounds, collegial laboratories, and commercial rearing operations. Widespread tuna culture in Japan is a goal soon to be realized. The Fishing Research Labs of Kinki University have raised bluefin tuna in open-water pens for 15 years. Some tunas are also commercially reared and marketed. But aquarium culture is still a goal that Tokyo Sea Life Park hopes to reach.

Complementing the keystone tuna exhibit are exhibits from the waters of Japan and the world. The Sea of Tokyo complex presents tropical fish from the rocky shores of Ogasawara Island, from Izu, and from Tokyo Bay. There are also exhibits on kelp forests and life in the deep sea.

Antarctic displays feature seldom-exhibited animals like krill, and notothenid fishes (a group limited to south polar seas with special blood chemistry permitting survival in very cold water), which must be kept in water temperatures below 38°F. The water is warmer in the exhibits on the Caribbean Sea, the Mediterranean Sea, the Red Sea, the Indian Ocean, the South Pacific, and the northwest Pacific.

Tokyo Sea Life Park has a strong commitment to educational programs. Seating areas in the Voyagers of the Sea exhibit space overlook the tuna schools, and individually controlled video monitors present varied information on tuna biology and fisheries science. A special Education Center is staffed with attendants to help children, families, and adults check out videos, books, and educational materials. All of the educational efforts and excellence in exhibitry depend on a strong, active staff of aquarium biologists. Tokyo Sea Life Park has dedicated substantial space to research and holding

aquariums. A significant part of the annual budget is devoted to travel, field research, and animal collection.

Each year, Tokyo Sea Life Park mounts an ambitious temporary exhibit aimed at international cooperation. These exhibits have focused on Monterey Bay (with help from their colleague aquarium), the Mediterranean (with help from the historic Naples Marine Laboratory and Barcelona Zoo), and the Sea of Cortez (again, with help from the Monterey Bay Aquarium).

Osaka Ring of Fire Aquarium
OSAKA, JAPAN

YEAR OPENED: 1991

APPROXIMATE ANNUAL ATTENDANCE: 4,000,000

AREA (IN SQUARE FEET): 150,000

TOTAL VOLUME OF TANKS (IN GALLONS): 2,000,000

Operated by: Port of Osaka; *Architect:* Cambridge Seven Associates; *Exhibit Designer:* Lyons/Zaremba; *Funded by:* Port of Osaka

When the Monterey Bay Aquarium chose to focus its exhibits on a single area—Monterey Bay and its habitats and ecosystems—it confirmed a trend among modern aquariums. The designers of the Osaka Ring of Fire Aquarium ambitiously chose as their regional theme the entire Pacific Ocean. The margin of this great sea is encircled by an area where the great geological plates of the sea floor meet the massive continents. These dynamic interfaces are marked by seismic movements, volcanic action, and the creation of new land.

The fire-ringed Pacific from Alaska to the Antarctic, Japan to Peru, is a rich ocean where diverse life abounds. The Osaka Aquarium has successfully met the challenge of conveying the dramatic richness of this half of the world to its audience.

As they enter the aquarium from a great sea-level plaza, visitors travel on a moving sidewalk while watching video portrayals of volcanic activity. After a long ascent by escalator to the top floor, almost seven stories above the harbor, visitors encounter the Japan Forest. This glass-roofed habitat features a green, tree-rich forest inhabited by river otters, birds, and freshwater fish. From this highland, visitors descend a spiraling corridor to the deeper regions of the sea. Nine areas of the Pacific Basin are re-created in 14 separate exhibits.

Modern aquariums display aquatic habitats from a great variety of ecosystems, not limited to ponds, lakes, and oceans. The Rain Forest exhibit at the Osaka Ring of Fire Aquarium features reptiles, insects, and amphibians as well as fishes, mammals, and plants. (Photo by Y. Matsumura; courtesy Cambridge Seven Associates.)

These include the Aleutian Islands, Monterey Bay, Gulf of Panama, Ecuadorian Rain Forest, Antarctica, Tasman Sea, Great Barrier Reef, Pacific Ocean, Seto Inland Sea, Kelp Forest, Coast of Chile, and Cook Strait. The central exhibit portrays the Pacific Ocean and offers perhaps the grandest view of open water in any aquarium. With a volume of 1.3 million gallons and a depth of 30 feet, this grand tank holds a world of fishes.

For years aquarists have discussed and debated the proper shape of an aquarium intended to hold schooling tuna and large sharks. Some argued for a circular tank, others for a dumbbell shape (two circles connected by a wide "raceway"). No one suggested the shape of a Maltese cross—the shape of Osaka's huge tank. The truth of the matter seems demonstrated here: It doesn't matter what shape the tank is as long as it is huge! The two whale sharks hosted at Osaka have shared the immense tank, calmly and leisurely swimming throughout it. In addition, this oceanic aquarium includes at least 50 other free-swimming species, including mahimahi, bluefin tuna, mackerel, eagle rays, groupers, sawfish, and jacks.

The Osaka Aquarium also has a strong educational program and an active research division. As part of the development of Osaka's harbor, which, in addition to being a commercial shipping center, also hosts cruise ships as big as the *Queen Elizabeth II,* the Ring of Fire Aquarium shares the harbor-front plaza with an extensive retail shopping center, Tempozan Marketplace. Thus it echoes architect Peter Chermayeff's first success on the Boston harbor front in 1969.

Port of Nagoya Public Aquarium
NAGOYA, JAPAN

YEAR OPENED: 1992

APPROXIMATE ANNUAL ATTENDANCE: 3,000,000

AREA (IN SQUARE FEET): 200,000

TOTAL VOLUME OF TANKS (IN GALLONS): 550,000

Operated by: Port of Nagoya; *Architect:* Dentsu Prox, Inc.; *Exhibit Designer:* K. Fukuda, Daiken Design Co.; *Funded by:* Port of Nagoya

The architecture of the Nagoya Aquarium presents the most futuristic appearance of any such institution. One approaches the appealing combination of glass cylinder, dome, triangles, and cubes from a graceful footbridge under sweeping arches. The structure's mirrored surface reflects the activity of the busy port. In the midst of the bustle, the aquarium building sits serenely in a spacious plaza, surrounded on three sides by water. The building complex looks like a habitat—a biosphere for creatures from another world—and indeed, it is just that. The aquarium houses almost 40,000 organisms of 540 kinds from the waters of tropical seas, the deep sea, Australia, and the Antarctic. The goal of the Port of Nagoya Aquarium is "to care for the earth and to raise up hearts with a will to do it."

The founding director was well chosen to lead this effort. Dr. Itaru Uchida is an internationally respected biologist with a long career dedicated to the study and conservation of the sea turtles of the world. Housed in an adjacent freestanding glass-roofed cylindrical structure is the Chelonian Institute, dedicated to research on sea turtles. Nagoya claims this as the world's foremost sea research facility where turtles are incubated, raised, and studied. Visitors can see how eggs are incubated and how turtles grow. The aquarium aims to introduce visitors to these endangered species and to help them realize how important it is to conserve nature.

Moored adjacent to the aquarium complex is the historic oceanographic ship *Fuji.* Now a museum, the ship once carried Japanese oceanographers and biologists to remote seas. Its travels, in part, inspired the exhibit theme. The aquarium introduces a variety of life and habitats while taking the visitor on a voyage from the oceans of Japan to antarctic waters, and to the waters of the deep sea. These expeditionary sites are arranged throughout three floors and almost 200,000 square feet, making Nagoya the largest international aquarium in Japan.

The living exhibits naturalistically portray habitats ranging from the frozen, blizzard-blown Antarctic penguin colony to the coral-reef exhibit, with beach, palm trees, and a transparent underwater tunnel. In addition, the designers employ display technology and "high-level image and sound technologies to enthrall all five senses."

Nagoya is at once accurate, naturalistic, and theatrical in its presentation. An IMAX theater occupies the great silver dome. A smaller "simulation theater" takes 30 visitors per trip to the deep-sea floor aboard the research submersible *Deep Sea 6,000.* Underwater volcanoes, benthic (deep-sea) fish, and abyssal creatures appear unexpectedly on the sub's enlarged viewing screen. The highlight of the aquarium exhibits is the giant Kuroshio Current Tank, which depicts the pelagic life of the great, rich ocean current that sweeps by Japan. This aquarium is 18 feet deep and 50 feet wide and holds 160,000 gallons.

If a traveler could visit only one aquarium in the world, and wished to see the grandest attempt to date to combine biology, technology, stagecraft, and conservation, the Port of Nagoya Public Aquarium would be the recommended choice.

The Nagoya Aquarium, which opened in October 1992, is the newest development in this busy and growing Japanese port. The aquarium includes an IMAX theater, a simulated submarine dive to the deep sea, an expansive antarctic exhibit, a coral reef, and many other state-of-the-art displays. It is also the home of the Chelonian Institute, noted internationally for its research on sea turtles. (Photo by Leighton Taylor.)

Asia

Throughout Southeast Asia, the aquarium fan will find many institutions that are satisfying to visit. In Hong Kong, the elaborate and extensive **Ocean Park,** founded by the Jockey Club, has hosted more than 25 million people since its opening in 1977. Although the park includes such attractions as water rides, a roller coaster, and a Chinese cultural museum (the Middle Kingdom), its most popular element is the aquarium complex. Highlights include a 440,000-gallon Atoll Reef, the million-gallon Ocean Theater with killer whales, por-

poises, and sea lions, and the 330,000-gallon wave cove, with seabirds and marine mammals.

Singapore offers **Underwater World** at Sentosa Island, and, in Central Park, the former Van Kleef Aquarium, recently refurbished and renamed **World of Aquariums**. On the island of Taiwan, the Republic of China has three large aquarium projects underway. The first to open, in 1995, will be on the P'eng-hu Islands west of Taiwan. The provincial government will operate this center to help people learn about the resources and marine environment of the China Sea. The project has been designed by an architect from Taipei, Joshua Jih Pan, with exhibit design by James Peterson of Bios, who also worked on the Monterey Bay Aquarium and the Aquarium of the Americas in New Orleans.

The second aquarium project in Taiwan will open after 1996 in a beautiful seaside location reminiscent of the rocky tropical shelf and mountain backdrops where Sea Life Park in Hawaii sits. The aquarium will be within Kenting National Park, a popular coastal resort adjacent to important ecological areas. The **National Museum of Marine Biology and Aquarium** is championed by outstanding scientists from Sun Yat Sen University in Kaoshiung. Financed by the national government, the planners have selected Charles Davis (Monterey Bay Aquarium) to design the building complex. Joe Wetzel has designed the exhibit program using the experience his firm gained from designing exhibits at the Texas State Aquarium, the Norwalk Maritime Center, and the Florida Aquarium.

The third aquarium-related project in Taiwan is planned for the northern coastal area near Taipei. Federally funded but guided by scientists from the National Taiwan Ocean University, this project is scheduled to open after 1997. It will include an existing fishing village and will focus on human relationships with the sea. The government of R.O.C. has planned to commit US$100 million to each of these three educational and research institutions. Their size and influence will be significant.

Other countries in Southeast Asia have or are considering aquariums. Indonesia is home to the richest marine fauna on the planet, and undoubtedly the best way to see marine life here is by snorkeling on the reef. Neighboring Brunei has an excellent small aquarium, the **Hassanal Bolkiah Aquarium** in the capital city. At least two aquarium projects are planned for Thailand.

Aquariums, whether existing or yet-to-be-built, in nations faced with developing economies and growing populations, can play essential roles. No matter how wealthy or frugal a people, they need to know the consequences of environmental and economic choices and the deep cultural values of their native plants and animals. Well-designed and -managed educational institutions like aquariums can be agents of social change even in nations faced with extreme choices.

Australia and New Zealand

Australia is a continent rich with living treasures, on both land and sea. The Great Barrier Reef, which extends almost 1,500 miles along its northeastern coast, is the larg-

est coral-reef complex in the world. The product of tiny plants and animals, the reef is one of the earth's few organic structures visible from orbiting spacecraft.

But *all* of Australia's coastline is rich with life; diversity is not limited to the upper-righthand corner. Even today, tourists on harbor cruise boats see fairy penguins in Sydney Harbor. Extensive river systems abound with life, from crocodiles to lungfish. Great white sharks share the waters of southern Australia with surfers and abalone divers.

The **Great Barrier Reef Aquarium** at Townsville affords the second-best look at the living corals and reef life of Australia. (The best look is through a face mask on the reef itself.) In Sydney, the **Taronga Park Zoo** has long maintained an important collection of Australian marine animals in its aquarium, where sharks have always been favorite species. In 1988 Taronga Park gained a neighbor, the **Sydney Aquarium,** on the city side of the harbor. In the west, Perth hosts **Underwater World,** which has its origins in Auckland.

In New Zealand, Auckland offers the original **Kelly Tarleton's Underwater World,** an opportunity to walk through a transparent acrylic tunnel as if on the sea floor itself. In Napier, **Hawke's Bay Marineland and Aquarium** presents an array of marine life.

Sydney Aquarium at Darling Harbor
SYDNEY, AUSTRALIA

YEAR OPENED: 1988

APPROXIMATE ANNUAL ATTENDANCE: 850,000

AREA (IN SQUARE FEET): 55,000

TOTAL VOLUME OF TANKS (IN GALLONS): 900,000

Operated by: Sydney Aquarium Corp., Ltd.; *Architect:* Philip Cox; *Exhibit Designers:* U. Erich Friese, Max Irvine; *Funded by:* commercial investment

The theme of the Sydney Aquarium is a journey across Australia's waterways and seacoast, an ambitious scope considering the size and diversity of the continent. The designers have met the challenge within the space of three connected structures. The main building lines the harbor front; the Sydney Harbour Oceanarium and the Open Ocean exhibit occupy two giant floating aquariums built on barges. In fact, the aquarium considers these the "largest floating oceanariums in the world." They have collectively received certification from the *Guinness Book of World Records* as the "largest aquarium, containing 3,315,398 litres of water" [about 850,000 gallons]. As with any superlative claim, there are undoubtedly other contenders for this title.

The aquarium visitor's trip through the water worlds of Australia at Sydney Aquarium begins with the continent's largest inland river complex, the Murray Darling System, home to Australia's largest freshwater fish. It continues through the estuaries and swamps of the northern rivers, where saltwater crocodiles abound. The Mangrove Habitat, Fishes of the Far North (that is, tropical freshwater), Rocky Shores, and The Great Barrier exhibits present the great diversity of aquatic Australia.

The Sydney Harbor Oceanarium uses a moving walkway within a transparent tunnel to transport the visitor on an excursion beneath the surface of Sydney Harbor. The actual harbor is rich, containing at least 570 species of fish. Such richness is due to the mixing of tropical, subtropical, and temperate waters that wash its sea grass, kelp, and rocky reefs. The adjacent Open Ocean exhibit features large, fast-swimming predators—the sharks and their relatives, the rays.

The Sydney Aquarium augments its fine aquarium displays with "sound sculptures" and multimedia presentations. Each exhibit area is filled with the natural sounds (both air- and waterborne) unique to the habitat and recorded there. Seabirds, frogs, insects, crabs, shrimp, and fish are soloists in the natural symphony replayed within the aquarium galleries. Overhead projections of natural images create a wild ambience in the Rocky Shore and Far North environments.

The aquarium also features five "microaquariums." These interactive exhibits feature small marine animals that can be viewed using magnifying video cameras on robotic arms.

Large exhibit or small, Sydney Aquarium offers a comprehensive look at the aquatic life of Australia.

It is fitting to end our global tour of aquariums on the continent where they found their first flowering—in Europe.

Europe

The aquariums of Europe are like an extensive bed of wonderful tulips. Many bloomed brightly in the early spring of the nineteenth century. The bloom of some has faded. Still others have blossomed with new vitality and brightness. The youngest blooms seem most vi-

brant. One has confidence that there is a new flowering to come.

To pretend to provide a comprehensive tour of European aquariums in this limited space would be folly. I will demur and invite the traveling aquarist to review the Directory and to be alert for wonderful new growth—perhaps in London, Naples, Barcelona, or Antwerp.

Europe is ready for a great renaissance of aquariums to equal the innovation and variety of its nineteenth-century efforts and to build on the achievements of European scientists and aquarists over the past three decades.

In the meantime, let us consider two of the continent's newer aquariums: Nausicaa in France and the Genoa Aquarium in Italy.

Nausicaa
BOULOGNE SUR MER, FRANCE

YEAR OPENED: 1991

APPROXIMATE ANNUAL ATTENDANCE: 800,000

AREA (IN SQUARE FEET): 210,000

TOTAL VOLUME OF TANKS (IN GALLONS): 200,000

Operated by: private society; *Architect:* J. Rougerie; *Exhibit Designer:* C. Le Comte; *Funded by:* government of France; EEC; private society

Avoiding the problem of what to name their institution—aquarium, oceanarium, marine museum, natural history center, or fisheries exhibition—the founders of this wonderful institution chose a unique and enlightened solution. They call their place *Nausicaa*. It is all the things I have listed and more, and it is certainly an aquarium by most definitions.

Nausicaa, in Homer's *Odyssey,* was the beautiful princess of a coastal kingdom who comforted Odysseus after he was shipwrecked, then sent him home on a magic ship. How French—to commemorate a lovely patroness of seafarers with a beautiful institution dedicated to helping others know and love the sea.

Nausicaa opened in the spring of 1991, after eight years of planning. The facility occupies the site and part of the original building of an old casino and public swimming complex. Living exhibits are based on excellent research and knowledge of marine biology. They appear in a context one must call "educational theatrics." This is no accident, because the exhibits were heavily influenced by an architect who is a theatrical specialist. Even the passageways are seen as contexts for teaching about and experiencing the sea, flooded with sounds and lighting effects. The mission of Nausicaa is to sensitize visitors to the many interactions that humankind has with the seas. The messages conveyed are positive—and fun.

Beyond viewing schools of fishes familiar to lovers of seafood, visitors can experience being caught in a trawl net—as if they were members of that school of fish. Mirrors, video, sounds, and lighting effects combine to create a convincing experience.

Other exhibits include underwater viewing domes, sharks, stingrays, and aquaculture demonstrations. A 50,000-gallon tropical lagoon displays living corals from the Red Sea and the Indian Ocean and giant clams from the Indo-Pacific.

Nausicaa and its sister aquariums at La Rochelle (the La Rochelle Aquarium) and Brest (Oceanopolis) are leading the way for Europe's new blooms of aquariums.

Nausicaa and its sister aquariums at La Rochelle (Coutant Aquarium) and Brest (Oceanopolis) are leading the way for Europe's new blooms of aquariums.

Genoa Aquarium
GENOA, ITALY

YEAR OPENED: 1992 (phase 1); 1993 (phase 2)

APPROXIMATE ANNUAL ATTENDANCE: 800,000

AREA (IN SQUARE FEET): 183,000

TOTAL VOLUME OF TANKS (IN GALLONS): 1,250,000

Operated by: private coventure of IDEA, Inc. (U.S.) and Italian investors; *Architect:* Aldo Piano and Cambridge Seven Associates; *Exhibit Designers:* Cambridge Seven Associates, Lyons/Zaremba; *Funded by:* government of Italy

The Genoa Aquarium joins the aquariums of the Old and New Worlds in two ways. First, its exhibits contrast the biology of Europe with the diversity of the New World waters into which Columbus sailed exactly five centuries before the aquarium opened. Italy chose 1992 to commemorate Columbus's voyages with a summer-long exposition in Genoa and the fall opening of the first phase of this aquarium.

Second, it was designed by two architects: Aldo Piano (Europe) and Peter Chermayeff (North America). Although its construction was financed by the Italian government, the aquarium is operated by a joint venture of Italian investors and an American firm founded by codesigner Chermayeff.

The site presented a challenging opportunity—the aquarium sits partly on an old pier that dates at least to the days when Christopher Columbus called the historic Italian commercial city his home port. Like most piers, this one is long and projects into the harbor. Thus, the visitor's path through exhibits is long, comes to a seaward stopping point, and reverses back to the shoreside.

The Genoa Aquarium presents a fascinating linear, three-level story line. Beginning, like Columbus, at the quayside, the visitor reviews the marine biology of the Mediterranean Sea, which, in the fifteenth century, was teeming with fish, shellfish, monk seals, dolphins, and seabirds. Today, the central sea of this Old World is dying through human disregard. The aim of the Genoa Aquarium is to educate and inspire the people of Europe who live by the sea to reverse this decline and restore the health of the Mediterranean. As the visitor continues, the focus of the exhibits shifts to the natural history of tropical America, a New World filled with wonderful, colorful animals and plants unknown to the Europeans of Columbus's time.

The Genoa Aquarium is wonderfully conceived. It provides exciting entertainment for both the Genoa visitor and resident. More importantly, it stimulates reflection on our own human place within the world's great ecosystems.

In the bright shallow waters of Indo-Pacific coral reefs, giant clams rely on the sun for food. Pigmented plant cells live within the clam's flesh. The food they photosynthetically produce helps nourish the large, colorful mollusc. (Photo by Thomas Kelley, Waikiki Aquarium.)

DIRECTORY OF WORLD AQUARIUMS

The following list of the world's aquariums may be useful to those wanting to visit aquariums in their area, or for planning a trip. Many aquariums have active education, membership, and volunteer programs and welcome your inquiries and support. Phone numbers are not available for some aquariums, but they are included here whenever possible so that visitors to those cities can inquire locally. The following sources were used in compiling this directory. Information was complete as of March 1992. It is possible that the status of some aquariums, particularly in Europe, may have changed. Every institution with "aquarium" (or some variant) in its name and zoos reporting collections of more than fifty species of fishes and other aquatic organisms have been included in this list.

Directory of the American Association of Zoological Parks and Aquariums

Reference Guide to Marine Parks and Aquaria of the United States (Pacheco and Smith, published by Lyons & Buford, New York, 1989)

Roster of the Japanese Association of Zoological Parks and Aquariums, 1992

Membership list of the European Union of Aquarium Curators, 1992

International Zoo Yearbook, Volume 28, 1989

United States and Canada

NORTHEASTERN

Oceans East
Box 760
87 Atlantic Avenue
Boothbay Harbor, ME 04538
207-633-3965

West Boothbay Harbor Aquarium
Bigelow Laboratory
McKown Point
West Boothbay Harbor, ME 04575
207-633-5572

Mount Desert Oceanarium
Clark Point Road
Southwest Harbor, ME 04679
207-244-7330

Kirkham Aquarium
Springfield Science Museum
236 State Street
Springfield, MA 01103
413-733-1194

Woods Hole Aquarium
Water Street
Woods Hole, MA 02543
508-548-5123

New England Aquarium
Central Wharf
Boston, MA 02110
617-973-5200

Mystic Marinelife Aquarium
55 Coogan Blvd.
Mystic, CT 06355-1997
203-536-3323

Maritime Center at Norwalk
112 Washington Street
South Norwalk, CT 06854
203-852-0700

Aquarium of Niagara Falls
701 Whirlpool Street
Niagara Falls, NY 14301
716-285-3575

New York Aquarium
Boardwalk and West 8th Street
Brooklyn, NY 11224
718-265-3474

Staten Island Zoo
614 Broadway
Staten Island, NY 10310
718-442-3101

New Jersey State Aquarium
Michel Boulevard
Camden, NJ 08102
609-365-3300

Pittsburgh Aqua Zoo
P.O. Box 5250
Pittsburgh, PA 15206
412-665-3640

National Aquarium in Baltimore
Pier 3, 501 E. Pratt Street
Baltimore, MD 21202
301-576-3800

SOUTHEASTERN

Virginia Marine Science Museum
717 General Booth Boulevard
Virginia Beach, VA 23451
804-425-3474

North Carolina Aquarium
Fort Fisher P.O. Box 130
Kure Beach, NC 28449
919-458-8257

North Carolina Aquarium
Pine Knoll Shores
Atlantic Beach, NC 28512
919-247-4003

North Carolina Aquarium
Roanoke Island
Manteo, NC 27954
919-473-3493

South Carolina Aquarium
116 Meeting Street
Charleston, SC 29401
803-724-3784

Riverbanks Zoological Park
500 Wildlife Parkway
P.O. Box 1060
Columbia, SC 29202
803-779-8717

Lowry Park Zoo
7530 North Blvd.
Tampa, FL 33604
813-935-8552

The Florida Aquarium
Harbor Island
P.O. Box 3434
Tampa, FL 33601
813-229-8861

Busch Gardens
P.O. Box 9158
3000 Busch Gardens Boulevard
Tampa, FL 33674
813-987-5082

Sea World of Florida
7007 Sea World Drive
Orlando, FL 32821
407-351-3600

Marineland of Florida
9507 Ocean Shore Boulevard
Marineland, FL 32086
904-471-1111

Miami Seaquarium
4400 Rickenbacker Causeway
Key Biscayne, FL 33149
305-361-5703

Theater of the Sea
P.O. Box 407
Islamorada, FL 33036
305-664-2431

SOUTH

Oklahoma City Zoological Park
2101 NE 50th Street
Oklahoma City, OK 73111
405-424-3344

Tulsa Zoological Park
5701 E. 36th Street North
Tulsa, OK 74115
918-596-2400

Sea World of Texas
10500 Sea World Drive
San Antonio, TX 78251
512-523-3611

San Antonio Zoological Gardens
 & Aquarium
3903 North St. Mary's Street
San Antonio, TX 78212
512-734-7184

Dallas Aquarium
First Ave. & Martin Luther
    King Blvd.
P.O. Box 26113
Dallas, TX 75226
214-670-8441

Fort Worth Zoological Park
2727 Zoological Park Drive
Fort Worth, TX 76110
817-871-7050

Houston Zoological Gardens
1513 N. MacGregor
Houston, TX 77030
713-525-3300

Texas State Aquarium
2710 N. Shore Dr.
Corpus Christi, TX 78402
512 881 1200

Aquarium of the Americas
Woldenberg Riverfront Park
New Orleans, LA 70130
504-861-2537

Louisville Zoological Garden
1100 Trevillian Way
Louisville, KY 40233
502-459-2181

Memphis Zoological Garden &
    Aquarium
2000 Galloway Avenue
Memphis, TN 38112
901-725-3400

The Tennessee Aquarium
Ross's Landing
Chattanooga, TN 37403
615-265-0695

Marine Life Oceanarium
P.O. Box 4078
Gulfport, MS 39502
601-863-0651

J.L. Scott Aquarium
115 Beach Boulevard
Biloxi, MS 39530
601-374-5550

MIDWEST

Omaha's Henry Doorly Zoo
3701 South 10th Street
Omaha, NE 68107-2200
402-733-8401

St. Louis Zoo
Forest Park
St. Louis, MO 63110
314-781-0900

Minnesota Zoological Garden
13000 Zoo Boulevard
Apple Valley, MN 55124
612-432-9000

Milwaukee County Zoological
    Gardens
10001 West Bluemound Road
Milwaukee, WI 53226
414-771-3040

John G. Shedd Aquarium
1200 South Lake Shore Drive
Chicago, IL 60605
312 939 2438

The New Indianapolis Zoo
1200 West Washington St.
Indianapolis, IN 46222
317-630-2030

Belle Isle Zoo & Aquarium
8450 West Ten Mile Road
Royal Oak, MI 48068
313-398-0903

Cincinnati Zoo & Botanical Garden
3400 Vine Street
Cincinnati, OH 45220
513-281-4701

Cleveland Aquarium at the
    Metroparks Zoo
3900 Brookside Park Drive
Cleveland, OH 44109
216-661-6500

Columbus Zoo
9900 Riverside Drive
Powell, OH 43065
614-645-3550

Toledo Zoological Gardens
2700 Broadway
Toledo, OH 43609
419-385-5721

Sea World of Ohio
1100 Sea World Drive
Aurora, OH 44202
216-562-8101

WESTERN

Seattle Aquarium
Pier 59, Waterfront Park
Seattle, WA 98010
206-386-4320

Point Defiance Zoo and Aquarium
5400 North Pearl Street
Tacoma, WA 98407
206-591-5335

Oregon Coast Aquarium
2820 SE. Ferry Slip Road
Newport, OR 97365
503-867-3474

Mark O. Hatfield Marine Science Center
2030 South Marine Science Drive
Newport, OR 97365
503-867-0100

Marine World Africa USA
2001 Marine World Parkway
Vallejo, CA 94589
707-644-4000

Steinhart Aquarium at California
    Academy of Sciences
Golden Gate Park
San Francisco, CA 94118
415-750-7145

Monterey Bay Aquarium
886 Cannery Row
Monterey, CA 93940
408-648-4888

Cabrillo Marine Museum
3720 Stephen White Dr.
San Pedro, CA 90731
310-548-7562

Steven Birch Aquarium-Museum
Scripps Institution of Oceanography
8602 La Jolla Shores Dr.
La Jolla, CA 92037
619-534-3474

Sea World of California
Sea World Drive
1729 S. Shores Rd.
San Diego, CA 92109
619-226-3901

Waikiki Aquarium, University of Hawaii
2777 Kalakaua Avenue
Honolulu, HI 96815
808-923-9741

Sea Life Park
Makapu'u Point
Waimanalo, HI 96815
808-923-1531

CANADA

Marineland of Canada
7657 Portage Road
Niagara Falls
Ontario L2E 6X8

Metro Toronto Zoo
P.O. Box 280
West Hill
Ontario M1E 4R5
416-392-5900

Aquarium du Québec
1675 Avenue du Parc
Sainte-Foy
Quebec GIW 453
418-659-5266

Vancouver Public Aquarium
Stanley Park
Vancouver
British Columbia V6B 3X8
604-685-3364

The Caribbean and Latin America
(listed alphabetically by country and city name)

ARGENTINA

Acuario del Museo Argentino de
  Ciencias Naturales
Angel Gallardo 470, Capital 1405
Buenos Aires
982-9410

Acuario del Inidep Sede Rosario
Cordiviola Paseo Ribereno
2000 Rosario
391698

Acuario Municipal de Mendoza
Ituzongo y Buenos Aires
Mendoza
253824

BERMUDA

Bermuda Aquarium, Natural
  History Museum & Zoo
P.O. Box FL 156
The Flatts FLBX
809-29-32727

CUBA

Havana Aquarium
Parque Lenin
Ciudad de La Habana

National Aquarium
Avenida 1 y Calle 60
Miramar Playa
Ciudad de La Habana
29-3504

FRENCH WEST INDIES

Aquarium de la Guadeloupe
Place Créole, La Marina
Bas-du-Fort 97190
590-90-92-38

VENEZUELA

Aquarium de Valencia:
  Juan Vicente Seijas
Avenida Fernanado Figueredo
Aptdo 1865
Valencia 2001
Carabobo
041-89222

Europe
(listed alphabetically by country and city name)

AUSTRIA

Aquarium Alpenzoo
Weiherburggasse 37
Innsbruck A-6020
512-892323

Haus der Natur
Museumplatz 5
Salzburg A-5020
662-842653

Haus de Meeres Vivarium Wien
Esterhazypark
Vienna A-1060
1-587-1417

Aquarium Schönbrunn Zoo
Maxingstrasse 13
Vienna A-1130
1-582-1236

BELGIUM

Aquarium Kon. My. Dierkunde
Koningin Astridplein 26
Antwerp B-2018
03-2311640

Aquarium Du Buisson de
  L'Universite de Liege
22 Quai Beneden
Liege B-4000
0-41-439918

DENMARK

Danmarks Akvarium
2920 Charlottenlund
DK-2920
3-62-3283

Fiskeri-og Sofartmuseet
Saltvandsakvariet
Esbjerg
DK-2920
75-150666

Aqua-Forskvands Akvarium
  & Museum
Vejlsovej 55
DK-6800 Silkeborg
89-222189

FINLAND

Aquarium Tampereen
  Sarkanniemi Oy
Sarkanniemi
Tampere SF-33230
31-231833

FRANCE

Marineland Antibes
Ave Mozart
Antibes 06600
93-334949

Musée Aquarium d'Arcachon
2 rue du Professeur Jolyet
Arcachon F-33120
56-83-10-22

Aquarium du Laboratoire Arago
1, avenue du Fontaulé
66650 Banyuls-sur-mer
68-88-00-40

Aquarium du Musée de la Mer
Esplanade des anciens combattants
Biarritz F-64200
59-24-02-59

Nausicaa Centre National de la Mer
Boulevard Sainte-Beuve
Boulogne-sur-Mer 62200
21-30-99-99

Oceanopolis
BP 411
Brest F29275
98-344040

Aquarium de Canet
1 Bd. de la Jetee
Canet et Roussillon F-66140
68-804964

Aquarium Coutant
Port des Minimes BP4
La Rochelle 17002
46-44-00-00

Musée de la Peche
La Ville Close
29181 Concarneau
98-97-10-20

Marinarium du College de France
Place de la Croix
29110 Concarneau
98-97-06-59

Océanarium du Croisic
Ave de St. Goustan BP 44
Le Croisic F-44490
40-23044

Aquarium du Laboratoire
  Maritime de Dinard
17, avenue George V
35801 Dinard
99-46-13-90

Aquarium Panoramique
Esplanade de la Capitainerie
22580 La Grande Motte
67-86-85-23

Musée Oceanographique le Roc
50400 Granville
33-50-19-10

Seaquarium-palais de la mer
BP 106
Le Grau du Roi F-30240
66-595757

Marseille Aquaforum
59 Georges Pompidou
Marseille F-13008
33-91-71-00-46

Aquarium de l'Univer. and Ville
34 rue Ste. Catherine
Nancy F-54000
83-329997

Aquarium du Musée des Arts
  Africains et Oceanicus à Paris
293 Avenue Daumesnil
Paris F-75012
1-43830747

Centre de la Mer et des Eaux
Institut Océanographique
195, rue Saint-Jacques
75005 Paris
1-46-33-08-61

Aquarium de St. Mâlo
Place Vauban
Saint Mâlo F-35400
99-81-64-34

Musée Aquarium
23, rue du Commandant Maratuel
24200 Sarlat
53-59-44-58

Aquarium Inst. Océ
anographique Ricard
Ile des Embiez
Six Fours les Plages F-83140
94-34-02-49

Aquarium Marin de la Cote
  de Granit Rose
Boulevard du Coz-Pers
22730 Tregastel
96-23-88-67

Aquarium Ecologique de Trouville
17, rue de Paris
14360 Trouville Sur Mer
21-88-46-04

GERMANY

Zoologischer Garten und
  Aquarium Berlin
Hardenbergplatz 8
Berlin 30 BRD-W1000
30-2540-10

Tierpark Berlin
Tierpark 125
Friedrichsfelde
Berlin BRD-O1136
30-5100111

Zoo am Meer
Am Weiserdeich
Bremerhaven BRD-W2850
471-5902516

Zoologischer Garten Dresden
Tiergartenstrasse
Dresden BRD-O8020
47-5445

Löbbecke Museum und Aquazoo
Kaiserwerther Strasse 380
Düsseldorf 30 BRD-W4000
211-8996152

Zoologischer Garten der Stadt
  Frankfurt am Main
Alfred-Brehm-Platz 16
Frankfurt am Main BRD-W6000
69-21233727

Troparium Hagenbeck's Zoo
Postfach 54-09-30
Hamburg 4 BRD-W2000
40-5400010

Aquarium des Niedersachsichs
  Landesmuseums Hanover
Am Maschpark 5
Hanover 1 BRD-W3000
0511-883051

Biologische Anstalt Helgoland Aquarium
Kurpromenade
Helgoland BRD-W2192
04725-291

Aquarium des Institut für Meereskunde
  an der Universitat Kiel
Dursternbrooker Weg 20
Kiel 1 BRD-W2300
431-5973912

Kölner Aquarium am Zoologischer Garten
Riehler Strasse 173
Köln 60 BRD-W5000
221-763066

Aquarium Zool. Garten Leipzig
Pfaffendorfer Strasse 29
Leipzig BRD-O7010
41-591742

Zoologischer Garten Leipzig
Dr. Kurt-Fischer Strasse 29
Leipzig BRD-O7010
41-291001

Münchener Tierpark
Tierparkstrasse 30
Munich 90 BRD-W8000
89-6258835

Allwetter Zoo
Santruper Strasse 315
Munster BRD-W4400
25-181533

Tiergarten der Stadt Nürnberg
Am Tiergarten 30
Nürnberg 30 BRD-W8500
911-543034

Zoologischer Garten Rostock
Rennbahnallee 21
Rostock BRD-O2500

Meeresmuseum Stralsund
Katherinenberg 14
Stralsund BRD-O2300

Wilhelma Zoologisch-Botanischer
  Garten
Postfach 50-12-27
Stuttgart BRD-W7000
711-5402109

Seewasseraquarium der Stadt
  Wilhelmshaven

Zoologischer Garten Wuppertal
Hubertusallee 30
Wuppertal-Elberfeld
0202-740075

GREAT BRITAIN

Aquarium of the Zoological
  Society of London
Regent's Park
London NW1 4RY
01-722-3333

Sea Life Centre
Barcaldine
Connel (Oban), Argyll PA37 1SE
063-172-586

North of England Zoological
  Society Zoological Gardens
Upton by Chester, Cheshire
024-438-0280

The Aquarium of the Marine
  Biological Association
The Laboratory, Citadel Hill
Plymouth, Devon
752-222772

Sea Life Park
Lodmoor Country Park
Weymouth, Dorset DT4 7SZ
305-761070

Marineland & Oceanarium
Morecambe, Lancashire
025-441-4727

Sea Life Centre
Blackpool, Lancashire FY1 5AA
0253-22445

Sea Life Centre
Scalby Mills Road
Scarborough, North Yorkshire
  YO12 6RP
0723-376125

Sea Life Centre
Rhyl, Olwyd LL18 3AF
0745-344660

Sea Life Centre
Clarence Esplanade
Southsea, Portsmouth PO5 3PB
0705-294443

Birdworld & Underwater World
Holt Pound Nr Farnham
Surrey

Sea Life Centre
Rock-A-Nore Road
Hastings, Sussex TN34 3DN
0424-718776

Sea Life Centre
Marine Parade/Madeira Drive
Brighton, Sussex BN2 1TB
0273-604234

Sea Life Centre
The Scores
St. Andrews, Fife KY16 9AS
Scotland

GREECE

Oceanographic Institute
Rhodos
241-27308

IRELAND

The Northern Ireland Aquarium
The Ropewalk–Castle Strand
Portaferry
County Down BT-221NZ
2477-28062

ITALY

Aquario di Genova
Ponte Spinola
Genova I-16123
10-247-1140

Aquario Civico
Viale Gadio 2
Milan I-20121
2-8690719

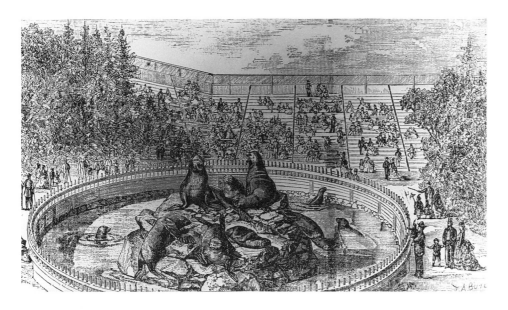

Naples Aquarium
Stazione Zoologica Di Napoli
Villa Comunale
Napoli I-80121
5833222

Adriatic Sea World–Delphinarium
    Riccione
Lungomare della Repubblica
Riccione I-47036
054-160-1712

Civico Aquario Marino
Riva Nazario Sauro
Trieste
040-306201

Giardino Zoologico della
    Citta di Torino
Corso Casale, Parco Michelotti
Torino I-10131

MADEIRA

Museu e Aquario Municipal
    do Funchal
Rua Da Mouraria 31
Funchal 9000
29761

MONACO

Musée Ocenographique de Monaco
Avenue Saint Martin
Monaco Ville
93-153600

NETHERLANDS

Aquarium Bergen aan Zee
Bergen aan Zee
2208-12928

Noorder Dierenpark Zoo
Hoofdstraat 18
7811 EP Emmen
059-101-8800

Ouwehands Zoo
Grebbeweg 109
Rhenen NL-3911
083-761-9110

Royal Rotterdam Zoological and
    Botanical Gardens
Van Aerssenlaan 49
3000 AM Rotterdam
010-465-4333

Amsterdam Aquarium, in
Stichting Koninkluk Zoologisch
    Genootschap Natura Artis
    Magistra
Plantage Kerklaan 38-40
1018 CZ Amsterdam
010-31-20-253931

Dolphinarium Harderwijk Holland
Strand Boulevard Oost 1
3840 GC Harderwijk
034-101-6041

NORWAY

Alesund Akvarium
Nedre Strandtgt. 4
Alesund N-6000
71-24123

Bergen Aquarium
Nordnesparken 2
P.O. Box 1870
Bergen N-5024
5-238500

Aquarium Norske Skogbruks Museum
Elverum N-2400
64-10299

University of Oslo/Akvarium
Blindern
Oslo

PORTUGAL

Aquario Vasco Da Gama
Rua Direita-Dafundo
Lisboa P-1495
1-419-8052

SPAIN

Aquarium of the Barcelona Zoo
Parc de La Ciutadela
Barcelona E-08003
93-309-25-00

Museu de la Ciencia Aquarium
Teodor Roviralta 55
Barcelona E-08022
3-2126066

SWEDEN

Malmö Museum of Natural History
Box 406
Malmö S-201
40-344414

Borasparken
Box 455
Boras S-501
33-13-55-80

Sjofartsmuseets Akvarium
Goteborg
Karl Johansgaten 1-3
Goteborg S-414
31-612912

Skansen-Akvariet
Stockholm
08-660-1082

SWITZERLAND

Aquarium Zoologischer Garten Basel
Basel CH-4054
061-2810000

Aquarium Zoo Zurich
Zurichbergstrasse
Zurich CH-8044
1-2515411

Eastern Europe and the Former Soviet Union
(listed alphabetically by country)

ARMENIA

Ervani Kentanabanakan Aigi
Prospekt Myasnikyana 20
Erevan-25

BULGARIA

Varna Aquarium
Research Institute of Fisheries
Blvd. Chervenoarmeisky 4
Varna

BYELORUSSIA

Grodznenskii Szyarzhauny
Zaalagichny Park
Timiryazeva 11

CZECHOSLOVAKIA

Vychodoceska Zoologicka
Zahrada Ve Dvore Kralove
Dvur Kralove

Oceanographic Museum
Al. Zjednoczenial
81345 Gdynia

Zoologicka Zahrada Mesta Brna
Brno
Bystre

ESTONIA

Tallinna Loomaaed
Paldiski Mnt. 145
Tallin

GEORGIA

Batumskii Oceanarium
Georgian Scientific Research Fish
Batumi Ul. Rustaveli 51

Tbilisis Zoologiuri Parki
Ul. Lenina 64
Tbilisi

HUNGARY

Budapest Fovaros Allat-Es
Novenykertje
H-1317
Budapest 5, Pf 469

KAZAKHSTAN

Alma-Atinskii Zoopark
Alma-Ata Ul. Jesenberlina 166

Chimkentskii Zoologicheskii Park
Chimkent Ul. Karla Marksa

LATVIA

Riga Zoologiskais Darzs
Mezhapark Prospekt 1
Riga

LITHUANIA

Jura Muziejus Ir Akvariumas
Klaipeda

Respublikinis Zoologijos
Sodas
16-Tos Divizijos Pl. 21
Kaunas

POLAND

Miejski Ogrod Zoologiczny W Lodzi
Ul. Konstantynowska
91-110 Lodz

Miejski Ogrod Zoologiczny
Ul. Wroblewskiego 1/5
51-618 Wroclaw

Miejski Ogrod Zoologiczny
Ul. Warszawska 30
09-402 Plock

Miejski Ogrod Zoologiczny
Ul. Warszawie
03-461 Warszawa, Ul. Ratuszowa

Miejski Park Ogrod Zoologiczny
Ul. Lesna 23
30-232 Krakow

Slaski Ogrod Zoologiczny
Silesian Zoological Garden
Katowice

Wielkopolski Park Zoologiczny
61-083 Poznan
Ul. Browarna 25

RUMANIA

Acvariu
B. dul 16 Februarie 1
Constanta

RUSSIA

Kaliningradskii Zoopark
Prospekt Mira 26
Kaliningrad 236000

Aquarium at Moskovskii
   Zoologicheski Park
Bolshaya Gruzinskaya
Ul. 1
Moscow

Rostovskii-Na-Donu
   Zoologicheskii Park
Zoologicheskaya Ul. 3
Rostov-Na-Donu

UKRAINE

Kharkovskii Zoologicheskii Park
Sumskaya Ul. 35
Khar'kov

Kievskii Zoologicheskii Park
Prospekt Pobedy 32
Kiev

Nikolaevskii Zoopark
Oktyabrskii Prospekt
Nikolaev

Sevastopolskii Morskoi Akvarium
Prospekt Nakhimova 2
Sevastopol

Australia and New Zealand

AUSTRALIA

Sydney Aquarium
Aquarium Pier
Darling Harbor
Sydney
NSW 2000
02-262-2300

Taronga Park Zoo
Post Box 20
Mosman
NSW
612-969-2777

NEW ZEALAND

Hawke's Bay Marineland and Aquarium
Napier
58-493

Kelly Tarleton's Underwater World
Auckland 1
764-785

Asia

BRUNEI

Hassanal Bolkiah Aquarium
P.O. Box 2161 Ministry of Development
Fisheries Department
Bandar Seri Begawan

HONG KONG

Ocean Park Ltd.
Wong Chuk Hang Road
Aberdeen

INDIA

Zoological Garden
Alipore
Calcutta 700027
West Bengal

Peshawe Park Zoological Garden
Sadashiv Peth
Pune 411 030
Maharashtra

INDONESIA

Kebun Binatang
Jalan Setail 1
Wonokromo
Surabaya

MALAYSIA

Zoo Negara
National Zoological Park
Ulu Kelang
Ampang 68000
Selangor

PAKISTAN

Karachi Municipal Aquarium
Clifton
Karachi

SINGAPORE

World of Aquariums (formerly
   Van Kleef Aquarium)
King George V Park
River Valley Road
0923

Underwater World and Coralarium
Sentosa Island

SRI LANKA

National Zoological Gardens
   of Sri Lanka
Anagrika Dharmapala Mawatha
Dehiwala

PEOPLE'S REPUBLIC OF CHINA

Fuzhou Zoological Gardens
Fuzhou
Aujian

Guangzhou Zoological Gardens
Guangzhou
Kwangtung

Nanshan Park
Yangchuan
Shanxi

Weipin Park
Zianyang
Shanxi

TAIWAN, REPUBLIC OF CHINA

National Museum of Marine
   Biology and Aquarium
Kenting National Park
c/o LrS. Fang
Sun YatSen University
Kaoshiung
886-7531

National Fisheries Center and Aquarium
National Taiwan Ocean University
Keelung 20224
886-2-7883463

P'eng-hu Aquarium
Makung
P'eng-hu Islands
02-708-7868

JAPAN (ALPHABETICALLY BY NAME)

Aburatsubo Marine Park Aquarium
Jonouchi 1082-2, Koajiro
Misaki-cho
Miura-shi
Kanagawa
046-881-6281

Amakusa Natural Aquarium in Bottom
Hirose 996, Hondo-Cho
Hondo-shi
Kumamoto
096-922-3161

Aomori Prefectural Asamushi Aquarium
Babayama 1-25, Asamushi
Aomori-shi
Aomori
017-752-3377

Ashizuri Kaiyokan
Imashiba 4032, Misaki
Tosashimizu-shi
Kochi
088-085-0635

Atagawa Banana-Crocodile
  Gardens
Atagawa, Higashiizu-cho
Kamo-gun
Shizuoka
055-723-1105

Awashima Marine Park
Shigedera 186, Uchiura
Numazu-shi
Shizuoka
055-943-2236

Biwako Bunkakan
Uchidehama 1-1
Otsu-shi
Shiga
077-522-8179

Echizen Matsushima Aquarium
Misaki, Mikuni-cho
Sakai-gun
Fukui
077-681-2700

Enoshima Aquarium
Katase-Kaigan 2-17-25
Fujisawa-shi
Kanagawa 251
046-622-8111

Futami Sea Paradise
Futami-cho
Watarai-gun
Mie
0594-3-4111

Gifu Park
Omiya-Cho 1-46
Gifu-shi
Gifu
058-262-3951

Hekinan Beach Aquarium
Hama-Cho 2-3
Hekinan-shi
Aichi
056-648-3761

Higashiyama Zoological &
  Botanical Gardens
Higashiyama-Motomachi
  3-70, Chigusa-ku
Nagoya-shi
Aichi
052-782-2111

Himeji City Aquarium
Tegarayama 440, Nishinobusue
Himeji-shi
Hyogo
079-297-0321

Hiyoriyama Park
Seto 1090
Toyooka-shi
Hyogo
079-628-2500

Inokashira Park Zoo
Gotenyama 1-17-6
Musashino-shi
Tokyo
042-246-1100

Inubosaki Marine Park
Inubosaki 9575-1
Choshi-shi
Chiba
047-924-0451

Izu Andyland
Hama-Hiraisoyama 405-2
Kawazu-cho
Kamo-gun
Shizuoka
055-834-0003

Izumito Sea Paradise
Nagahama 3-1, Uchiura
Numazu-shi
Shizuoka
055-943-2331

Joetsu City Aquarium
Nishimoto-cho 4-19-27
Joetsu-shi
Niigata
0255-43-2449

Kamogawa Sea World
Higashi-cho 1464-18
Kamogawa-shi
Chiba 296
047-092-2121

Kanazawa Aquarium
Higashimikage-cho 450
Kanazawa-shi
Ishikawa
076-252-5234

Katsurahama Aquarium
Urato 778
Kochi-shi
Kochi
088-841-2437

Keikyu Aburatsubo Marine Park
Koajiro 1082
Miura-shi
Kanagawa 238-02
046-881-6281

Kiryugaoka Park Zoo
Miyamoto-cho 2-1-40
Kiryu-shi
Gumma
027-722-4442

Kushimoto Marine Park
  Center Aquarium
Arita, Kushimoto
Wakayama 649-34
073-562-1122

Marine Palace Oita
  Ecological Aquarium
Takazakiyamashita
Oita-shi 870
097-534-1010

Marine Science Museum
Tokai University
Miho 2389
Shimizu-shi
Shizuoka-ken 424
054-334-2385

Marinepia Matsushima Aquarium
Namiuchihama 16,
  Matsushima-Machi
Miyagi-gun
Miyagi
0235-4-2020

Marineworld Umino-nakamichi
Nishitosaki 18-28
Higashi-ku
Fukuoka-shi
Fukuoka
092-603-0400

Matsushima Aquarium
Namiuchihama 16
Matsushima-cho
Miyagi-gun
Miyagi 981-02
022-354-2020

Minamichita Beach Land Aquarium
Okuda, Mihama-cho
Chita-gun
Aichi 470-32
056-987-2000

Misaki Park Zoo & Aquarium
Tannowa 3990, Misaki-cho
Sennan-gun
Osaka
072-492-1005

Miyajima Aquarium
Miyajima-cho 10-3
Saeki-gun
Hiroshima 739-05
082-944-2010

Miyazu E.L. Aquarium
Odashukuno 1001
Miyazu-shi
Kyoto
077-225-0003

Muroran Aquarium
Shukutsu-cho 3-3-12
Otaru-shi
Hokkaido
014-327-1638

Nagasaki Aquarium
Shuku-machi 3
Nagasaki-shi
Nagasaki 851-01
095-838-3131

Nagasaki Bio Park
Nakayama 2291-1, Saiki-cho
Nishisongi-gun
Nagasaki
095-927-1247

Nanki Shiraham Adventure World
Katada, Shirahama-shi
Nishimuro-gun
Wakayama
073-943-3333

Niigata Aquarium
Nishifunami-machi 5932-445
Niigata-shi
Niigata
025-222-7500

Noboribetsu Marine Park
Higashi-machi 1-22, Noboribetsu
Noboribetsu-shi
Hakkaido
014-383-3800

Noshappu Kanryu Aquarium
Noshappu 2-Chome
Wakkanai-shi
Hakkaido
016-223-6278

Notojima Beach Park Aquarium
Magri 15-40, Notojima-Machi
Kashima-gun
Ishikawa-ken 926-02
076-784-1271

Oarai Aquarium
Isohama-cho 8252-3
Oarai-shi
Higashibaragi-gun 311-13
Ibaragi
0292-67-5151

Oga Aquarium
Toga
Oga-shi
Akita-ken 010-06
018-537-2131

Oita Ecological Aquarium
Uto 3078-6, Kanzaki
Oita-shi
Oita
097-534-1010

Okhotsk Aquarium Foundation
Futatsuiwa 1
Abashiri-shi
Hokkaido
015-243-2973

Okinawa Expo Park Aquarium
Motobu-cho
Okinawa 905-03
098-048-2742

Okinawa-Kodomonokuni
    Zoo & Aquarium
Koya 5-7-1
Okinawa-shi
Okinawa
098-933-4190

Osaka Ring of Fire Aquarium
Kaigandori 1-1-10
Minato-ku
Osaka 552
06-576-5545

Otaru Aquarium
Kita Shukuzu-cho 210
Otaru
Hokkaido 047
013-433-1400

Oyama Marine Aquarium
Yoshizawa 1475
Oyama
Tochigi
028-522-9068

Port of Nagoya Aquarium
1-3 Minato-machi
Minato-ku Nagoya 455
052-654-7000

Saitama Municipal Aquarium
Hozoji 751-1, Mitagaya
Hanyu-shi
Saitama
048-565-1010

Sakaigahama Marine Park Aquarium
Urasaki-cho 1359
Onomichi-shi
Hiroshima
084-987-3677

Seaside Park Hiroo Aquarium
Nozuka 989, Hiroo-cho
Hiroo-gun
Hokkaido
015-582-3707

Shima Marineland
Kashiki 723-1, Myojin
Ago-machi
Shima-gun
Mie
059-943-1225

Shimoda Floating Aquarium
Shimoda-shi 3-22-31
Shizuoka 415
055-822-3567

Shimonoseki Municipal Aquarium
Chofusotoura-cho
Shimonoseki-shi
Yamaguchi 752
083-245-1196

Shirahama Aquarium
Kyoto University
Shirahama-shi
Nishimuro-gun
Wakayama 649-22
073-942-3515

Shonai-Beach Kamo Aquarium
Okubo 560-2
Imaizumi
Tsuruoka-shi
Yamagata
023-533-3036

Suma Aqualife Park
Wakamiya-cho 1-3-5, Suma-ku
Kobe-shi
Hyogo
078-731-7301

Sun Plaza Aquarium
Nijo 5-7-5, Atsubetsu-Chuo
Atsubetsu-ku
Sapporo-shi
Hokkaido
011-890-2455

Sunshine International Aquarium
Higashiikebukuro 3-1-3
Toshima-ku
Tokyo
033-989-3466

Suzaka Zoo
Koyama 663
Suzaka-shi
Nagano
026-245-1770

Taiji Whales Museum
Joto 2934-2, Tiji, Taiji-cho
Higashimuro-gun
Wakayama
073-559-2400

Takarazuka Zoological &
    Botanical Gardens
Sakae-Cho 1-1-57
Takarazuka-shi
Hyogo
079-785-6301

Takeshima Aquarium
Takeshima-cho 1-6
Gamagori-shi
Aichi
053-368-2059

Tama Zoological Park
Hodokubo 7-1-1
Hino-shi
Tokyo
042-591-1611

Tamano Marine Museum
Shibukawa 2-6-1
Tamano-shi
Okayama
086-381-8111

Teradomari Aquarium
Hanatate 9353 Teradomari
Teradomari-cho
Mishima-gun
Niigata
025-875-4936

Toba Aquarium
Toba 3-3-6
Toba-shi
Mie
059-925-2555

Tokyo Sea Life Park
Rinkai-cho 6-2-3
Edogawa-ku
Tokyo 134
03-3-869-5153

Toyama Family Park Zoo
Furusawa 254
Toyama-shi
Toyama
076-434-1234

Ueno Zoological Gardens
Ueno Park
Taito-ku
Tokyo 110
03-828-5171

Uozu Aquarium
Sanko 1390
Uozu-shi
Toyama
076-524-4100

Wakayama Municipal Natural
    Science Museum
Funao 370-1
Kainan-shi
Wakayama
073-483-1777

Yambaru Wildlife Park
Nago 4607-41
Nago-shi
Okinawa
098-052-6348

Yashima Sea Palace
Yashima-Higashicho 1785-1
Takamatsu-shi
Kagawa
087-841-2678

Yomiyuriland Marine Aquarium
Yanokuchi Inagi-shi
Tokyo 206
044-966-1111

The Middle East and Africa

UNITED ARAB EMIRATES

Al Ain Zoo and Aquarium
POB 1204
Al Ain
Abu Dhabi
971-3-828188

Dubai Municipality Zoo and Aquarium
POB 67
Dubai
229161

ISRAEL

Coral World Underwater Observatory
    and Aquarium
P.O. Box 829
Eilat
059-76666

SOUTH AFRICA

East London Aquarium
Esplanade
East London 25151

National Zoological Gardens
    of South Africa
Box 754
Boom Street
Pretoria 0001
012-283265

Port Elizabeth Museum and
    Oceanarium
Box 13147
Humewood 6013

Sea World Durban
2 West Street
Durban 4001
Natal
031-373536

BIBLIOGRAPHY

"The Aquarium." *The Atlantic Monthly* (1861) 8: 322–37.

Atkinson-Grosjean, J. *Values and Visions: A Study of Cetaceans at the Vancouver Aquarium.* Vancouver Aquarium, 1992.

Barber, L. *The Heyday of Natural History 1820–1870.* Garden City, N.Y.: Doubleday & Company, Inc., 1980.

Bateman, G. C. and R. A. R. Bennett. *The Book of Aquaria: Practical Guide to Construction, Arrangement, and Management of Fresh-water and Marine Aquaria.* New York: Charles Scribner's Sons, 1902.

Beasley, W. L. "The New York Aquarium." *Scientific American,* May 27, 1905, 391–95.

Boulenger, E. G. *The Aquarium Book* [*New York Aquarium*]. New York: D. Appleton, 1926.

Breen, A., Rigby, R., editors. *Resource Book: Aquarium Planning and Management Workshop II.* Monterey, Cal.: The Waterfront Center, 1991.

Bristol, C. L. "Treasures of the New York Aquarium." *The Century,* May 1900, 553–60.

Browne, W. P. *Barnum's Own Story: The autobiography of P. T. Barnum combined and condensed from the various editions published during his lifetime.* New York: Dover Publications, Inc., 1961.

Butler, H. D. *The Family Aquarium; or, Aqua-vivarium, a new pleasure for the domestic circle.* New York: Dick and Fitzgerald, 1858.

Carlson, B. "Aquarium systems for living corals." *International Zoo Yearbook 1986.* London: Zoological Society of London, 1–9, 1987.

Catala, R. L. A. *Carnival of the Sea.* Nouméa: Editions Pacifique,1956.

Chermayeff, Peter, "The Age of Aquariums." *World Monitor,* August 1992, 54–57.

Crow, G. L. and J. D. Hewitt, IV. "Longevity records for captive tiger sharks (*Galeocerdo cuvier*) with notes on behaviour and management." *International Zoo Yearbook 1988.* London: Zoological Society of London, 237–40, 1989.

Dean, B. "Public Aquariums in Europe." *Appleton's Public Science Monthly* 50: 13–27, 1896.

Dietsch, Deborah K. "Coastal Education, the Oregon Coast Aquarium." *Architecture,* September 1992, 72–75.

Edwards, A. M. *Life Beneath the Waters: or, The Aquarium in America.* London: Baillere, 1858.

Findling, J. E. and K. D. Pelle, eds. *Historical Dictionary of World's Fairs and Expositions, 1851–1988.* New York and London: Greenwood Press, 1990.

Freeman, R. B. *British Natural History Books: A Handlist 1495–1900.* Hamden, Conn.: Archon Books, The Shoe String Press, Inc., 1980.

Gosse, P. H. *The Aquarium: An Unveiling of the Wonders of the Deep Sea.* London: John Van Voorst, 1854.

———. *Actinologica Britannica: A History of the British Sea-Anemones and Corals.* London: Van Voorst, 1860.

Gradenwitz, A. "The New Berlin Aquarium; the Old Establishment Resuscitated on a New Site." *Scientific American Supplement* 76: 276, 1913.

Gunts, Edward. "Age of Aquariums." *Architecture,* September 1992, 58–72.

Hill, R. N. *Window in the Sea.* New York: Rinehart and Company, 1956.

Huxley, J. S. "L'Acquario." *The Forum* 49: 729–33, 1913.

Innes, W. T. *Goldfish Varieties and Tropical Aquarium Fishes.* Philadelphia: Innes & Sons, 1917.

Klös, H.-G. and J. Lange. "The modernisation of the Aquarium at Berlin Zoo." *International Zoo Yearbook 1985.* London: Zoological Society of London, 322–32, 1986.

Kourist, W. *400 Jahre Zoo.* Cologne: Rheinland-Verlag GmbH, 1976.

Kuroyanagi, A., et al. "Composition of Oceanic Architecture." *Process: Architecture* 96: 1–165, 1991.

Maitland, P. S. and D. Evans. "The role of captive breeding in the conservation of fish species." *International Zoo Yearbook 1985*. London: Zoological Society of London, 66–74, 1986.

McCosker, J. E. "Flashlight Fishes." *Scientific American* 236(3): 106–14, 1977.

———. and E. E. Miller. "The Steinhart Aquarium Fish Roundabout: A decade later." *International Zoo Yearbook 1986*. London: Zoological Society of London, 48–53, 1987.

Newman, M. A. and S. I. Hewlett. "The Graham Amazon Gallery at the Vancouver Aquarium." *International Zoo Yearbook 1986*. London: Zoological Society of London, 81–90, 1987.

Norris, K. S. *Dolphin Days: The Life and Times of the Spinner Dolphin*. New York and London: W. W. Norton, 1991.

Olney, P. J. S. et al., eds. "Zoos and Aquaria of the World." *International Zoo Yearbook 1988*. London: Zoological Society of London, 284–379, 1989.

Pacheco, A. L. and S. E. Smith. *Marine Parks and Aquaria of the United States*. New York: Lyons & Burford, 1989.

Phillips, C. *The Captive Sea: Life Behind the Scenes of the Great Modern Oceanariums*. Philadelphia and New York: Chilton Books, 1964.

Pindar, G. N. *Guide to the Nature Treasures of New York City* [*New York Aquarium*]. New York: American Museum of Natural History by Charles Scribner's Sons, 1917.

Pryor, K. and K. S. Norris, eds. *Dolphin Societies: Discoveries and Puzzles*. Berkeley: University of California Press, 1991.

Rutherford, J. *Aquarium exhibit view windows: plastic or glass?* American Association of Zoological Parks and Aquariums, Annual Conference Proceedings. Portland, Oregon, September, 20–24, 210–41, 1987.

"The Salt Water Aquarium at the Paris Exposition." *Scientific American Supplement* (1900) 1300: 208.

Saxon, A. H., ed. *Selected Letters of P. T. Barnum*. New York: Columbia University Press, 1983.

Shallenberger, E. W. *The Status of Hawaiian Cetaceans*. U.S. Marine Mammal Commission, 1979.

Simmons, W. E., Jr. "The Aquarium." *The Popular Science Monthly* (May 1874): 687–95.

Solomon, Nancy B. "Aquatic Anchor, the New Jersey State Aquarium." *Architecture*, September 1992, 76–81.

Taylor, J. E. *The Aquarium: Its Inhabitants, Structure, and Management*. London: Hardwicke, 1876.

Todd, F. S. "The Penguin Encounter at Sea World, San Diego." *International Zoo Yearbook 1986*. London: Zoological Society of London, 104–109, 1987.

———. "Techniques for propagating King and Emperor penguins (*Aptenodytes patagonica* and *A. forsteri*) at Sea World, San Diego." *International Zoo Yearbook 1986*. London: Zoological Society of London. 110–24, 1987.

Uchida, S. et al. "Reproduction of elasmobranchs in captivity," *Elasmobranchs as Living Resources*. National Oceans and Atmospheric Administration Tech Report 90., ed. by H.L. Pratt, Jr. et al. Washington, D.C. 211–37, 1990.

Ulmer, J. G. and S. Gower. *Lions and Tigers and Bears: A Guide to Zoological Parks, Visitor Farms, Nature Centers, and Marine Life Displays in the United States and Canada*. New York and London: Garland Publishing, 1985.

Wallace, I. *The Fabulous Showman: The Life and Times of P. T. Barnum*. New York: Alfred A. Knopf, 1959.

Ward, Nathaniel Bagshaw. *On the growth of plants in closely glazed cases*. London: Van Voorst, 1842.

Williams, T. D. "Sea Otter Biology and Medicine." In *Handbook of Marine Mammal Medicine: Health, Disease, and Rehabilitation*. Boca Raton: CRC Press, 1990.

———. and J. Hymer (1992). "Raising orphaned sea otter pups." Journal of the American Veterinary Association 201 (5): 688–691.

Wood, J. B. *The Fresh and Salt-Water Aquarium*. London and New York: George Routledge and Sons, 1868.

Yoshida, H. International Symposium on Aquariums. *The Roles and Activities of the Aquariums in the 21st Century*. Tokyo: Uneo Zoological Garden, 1990.

INDEX

Note: Photo/illustration pages indicated in bold face; all scientific names in italic as noted.